VICTOR LaVALLE'S
DESTROYER™

BOOM!
STUDIOS

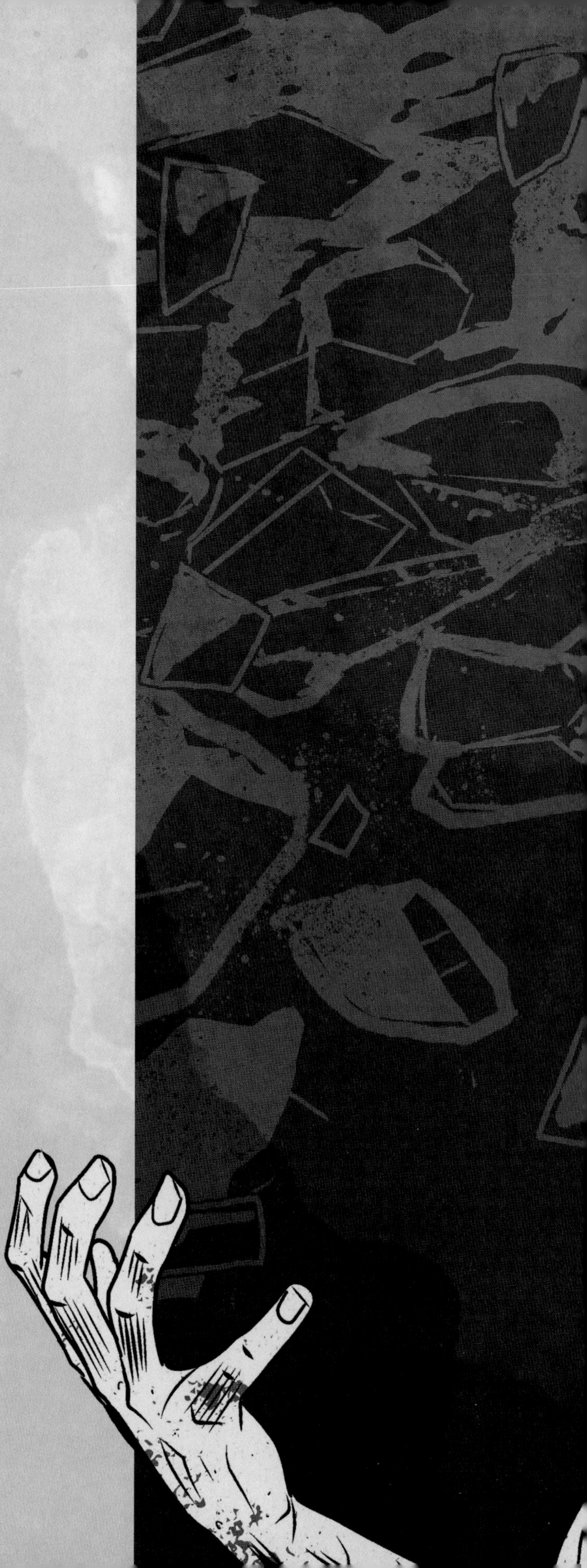

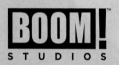

VICTOR LaVALLE'S DESTROYER, October 2018. Published by BOOM! Studios, a division of Boom Entertainment, Inc. Victor LaValle's Destroyer is ™ & © 2018 Victor LaValle. Originally published in single magazine form as VICTOR LaVALLE'S DESTROYER No. 1-6. ™ & © 2017 Victor LaValle. All rights reserved. BOOM! Studios™ and the BOOM! Studios logo are trademarks of Boom Entertainment, Inc., registered in various countries and categories. All characters, events, and institutions depicted herein are fictional. Any similarity between any of the names, characters, persons, events, and/or institutions in this publication to actual names, characters, and persons, whether living or dead, events, and/or institutions is unintended and purely coincidental. BOOM! Studios does not read or accept unsolicited submissions of ideas, stories, or artwork.

For information regarding the CPSIA on this printed material, call: (203) 595-3636 and provide reference #RICH - 819683.

BOOM! Studios, 5670 Wilshire Boulevard, Suite 400, Los Angeles, CA, 90036-5679. Printed in USA. Second Printing.

ISBN: 978-1-68415-055-7, eISBN: 978-1-61398-732-2

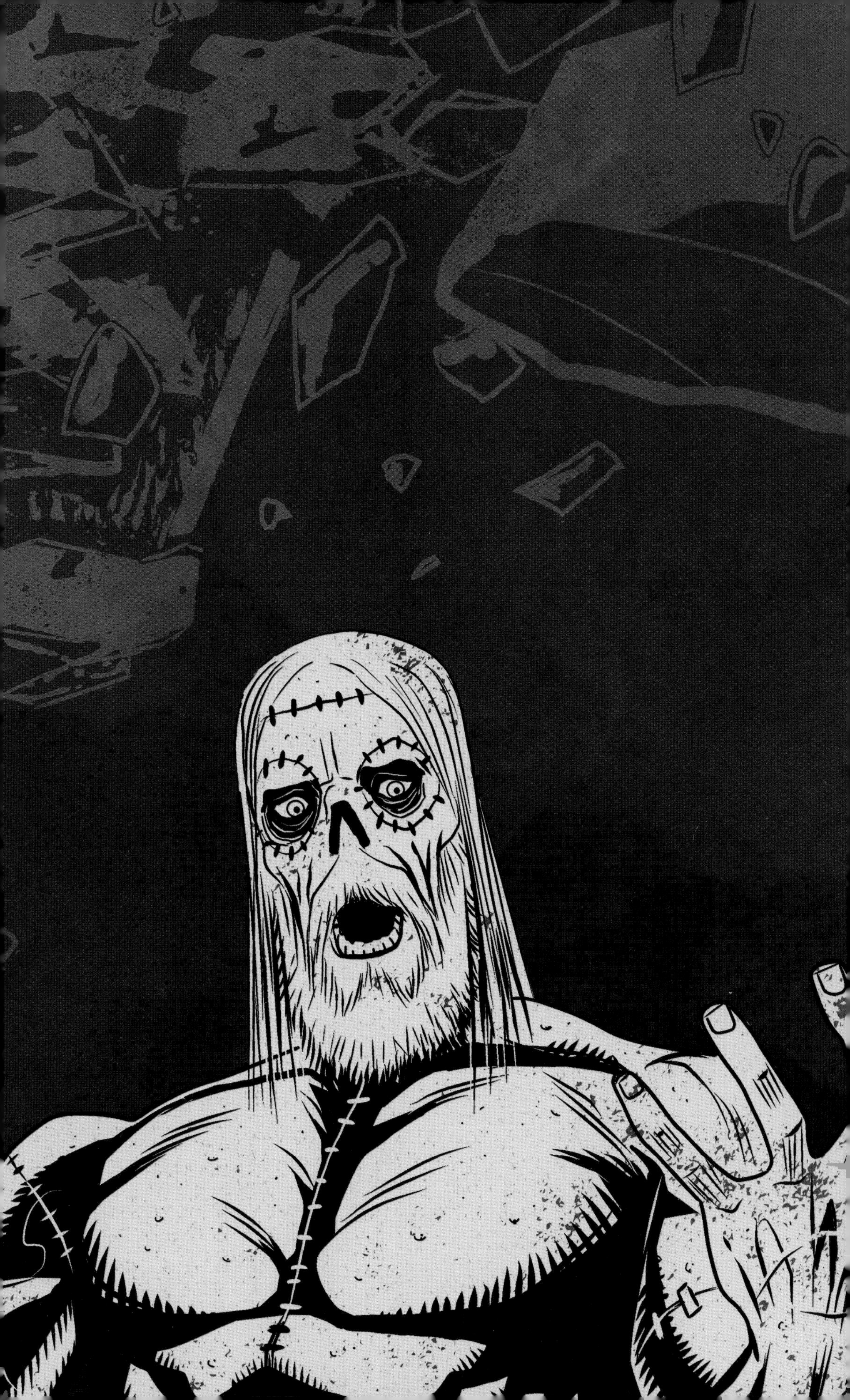

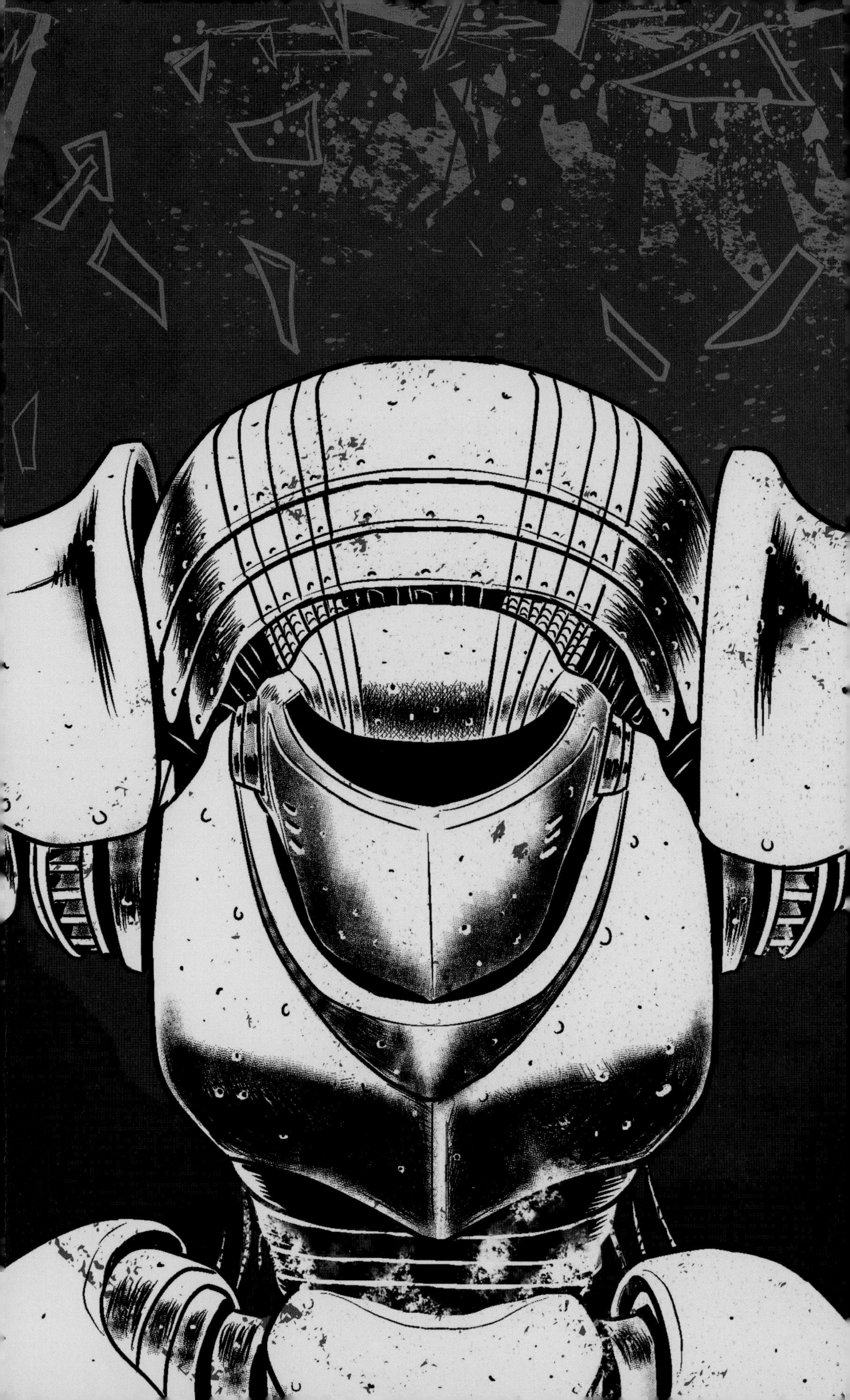

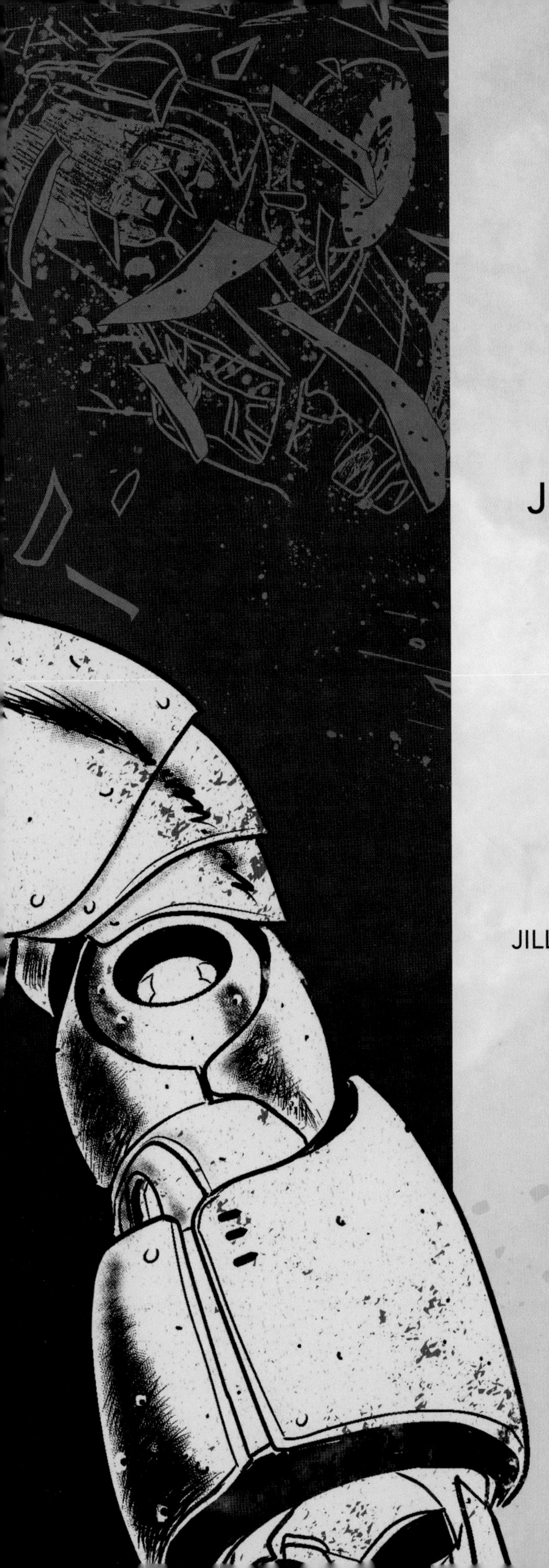

WRITTEN BY
VICTOR LAVALLE

ILLUSTRATED BY
DIETRICH SMITH

COLORED BY
JOANA LAFUENTE

LETTERED BY
JIM CAMPBELL

COVER BY
MICAELA DAWN

CHARACTER DESIGNS BY
DAN MORA &
DIETRICH SMITH

DESIGNERS
JILLIAN CRAB & MARIE KRUPINA

ASSOCIATE EDITOR
CHRIS ROSA

EDITOR
ERIC HARBURN

VICTOR LAVALLE'S DESTROYER™

CREATED BY VICTOR LAVALLE
& DIETRICH SMITH

CHAPTER
ONE

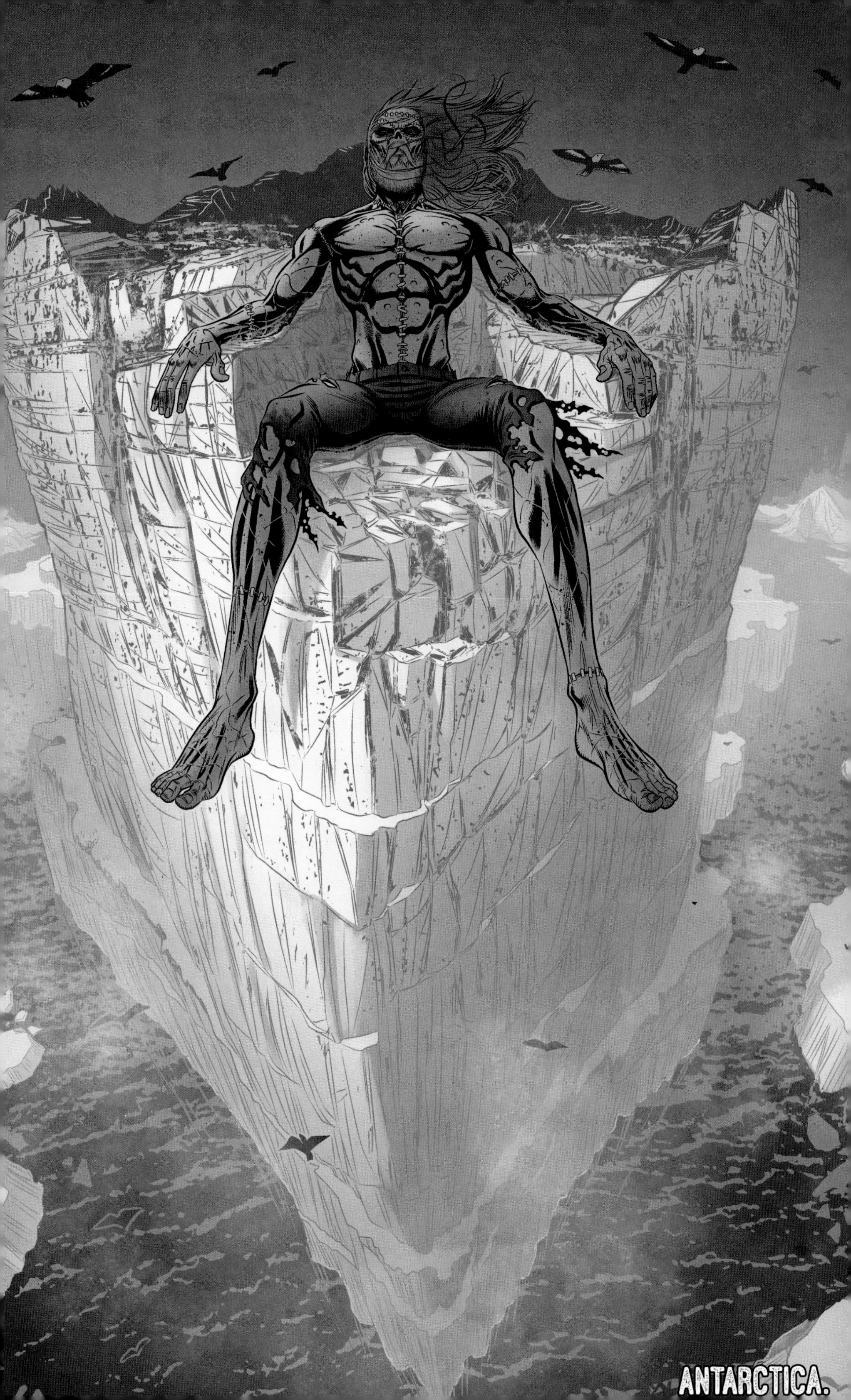
ANTARCTICA.

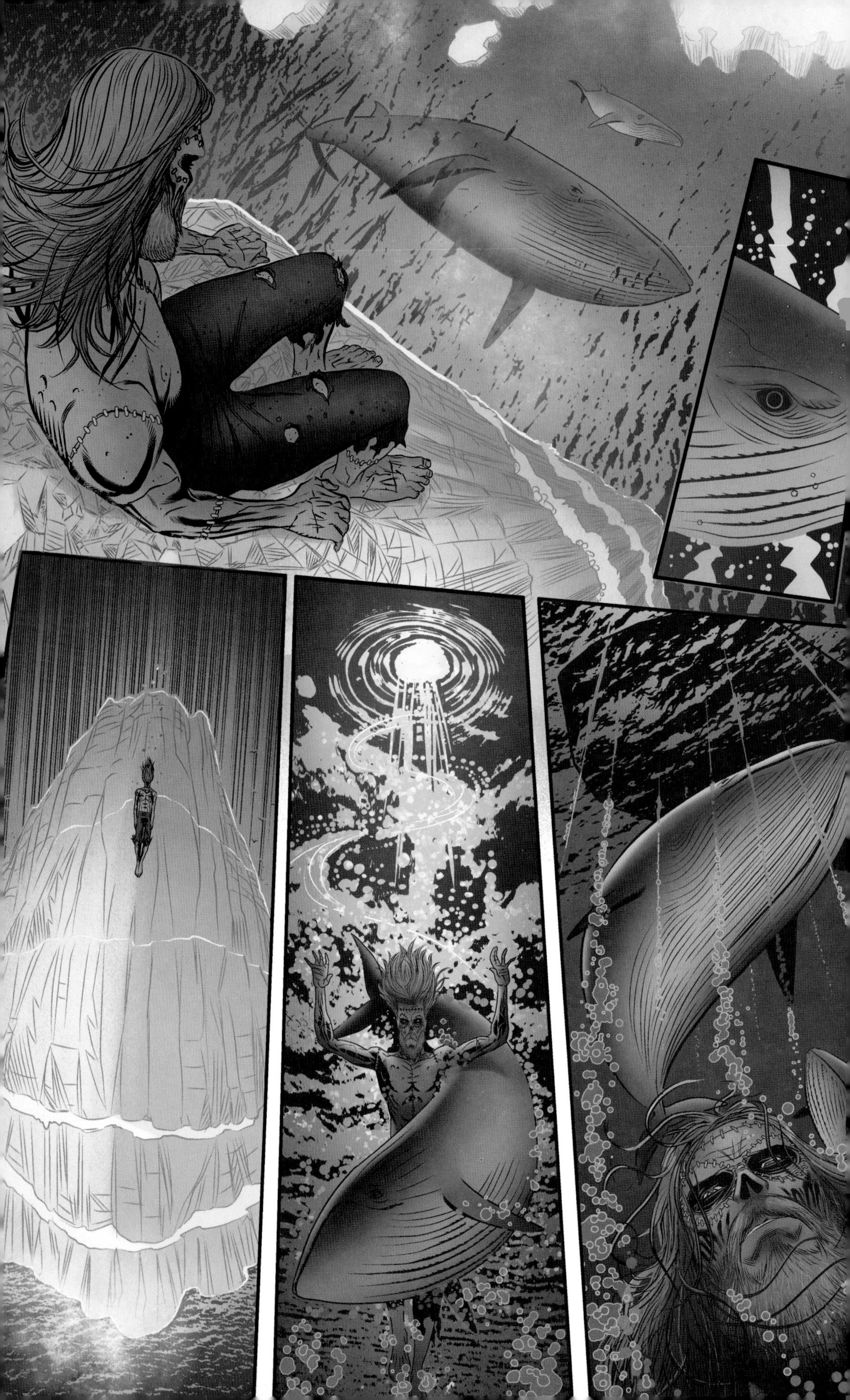

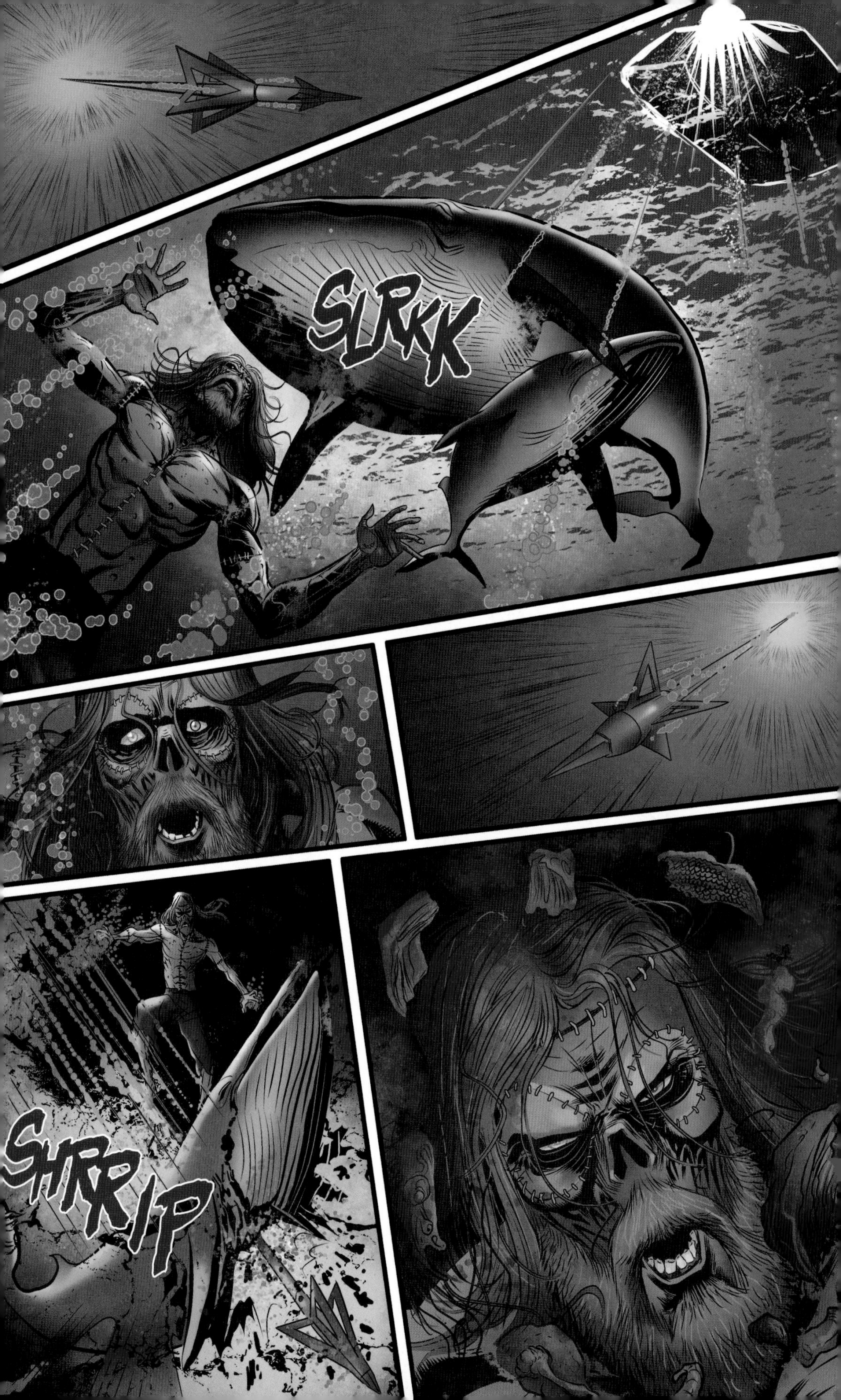
SLRKK
SHRRIP

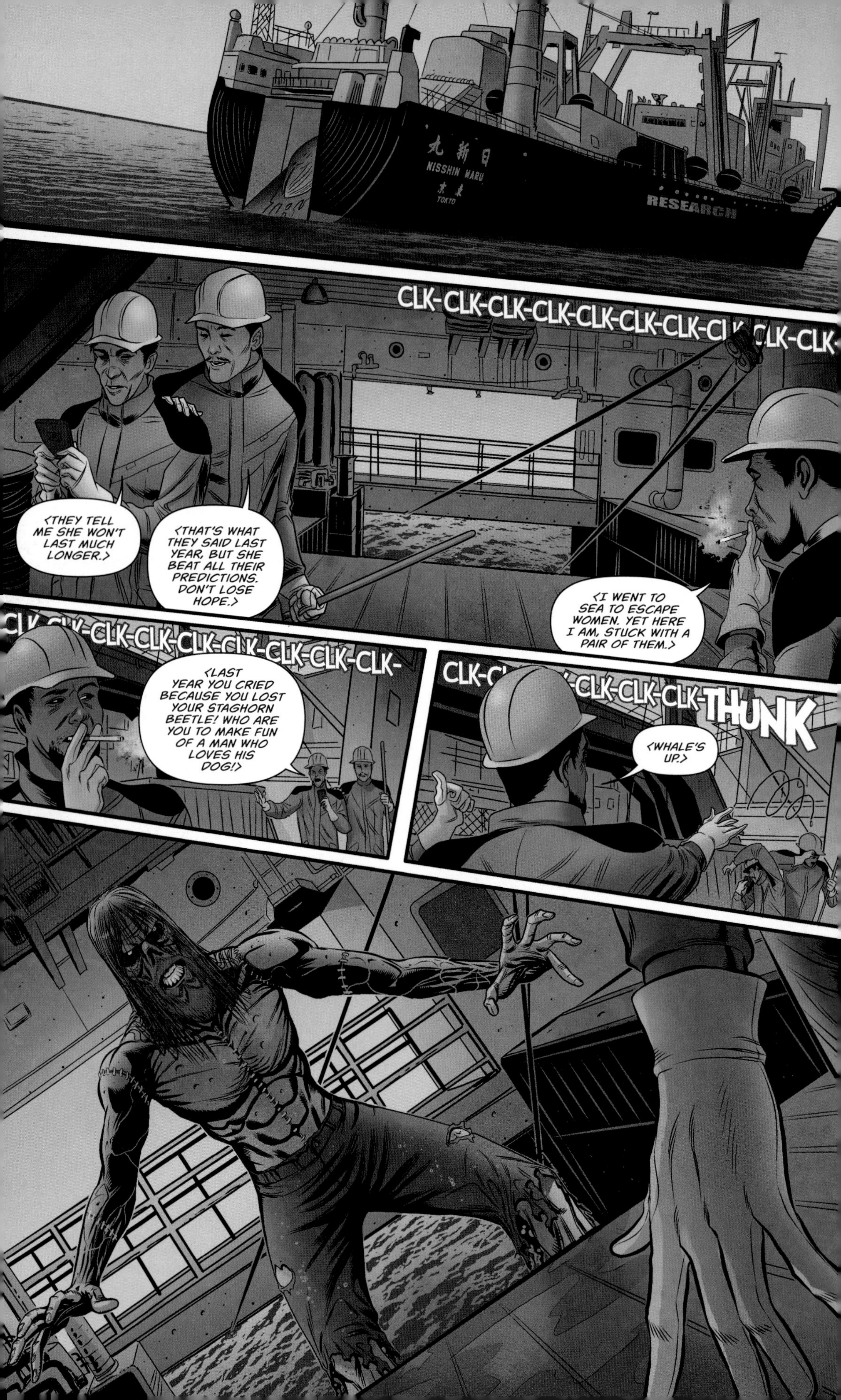
丸新日
NISSHIN MARU
東京
TOKYO
RESEARCH
CLK-CLK-CLK-CLK-CLK-CLK-CLK-CLK-CLK-
<THEY TELL ME SHE WON'T LAST MUCH LONGER.>
<THAT'S WHAT THEY SAID LAST YEAR, BUT SHE BEAT ALL THEIR PREDICTIONS. DON'T LOSE HOPE.>
<I WENT TO SEA TO ESCAPE WOMEN. YET HERE I AM, STUCK WITH A PAIR OF THEM.>
CLK-CLK-CLK-CLK-CLK-CLK-CLK-CLK-
<LAST YEAR YOU CRIED BECAUSE YOU LOST YOUR STAGHORN BEETLE! WHO ARE YOU TO MAKE FUN OF A MAN WHO LOVES HIS DOG!>
CLK-CLK-CLK-CLK-THUNK
<WHALE'S UP.>

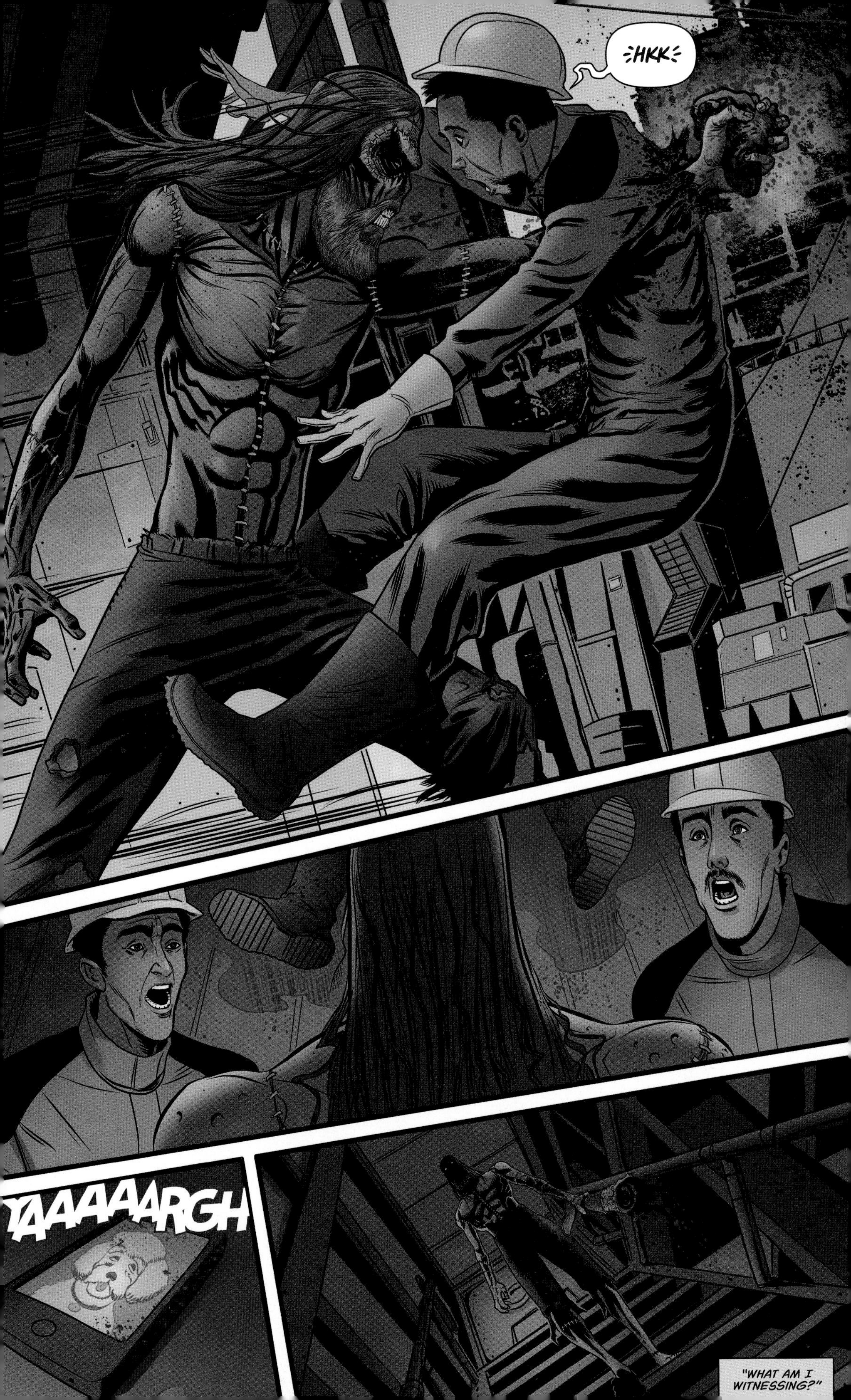
HKK
YAAAAARGH
"WHAT AM I WITNESSING?"

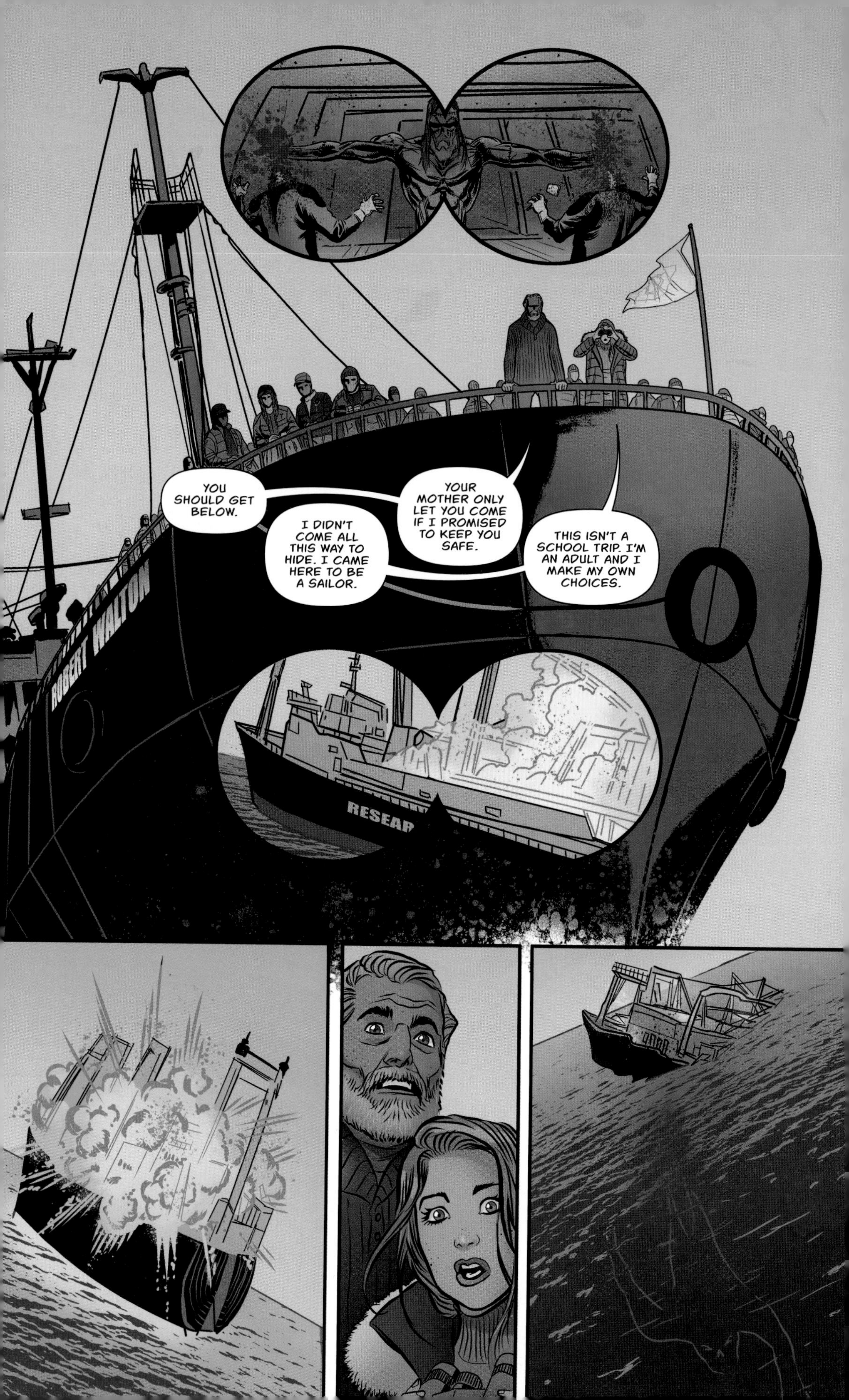
YOU SHOULD GET BELOW.
YOUR MOTHER ONLY LET YOU COME IF I PROMISED TO KEEP YOU SAFE.
I DIDN'T COME ALL THIS WAY TO HIDE. I CAME HERE TO BE A SAILOR.
THIS ISN'T A SCHOOL TRIP. I'M AN ADULT AND I MAKE MY OWN CHOICES.
ROBERT WALTON
RESEAR

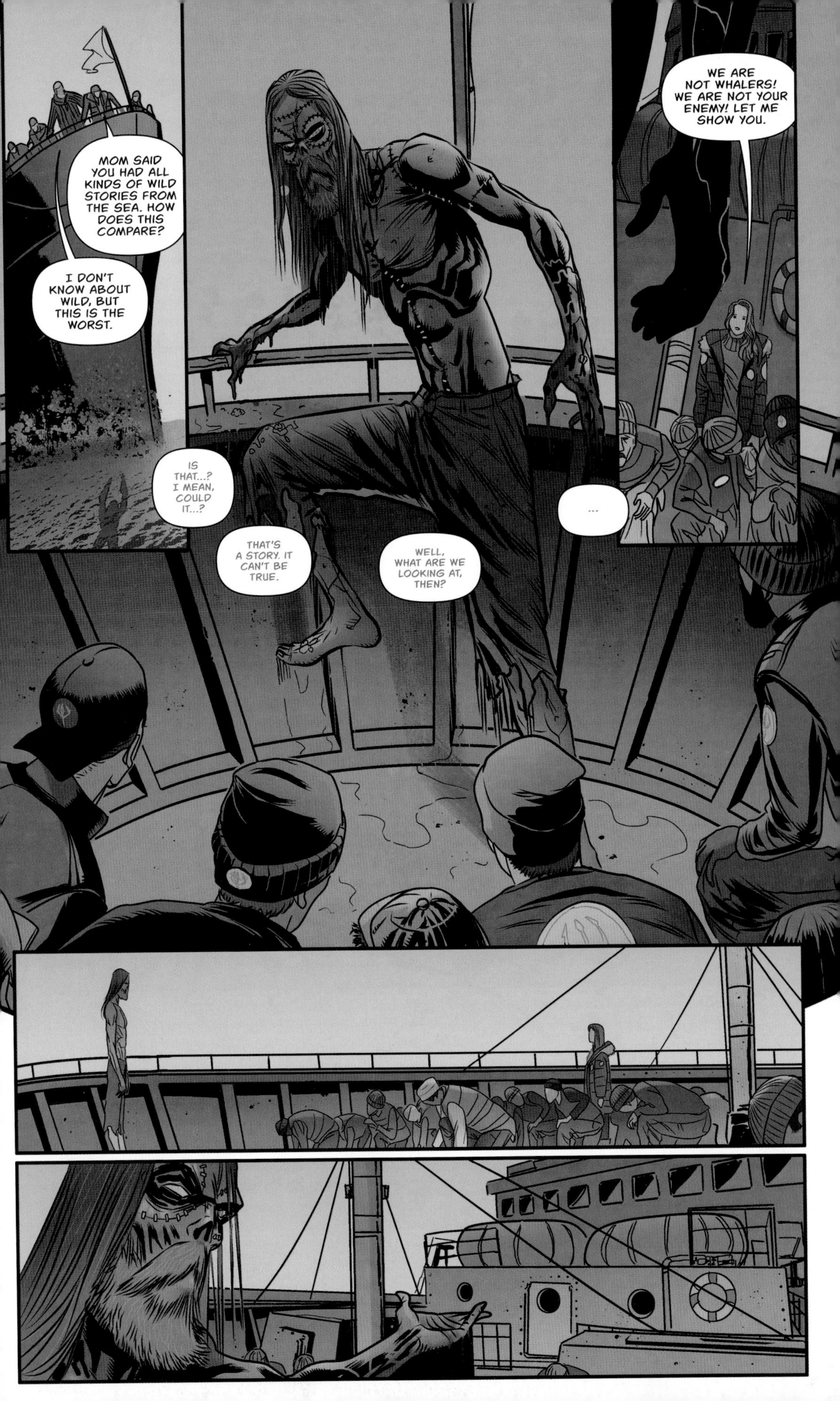
MOM SAID YOU HAD ALL KINDS OF WILD STORIES FROM THE SEA. HOW DOES THIS COMPARE?
I DON'T KNOW ABOUT WILD, BUT THIS IS THE WORST.
WE ARE NOT WHALERS! WE ARE NOT YOUR ENEMY! LET ME SHOW YOU.
IS THAT...? I MEAN, COULD IT...?
THAT'S A STORY. IT CAN'T BE TRUE.
WELL, WHAT ARE WE LOOKING AT, THEN?
...

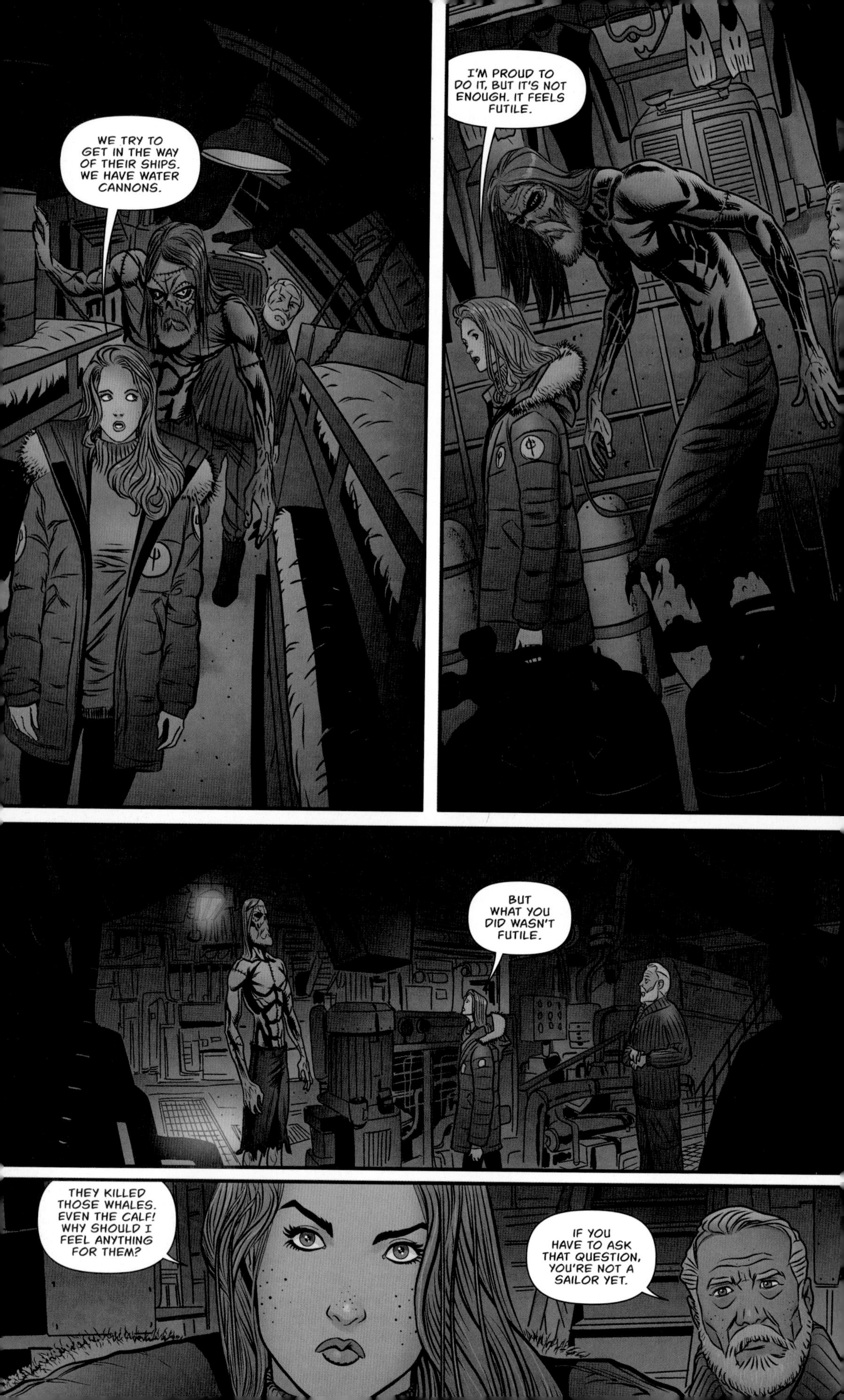
WE TRY TO GET IN THE WAY OF THEIR SHIPS. WE HAVE WATER CANNONS.
I'M PROUD TO DO IT, BUT IT'S NOT ENOUGH. IT FEELS FUTILE.
BUT WHAT YOU DID WASN'T FUTILE.
THEY KILLED THOSE WHALES. EVEN THE CALF! WHY SHOULD I FEEL ANYTHING FOR THEM?
IF YOU HAVE TO ASK THAT QUESTION, YOU'RE NOT A SAILOR YET.

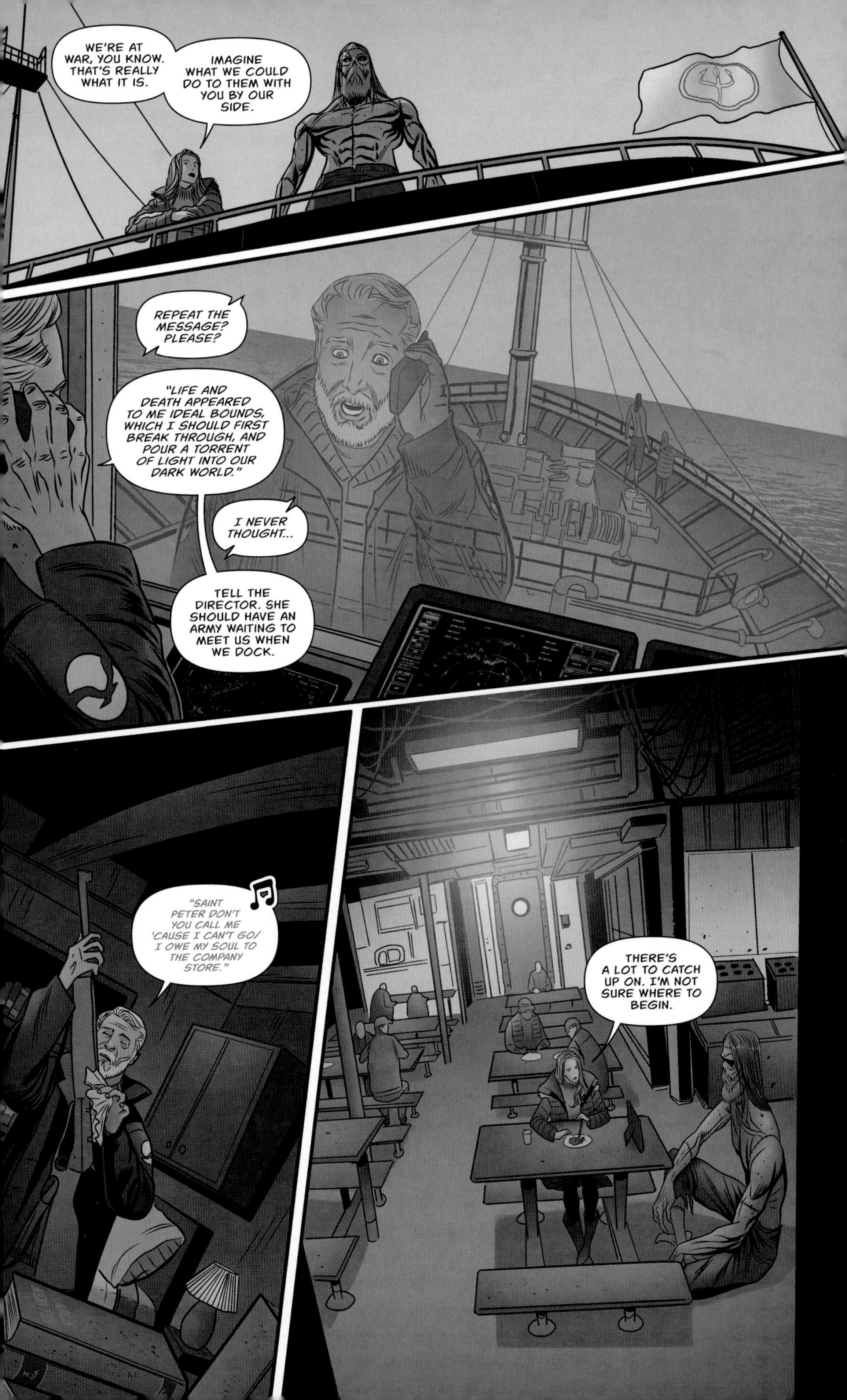
WE'RE AT WAR, YOU KNOW. THAT'S REALLY WHAT IT IS.
IMAGINE WHAT WE COULD DO TO THEM WITH YOU BY OUR SIDE.
REPEAT THE MESSAGE? PLEASE?
"LIFE AND DEATH APPEARED TO ME IDEAL BOUNDS, WHICH I SHOULD FIRST BREAK THROUGH, AND POUR A TORRENT OF LIGHT INTO OUR DARK WORLD."
I NEVER THOUGHT...
TELL THE DIRECTOR. SHE SHOULD HAVE AN ARMY WAITING TO MEET US WHEN WE DOCK.
"SAINT PETER DON'T YOU CALL ME 'CAUSE I CAN'T GO/ I OWE MY SOUL TO THE COMPANY STORE."
THERE'S A LOT TO CATCH UP ON. I'M NOT SURE WHERE TO BEGIN.

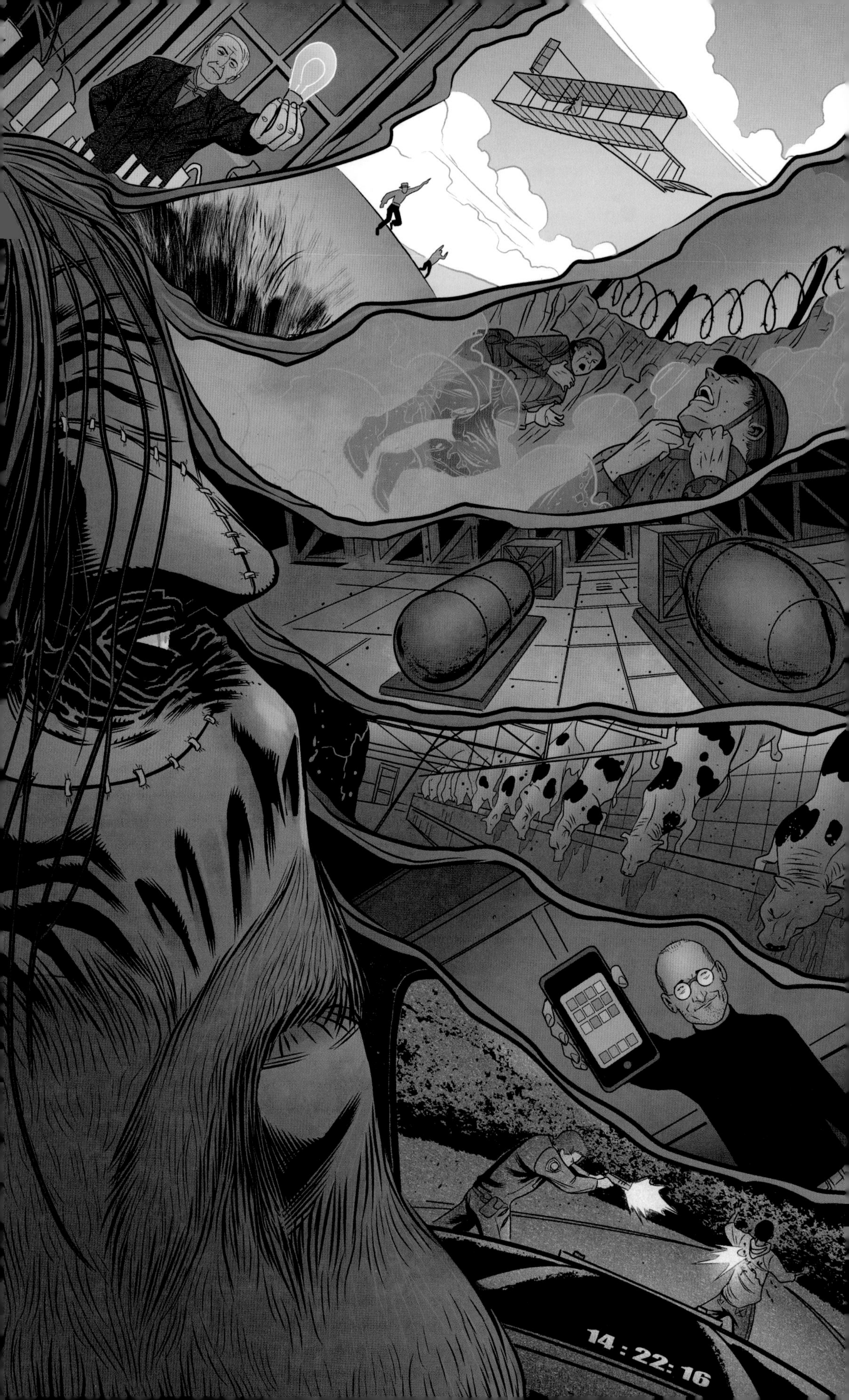
14 : 22: 16

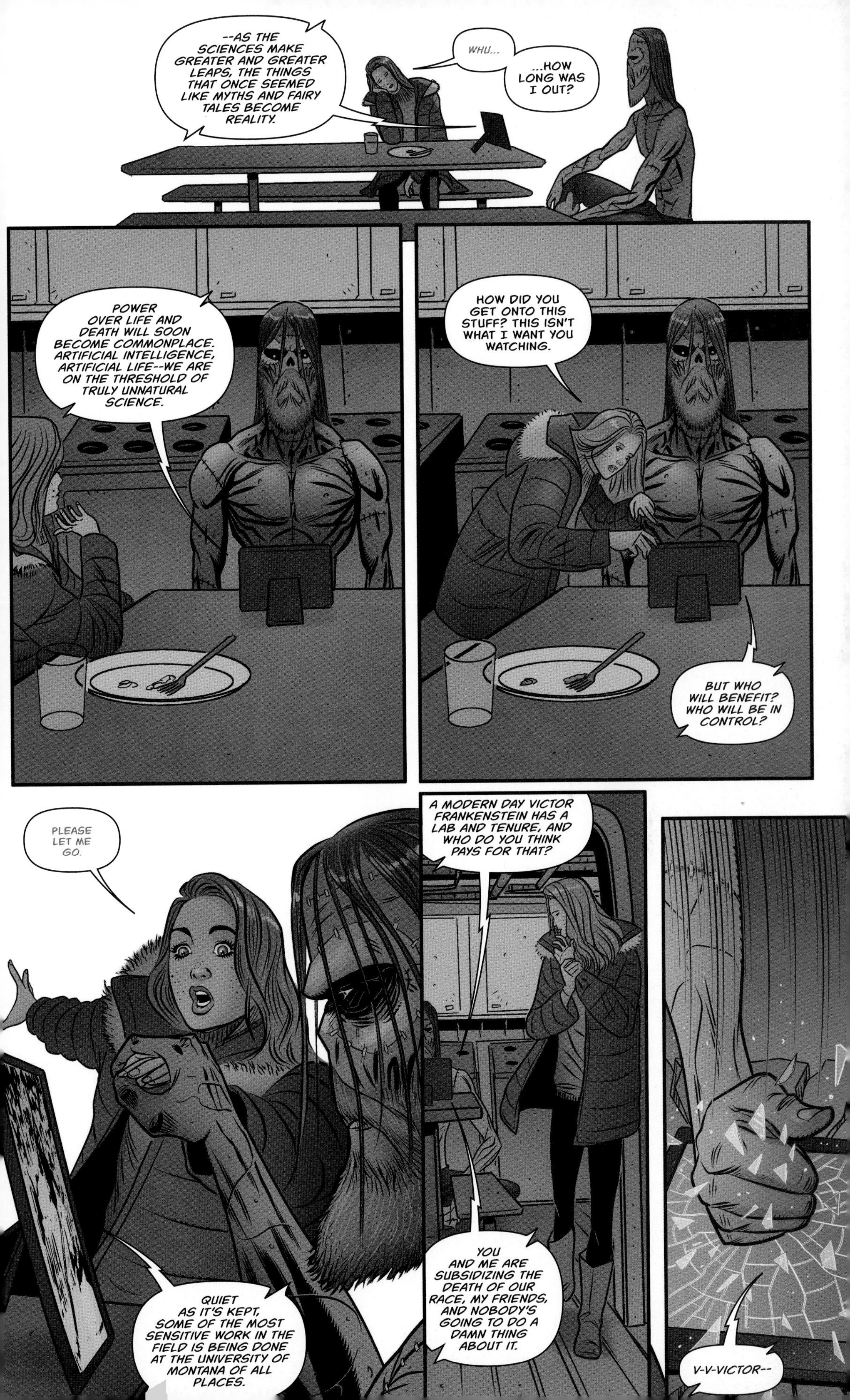
--AS THE SCIENCES MAKE GREATER AND GREATER LEAPS, THE THINGS THAT ONCE SEEMED LIKE MYTHS AND FAIRY TALES BECOME REALITY.
WHU...
...HOW LONG WAS I OUT?
POWER OVER LIFE AND DEATH WILL SOON BECOME COMMONPLACE. ARTIFICIAL INTELLIGENCE, ARTIFICIAL LIFE--WE ARE ON THE THRESHOLD OF TRULY UNNATURAL SCIENCE.
HOW DID YOU GET ONTO THIS STUFF? THIS ISN'T WHAT I WANT YOU WATCHING.
BUT WHO WILL BENEFIT? WHO WILL BE IN CONTROL?
PLEASE LET ME GO.
QUIET AS IT'S KEPT, SOME OF THE MOST SENSITIVE WORK IN THE FIELD IS BEING DONE AT THE UNIVERSITY OF MONTANA OF ALL PLACES.
A MODERN DAY VICTOR FRANKENSTEIN HAS A LAB AND TENURE, AND WHO DO YOU THINK PAYS FOR THAT?
YOU AND ME ARE SUBSIDIZING THE DEATH OF OUR RACE, MY FRIENDS, AND NOBODY'S GOING TO DO A DAMN THING ABOUT IT.
V-V-VICTOR--

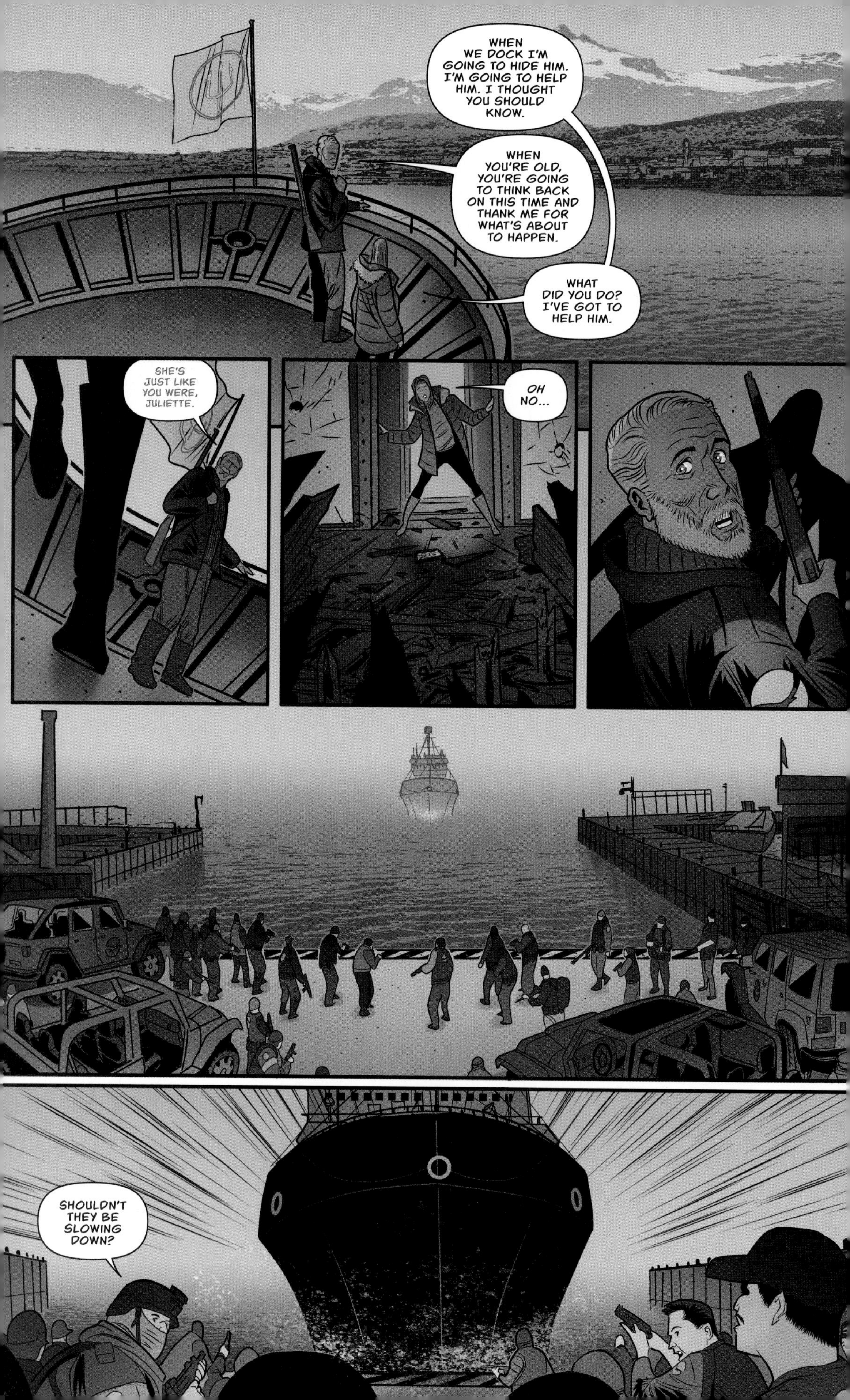
WHEN WE DOCK I'M GOING TO HIDE HIM. I'M GOING TO HELP HIM. I THOUGHT YOU SHOULD KNOW.
WHEN YOU'RE OLD, YOU'RE GOING TO THINK BACK ON THIS TIME AND THANK ME FOR WHAT'S ABOUT TO HAPPEN.
WHAT DID YOU DO? I'VE GOT TO HELP HIM.
SHE'S JUST LIKE YOU WERE, JULIETTE.
OH NO...
SHOULDN'T THEY BE SLOWING DOWN?

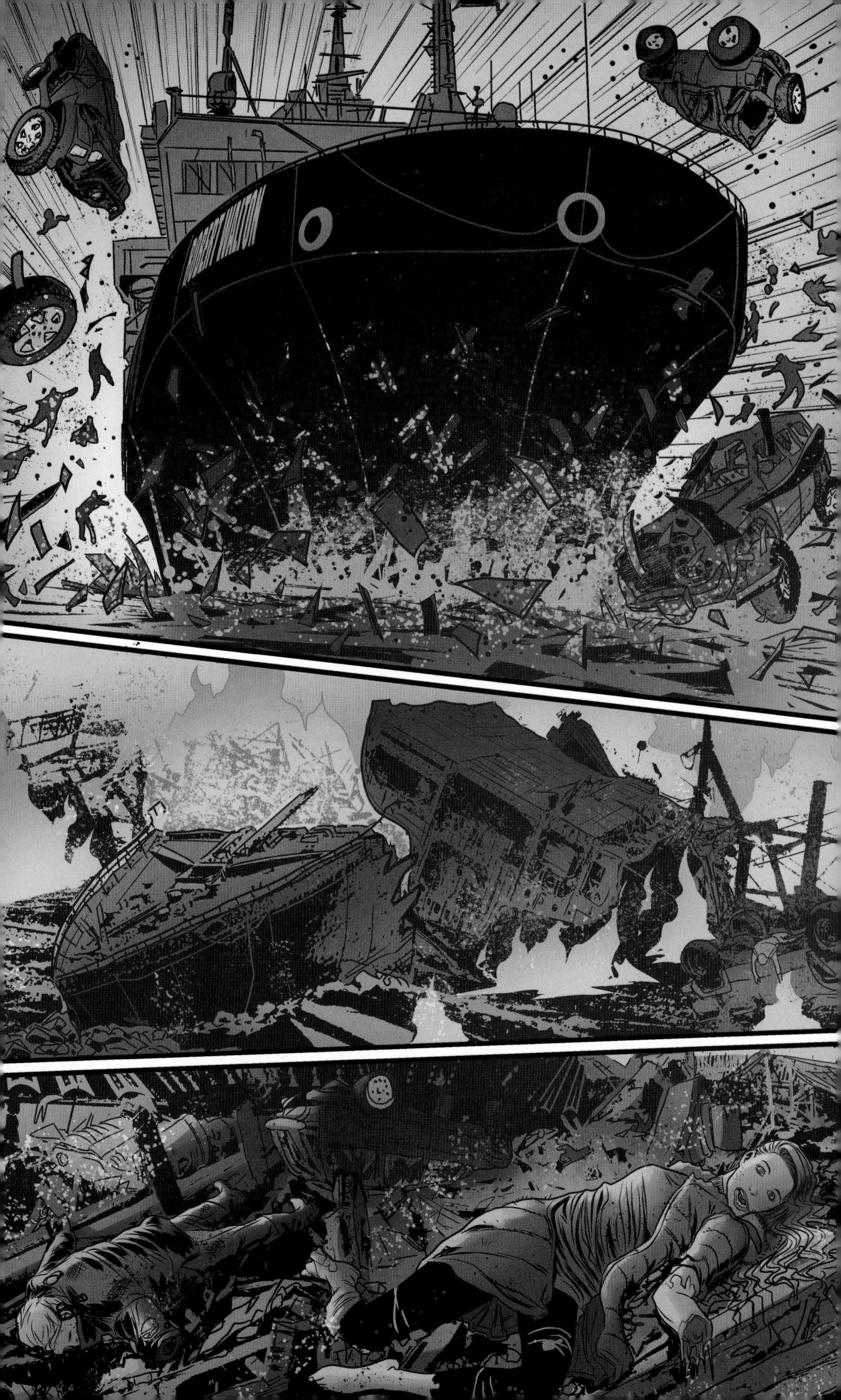

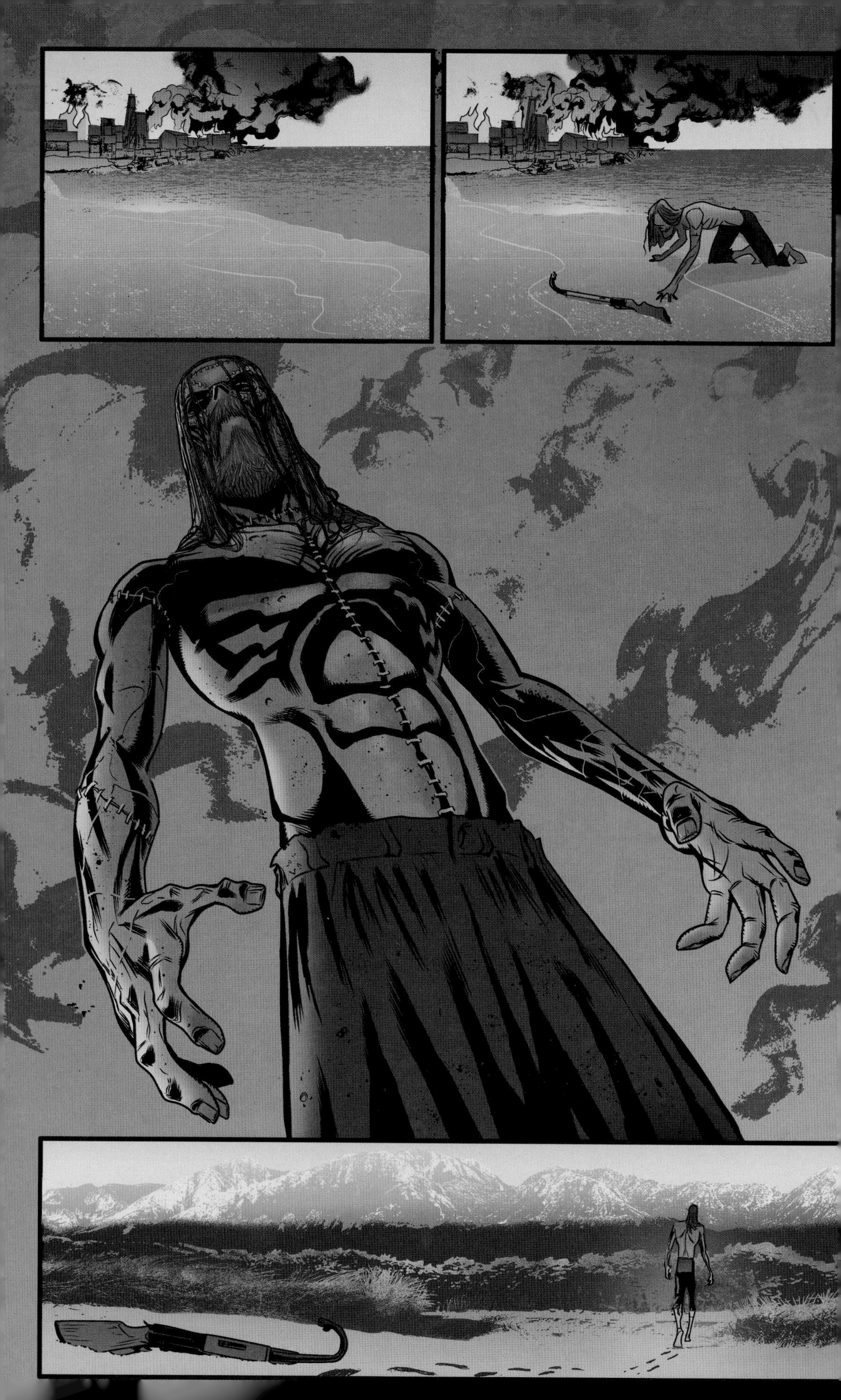

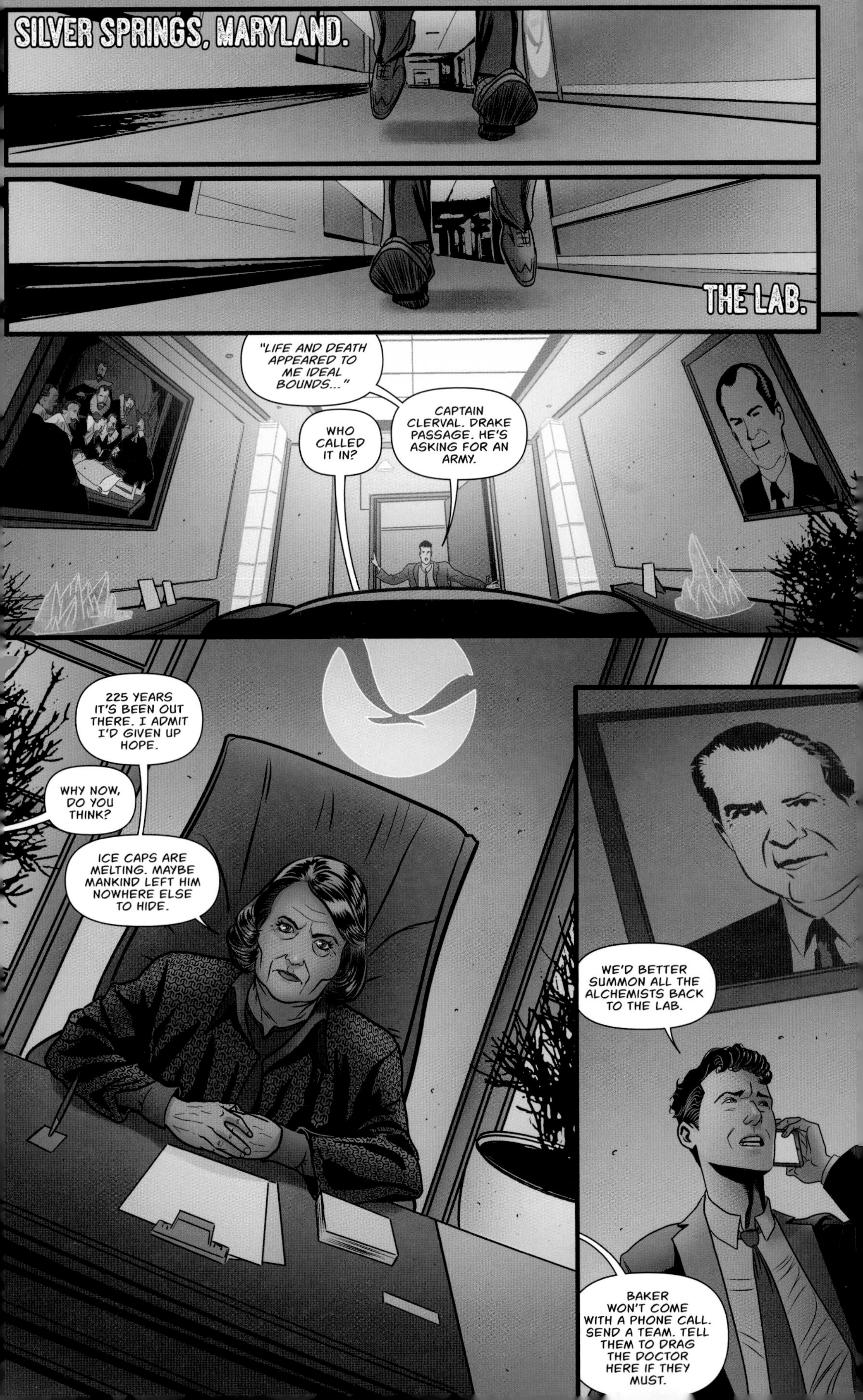
SILVER SPRINGS, MARYLAND.
THE LAB.
"LIFE AND DEATH APPEARED TO ME IDEAL BOUNDS..."
WHO CALLED IT IN?
CAPTAIN CLERVAL. DRAKE PASSAGE. HE'S ASKING FOR AN ARMY.
225 YEARS IT'S BEEN OUT THERE. I ADMIT I'D GIVEN UP HOPE.
WHY NOW, DO YOU THINK?
ICE CAPS ARE MELTING. MAYBE MANKIND LEFT HIM NOWHERE ELSE TO HIDE.
WE'D BETTER SUMMON ALL THE ALCHEMISTS BACK TO THE LAB.
BAKER WON'T COME WITH A PHONE CALL. SEND A TEAM. TELL THEM TO DRAG THE DOCTOR HERE IF THEY MUST.

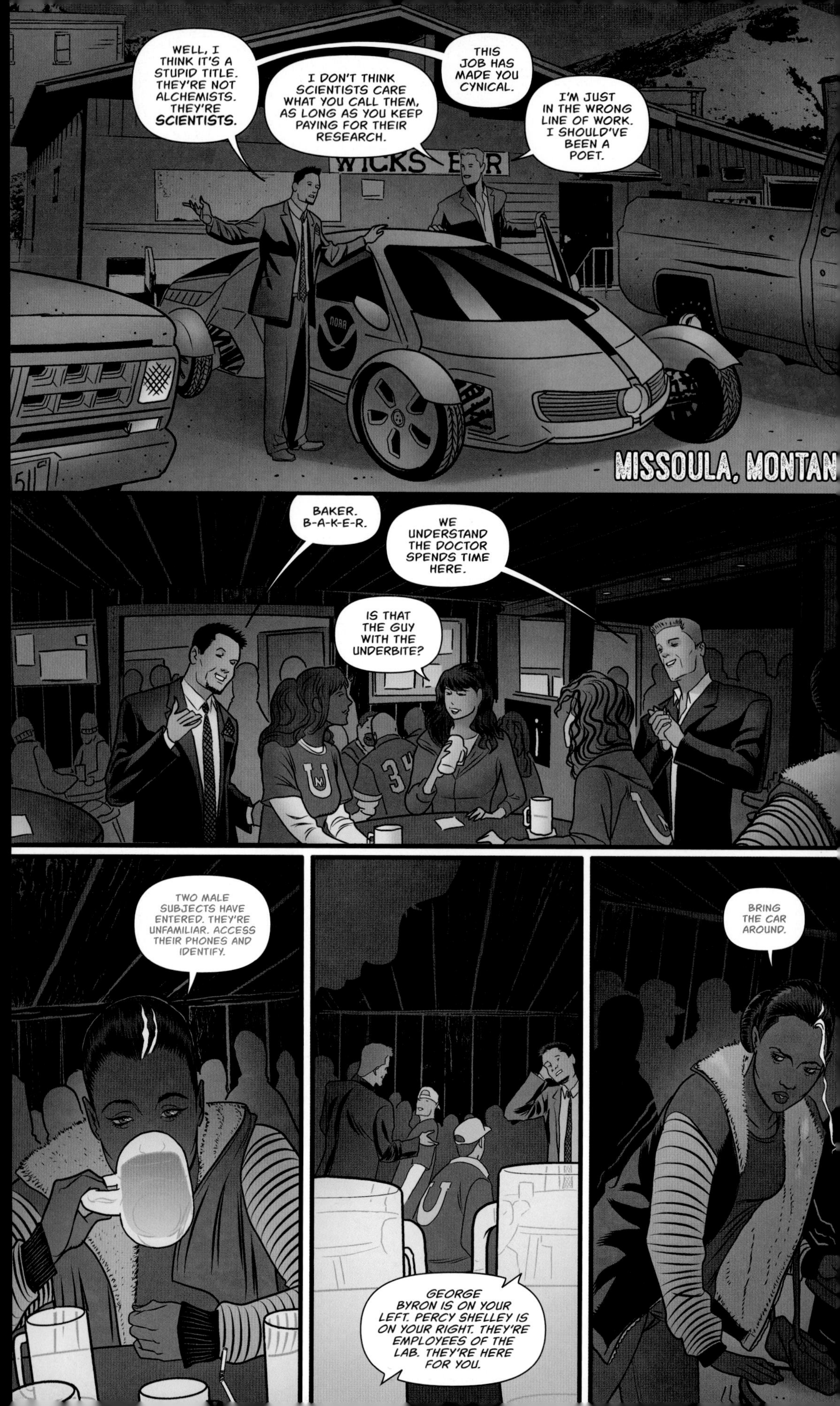
WELL, I THINK IT'S A STUPID TITLE. THEY'RE NOT ALCHEMISTS. THEY'RE SCIENTISTS.
I DON'T THINK SCIENTISTS CARE WHAT YOU CALL THEM, AS LONG AS YOU KEEP PAYING FOR THEIR RESEARCH.
THIS JOB HAS MADE YOU CYNICAL.
I'M JUST IN THE WRONG LINE OF WORK. I SHOULD'VE BEEN A POET.
MISSOULA, MONTAN
BAKER. B-A-K-E-R.
WE UNDERSTAND THE DOCTOR SPENDS TIME HERE.
IS THAT THE GUY WITH THE UNDERBITE?
TWO MALE SUBJECTS HAVE ENTERED. THEY'RE UNFAMILIAR. ACCESS THEIR PHONES AND IDENTIFY.
GEORGE BYRON IS ON YOUR LEFT. PERCY SHELLEY IS ON YOUR RIGHT. THEY'RE EMPLOYEES OF THE LAB. THEY'RE HERE FOR YOU.
BRING THE CAR AROUND.

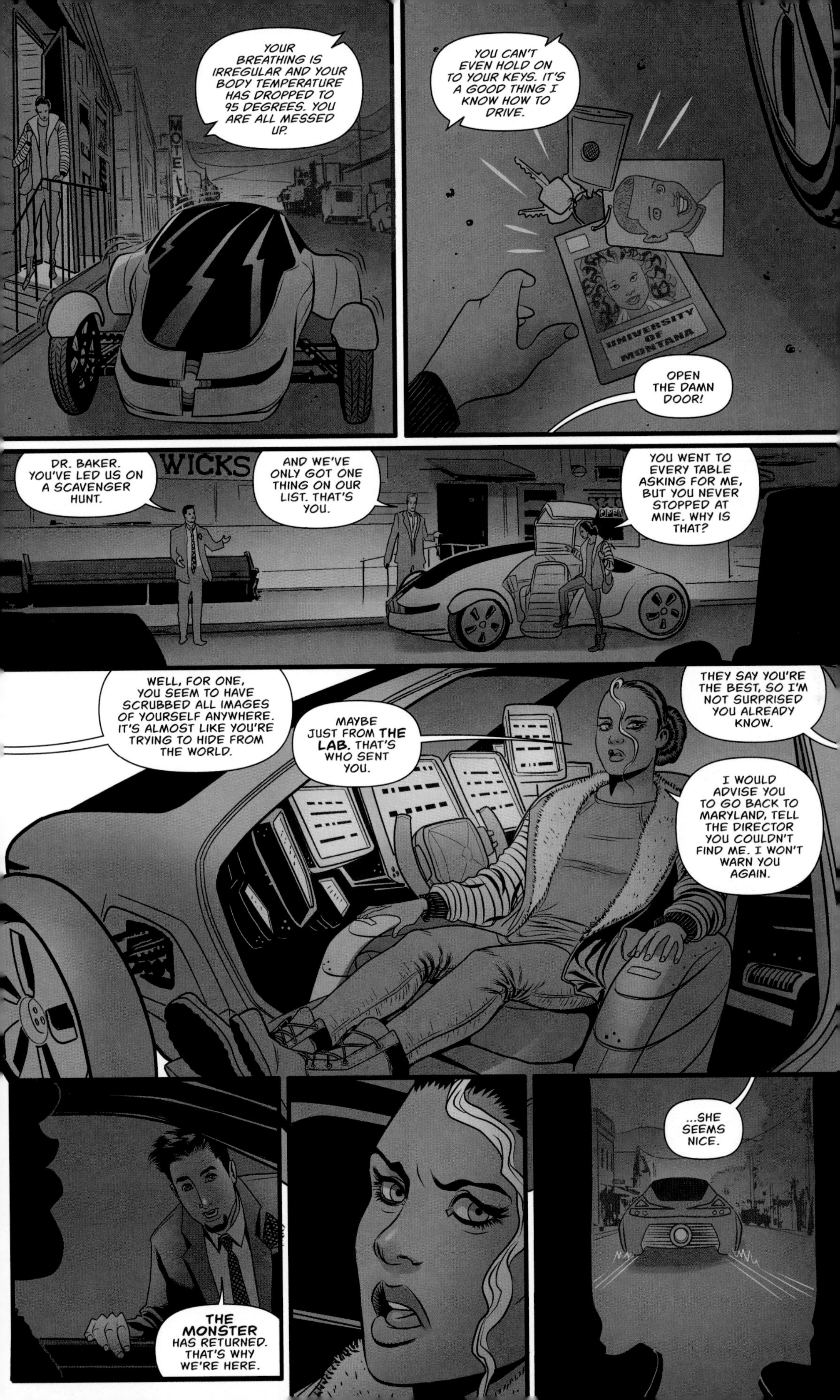

YOUR BREATHING IS IRREGULAR AND YOUR BODY TEMPERATURE HAS DROPPED TO 95 DEGREES. YOU ARE ALL MESSED UP.
MOTE
YOU CAN'T EVEN HOLD ON TO YOUR KEYS. IT'S A GOOD THING I KNOW HOW TO DRIVE.
UNIVERSITY OF MONTANA
OPEN THE DAMN DOOR!
WICKS
DR. BAKER. YOU'VE LED US ON A SCAVENGER HUNT.
AND WE'VE ONLY GOT ONE THING ON OUR LIST. THAT'S YOU.
YOU WENT TO EVERY TABLE ASKING FOR ME, BUT YOU NEVER STOPPED AT MINE. WHY IS THAT?
OPEN
WELL, FOR ONE, YOU SEEM TO HAVE SCRUBBED ALL IMAGES OF YOURSELF ANYWHERE. IT'S ALMOST LIKE YOU'RE TRYING TO HIDE FROM THE WORLD.
MAYBE JUST FROM THE LAB. THAT'S WHO SENT YOU.
THEY SAY YOU'RE THE BEST, SO I'M NOT SURPRISED YOU ALREADY KNOW.
I WOULD ADVISE YOU TO GO BACK TO MARYLAND, TELL THE DIRECTOR YOU COULDN'T FIND ME. I WON'T WARN YOU AGAIN.
THE MONSTER HAS RETURNED. THAT'S WHY WE'RE HERE.
...SHE SEEMS NICE.

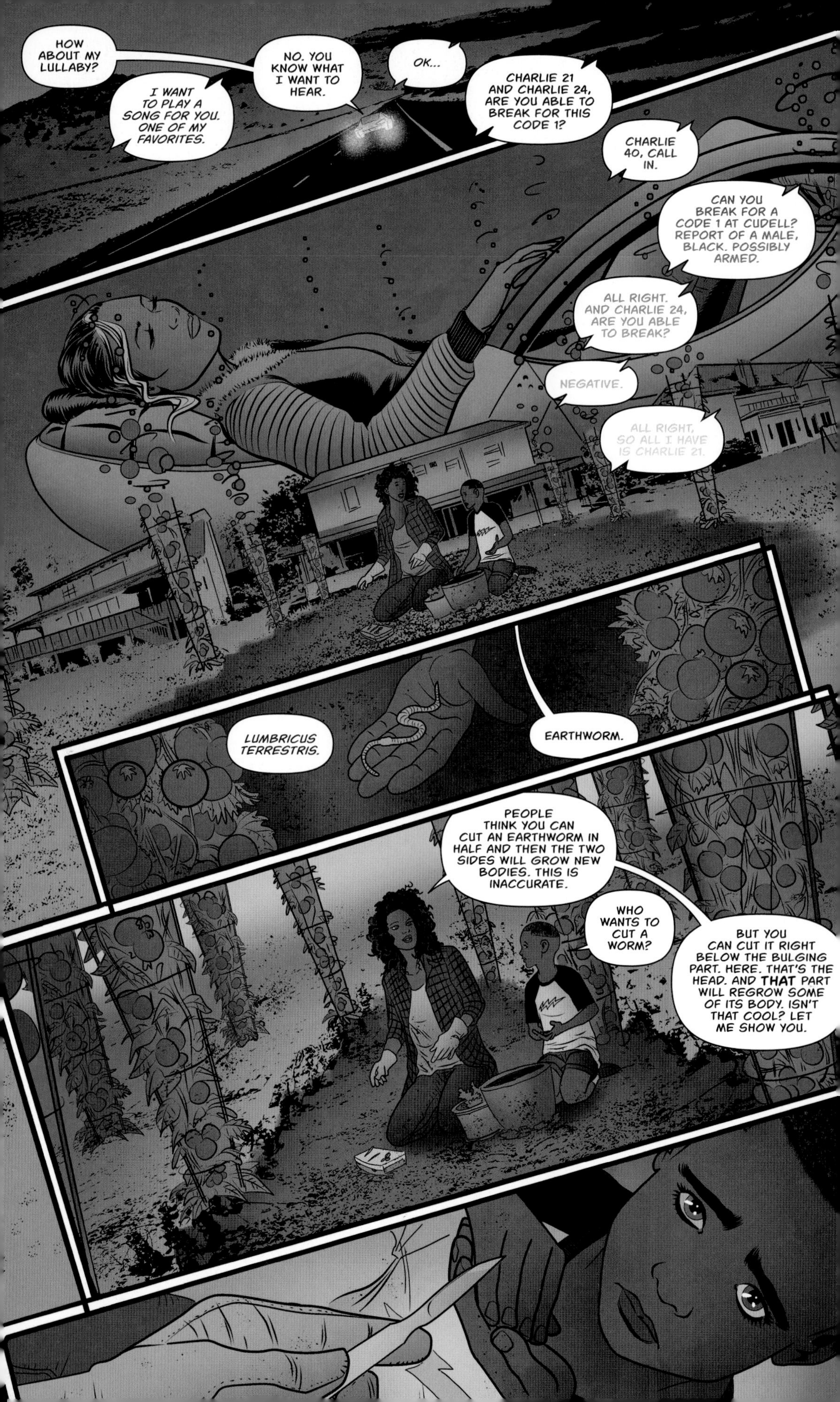
HOW ABOUT MY LULLABY?
I WANT TO PLAY A SONG FOR YOU. ONE OF MY FAVORITES.
NO. YOU KNOW WHAT I WANT TO HEAR.
OK...
CHARLIE 21 AND CHARLIE 24, ARE YOU ABLE TO BREAK FOR THIS CODE 1?
CHARLIE 40, CALL IN.
CAN YOU BREAK FOR A CODE 1 AT CUDELL? REPORT OF A MALE, BLACK. POSSIBLY ARMED.
ALL RIGHT. AND CHARLIE 24, ARE YOU ABLE TO BREAK?
NEGATIVE.
ALL RIGHT, SO ALL I HAVE IS CHARLIE 21.
LUMBRICUS TERRESTRIS.
EARTHWORM.
PEOPLE THINK YOU CAN CUT AN EARTHWORM IN HALF AND THEN THE TWO SIDES WILL GROW NEW BODIES. THIS IS INACCURATE.
WHO WANTS TO CUT A WORM?
BUT YOU CAN CUT IT RIGHT BELOW THE BULGING PART. HERE. THAT'S THE HEAD. AND THAT PART WILL REGROW SOME OF ITS BODY. ISN'T THAT COOL? LET ME SHOW YOU.

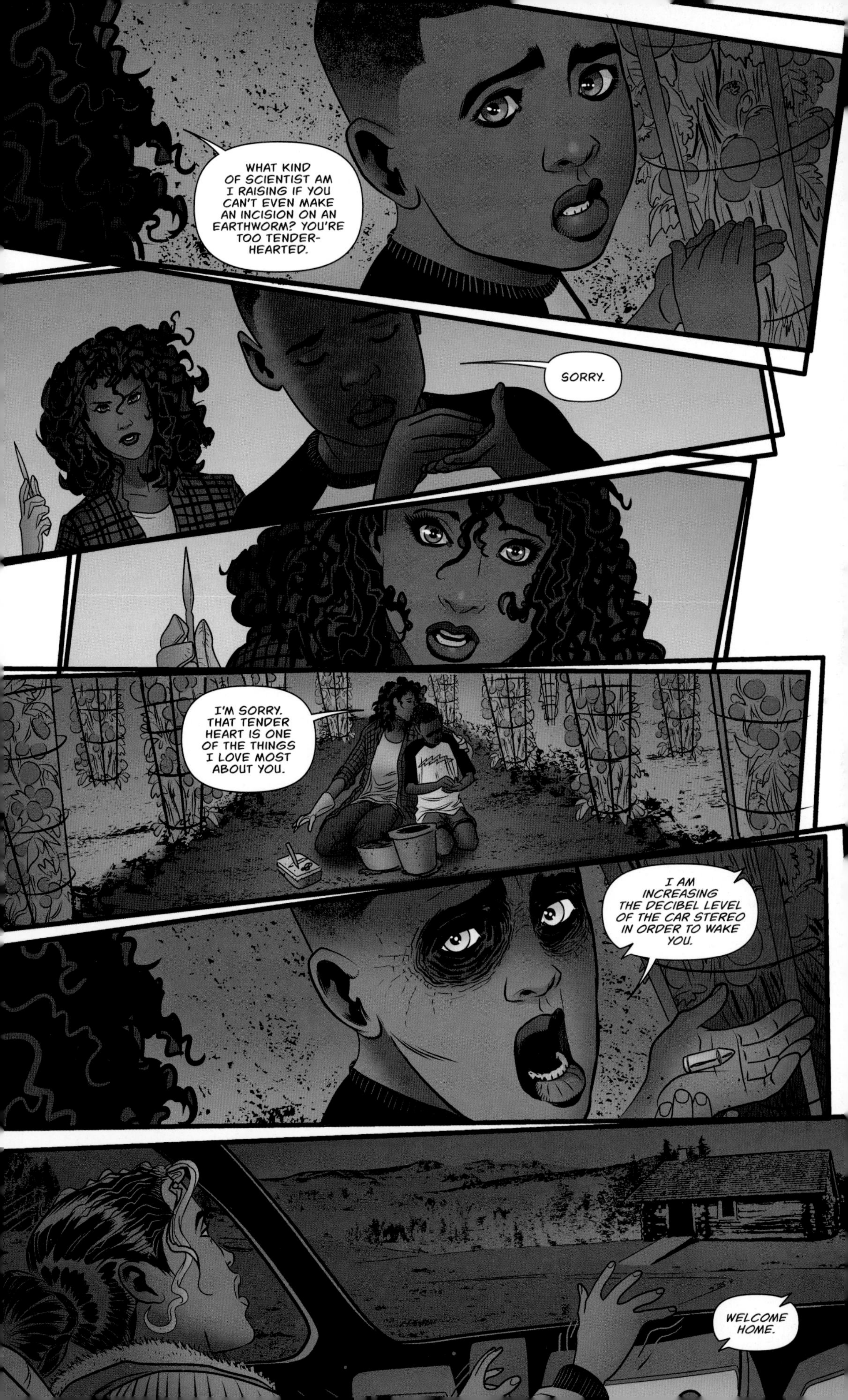
WHAT KIND OF SCIENTIST AM I RAISING IF YOU CAN'T EVEN MAKE AN INCISION ON AN EARTHWORM? YOU'RE TOO TENDER-HEARTED.
SORRY.
I'M SORRY. THAT TENDER HEART IS ONE OF THE THINGS I LOVE MOST ABOUT YOU.
I AM INCREASING THE DECIBEL LEVEL OF THE CAR STEREO IN ORDER TO WAKE YOU.
WELCOME HOME.

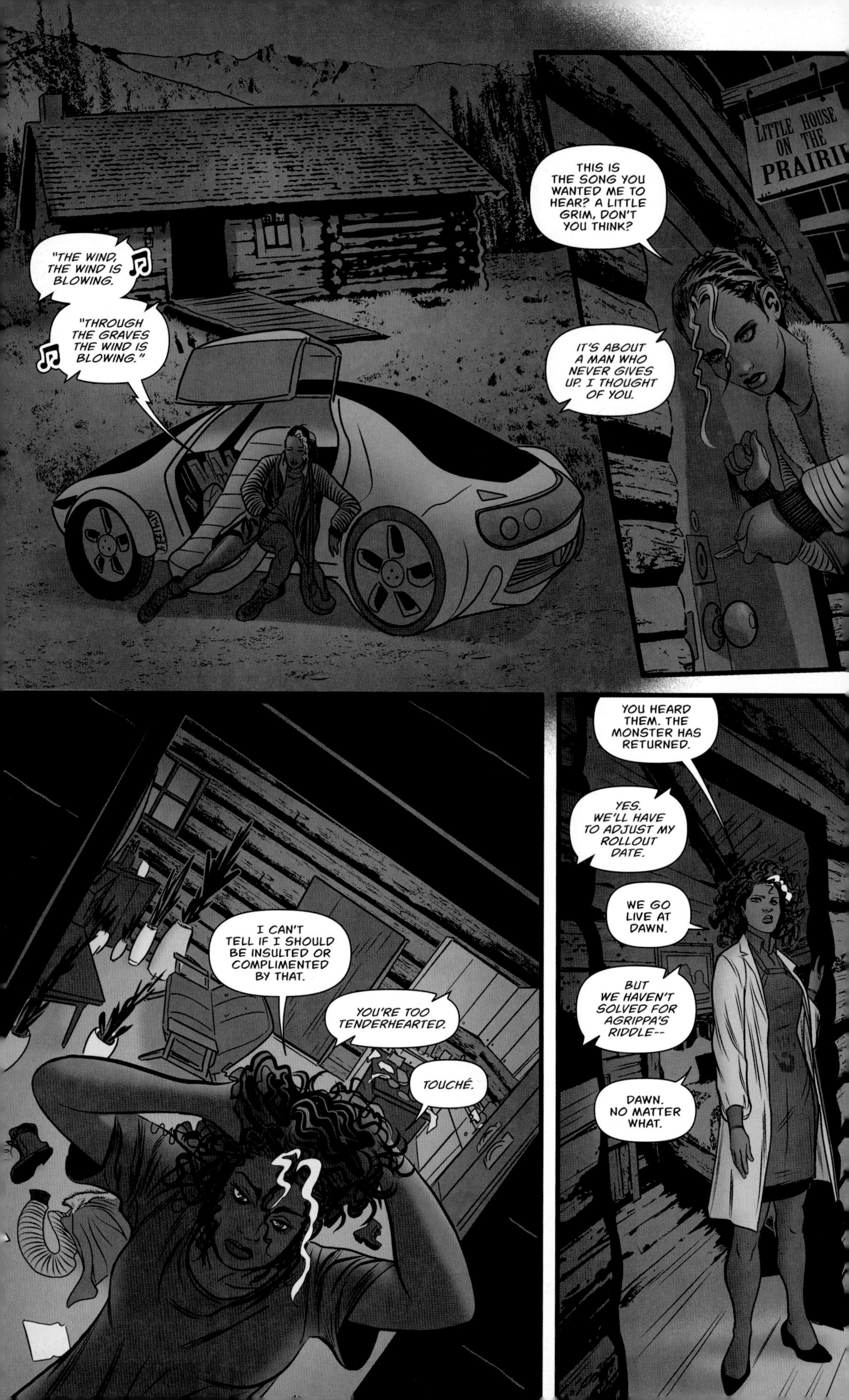
LITTLE HOUSE ON THE PRAIRIE
"THE WIND, THE WIND IS BLOWING.
"THROUGH THE GRAVES THE WIND IS BLOWING."
THIS IS THE SONG YOU WANTED ME TO HEAR? A LITTLE GRIM, DON'T YOU THINK?
IT'S ABOUT A MAN WHO NEVER GIVES UP. I THOUGHT OF YOU.
I CAN'T TELL IF I SHOULD BE INSULTED OR COMPLIMENTED BY THAT.
YOU'RE TOO TENDERHEARTED.
TOUCHÉ.
YOU HEARD THEM. THE MONSTER HAS RETURNED.
YES. WE'LL HAVE TO ADJUST MY ROLLOUT DATE.
WE GO LIVE AT DAWN.
BUT WE HAVEN'T SOLVED FOR AGRIPPA'S RIDDLE--
DAWN. NO MATTER WHAT.

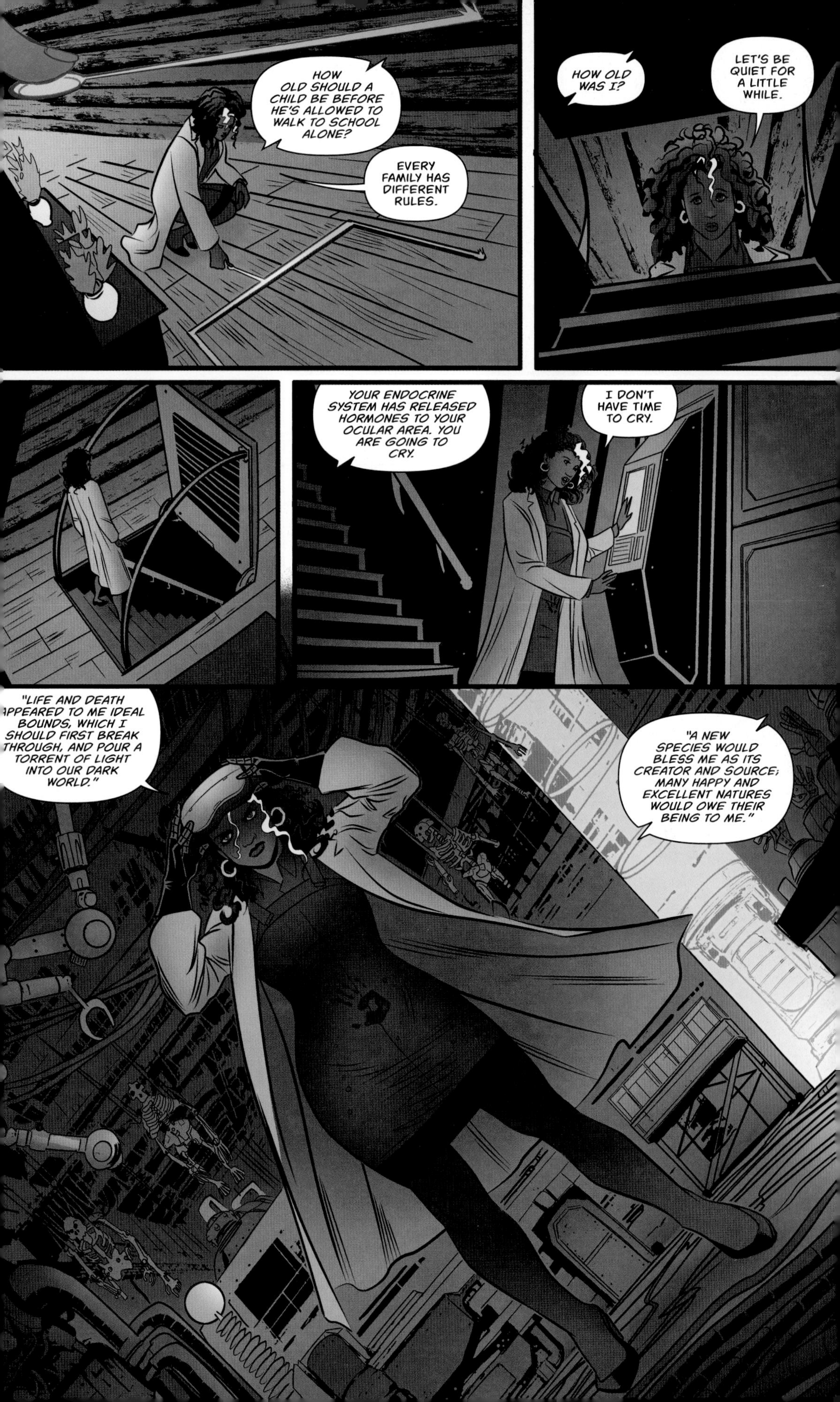
HOW OLD SHOULD A CHILD BE BEFORE HE'S ALLOWED TO WALK TO SCHOOL ALONE?
EVERY FAMILY HAS DIFFERENT RULES.
HOW OLD WAS I?
LET'S BE QUIET FOR A LITTLE WHILE.
YOUR ENDOCRINE SYSTEM HAS RELEASED HORMONES TO YOUR OCULAR AREA. YOU ARE GOING TO CRY.
I DON'T HAVE TIME TO CRY.
"LIFE AND DEATH APPEARED TO ME IDEAL BOUNDS, WHICH I SHOULD FIRST BREAK THROUGH, AND POUR A TORRENT OF LIGHT INTO OUR DARK WORLD."
"A NEW SPECIES WOULD BLESS ME AS ITS CREATOR AND SOURCE; MANY HAPPY AND EXCELLENT NATURES WOULD OWE THEIR BEING TO ME."

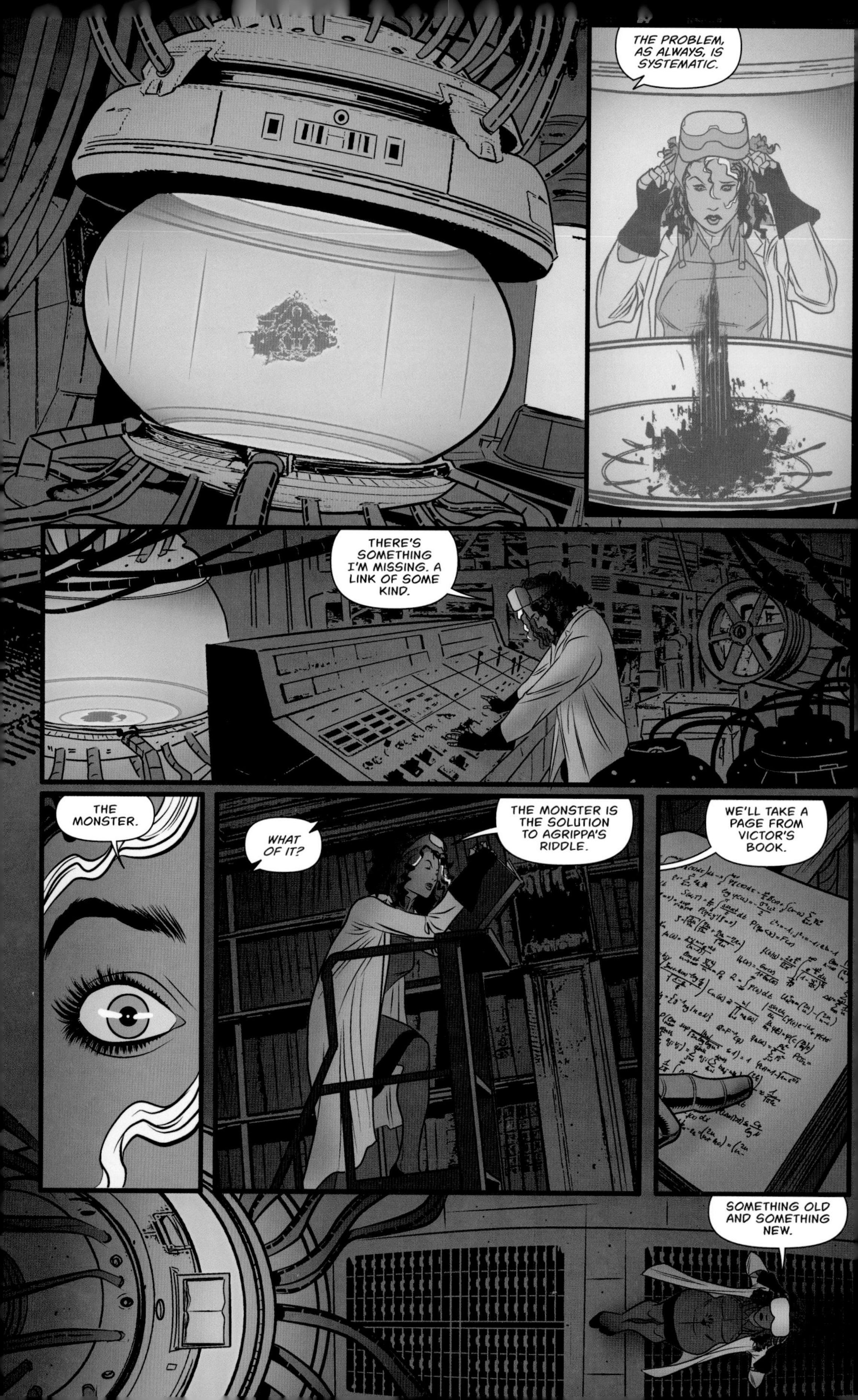
THE PROBLEM, AS ALWAYS, IS SYSTEMATIC.
THERE'S SOMETHING I'M MISSING. A LINK OF SOME KIND.
THE MONSTER.
WHAT OF IT?
THE MONSTER IS THE SOLUTION TO AGRIPPA'S RIDDLE.
WE'LL TAKE A PAGE FROM VICTOR'S BOOK.
SOMETHING OLD AND SOMETHING NEW.

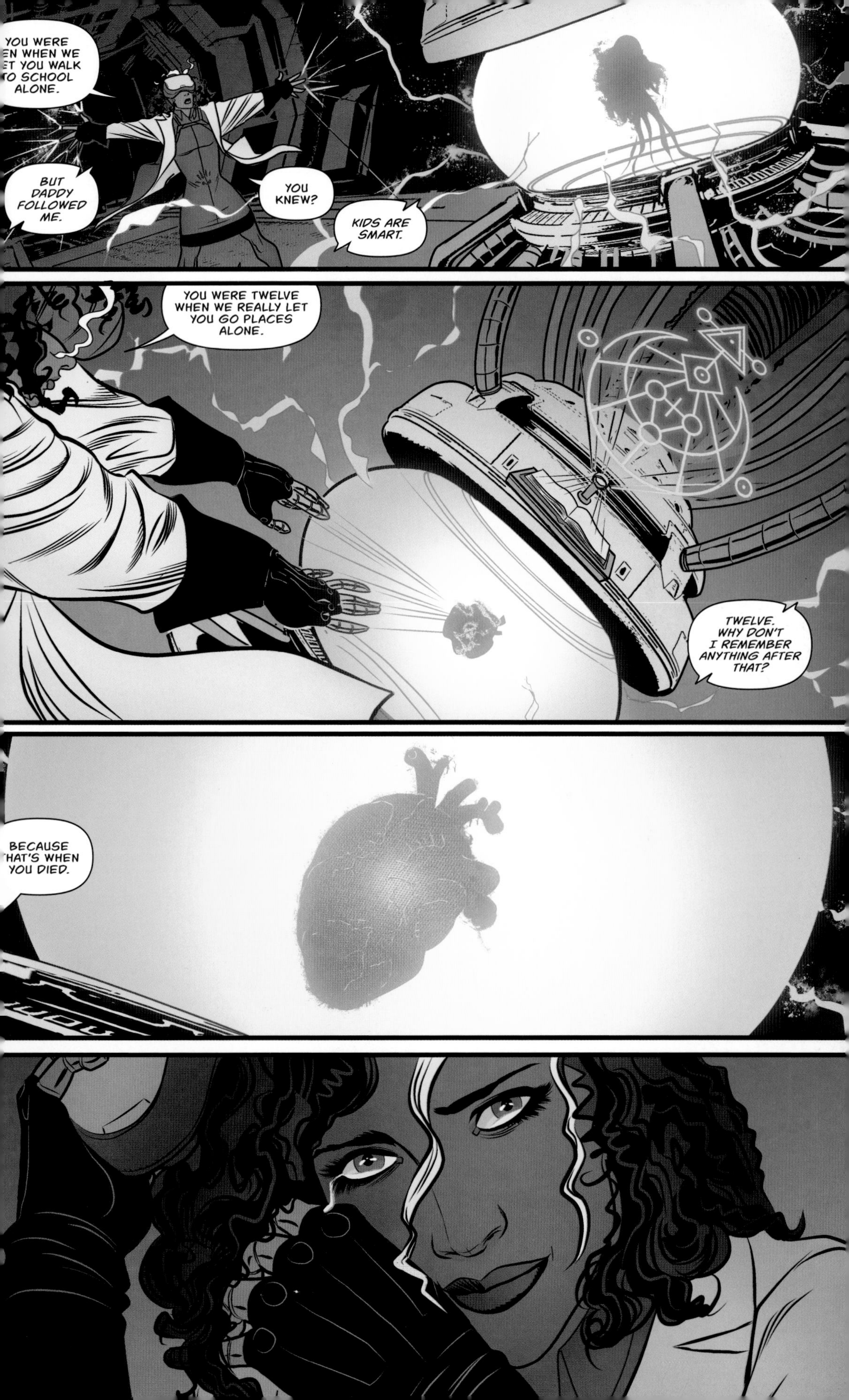
YOU WERE EN WHEN WE ET YOU WALK O SCHOOL ALONE.
BUT DADDY FOLLOWED ME.
YOU KNEW?
KIDS ARE SMART.
YOU WERE TWELVE WHEN WE REALLY LET YOU GO PLACES ALONE.
TWELVE. WHY DON'T I REMEMBER ANYTHING AFTER THAT?
BECAUSE HAT'S WHEN YOU DIED.

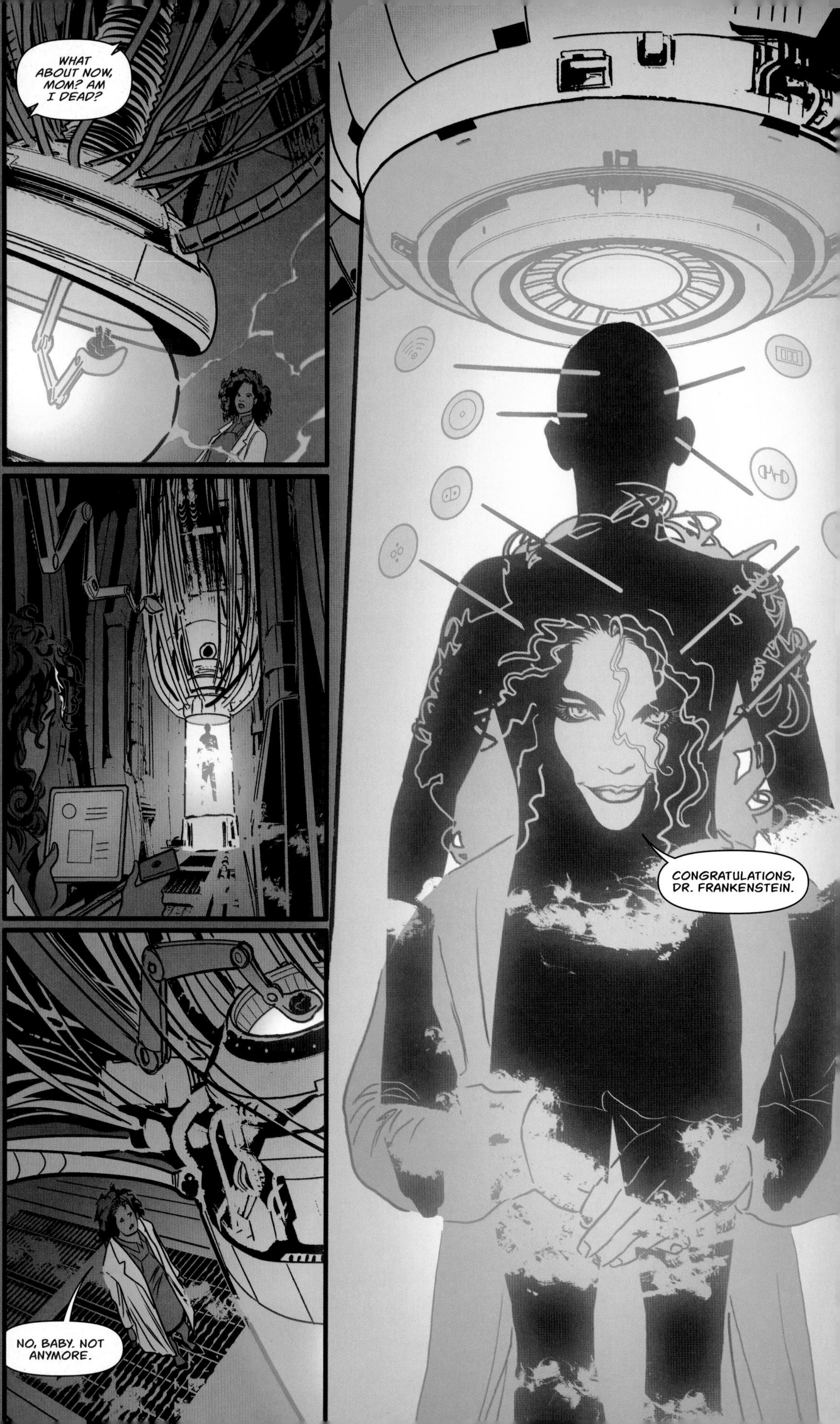
WHAT ABOUT NOW, MOM? AM I DEAD?
NO, BABY. NOT ANYMORE.
CONGRATULATIONS, DR. FRANKENSTEIN.

- This creature is not bad as Frankenstein's creature wasn't not just wants the whales protected.
- No one understands him
- One woman on the ship wanted to help him but the ship crashed + everyone died.
- Dr. Baker seems to be scarred when she hears the monster is back.
- How is she talking to her son if he died?
- Did she make the monster to replace him?

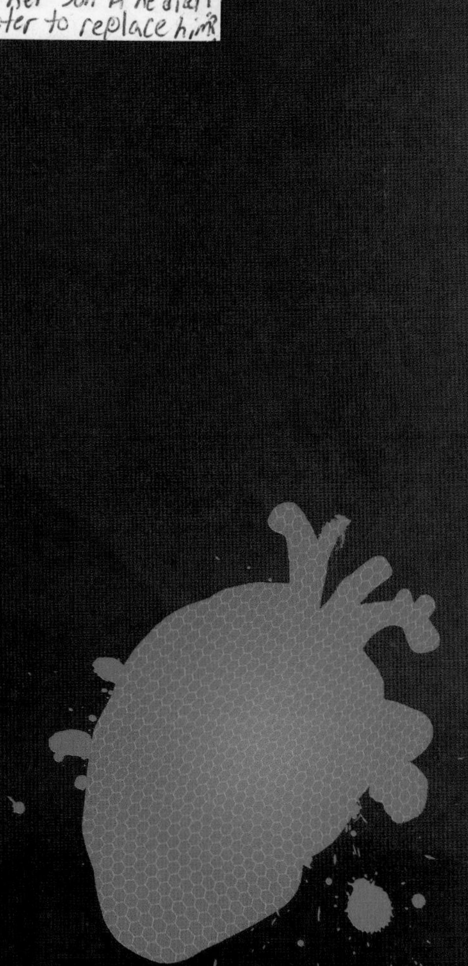

CHAPTER
TWO

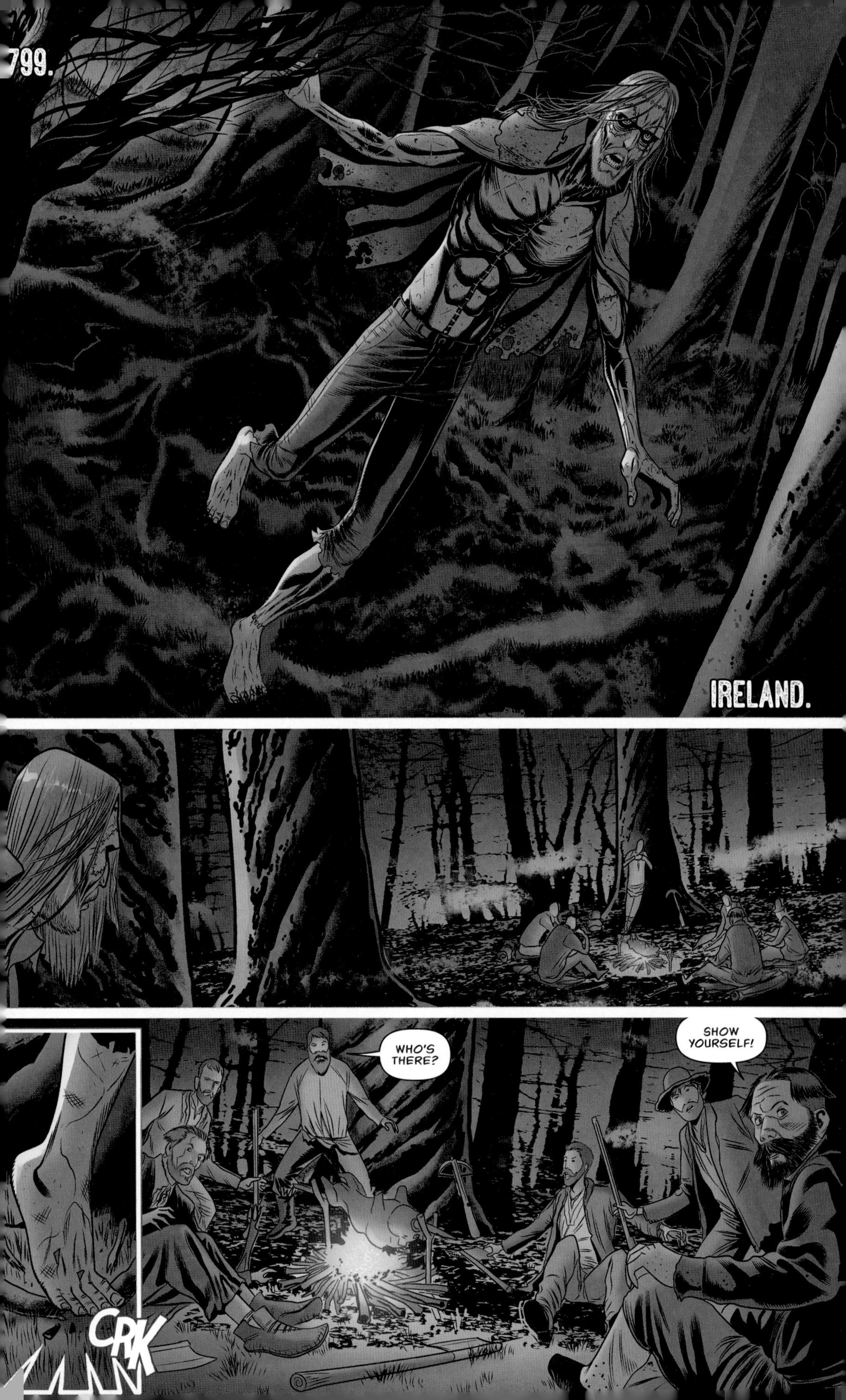
1799.
IRELAND.
WHO'S THERE?
SHOW YOURSELF!
CRK

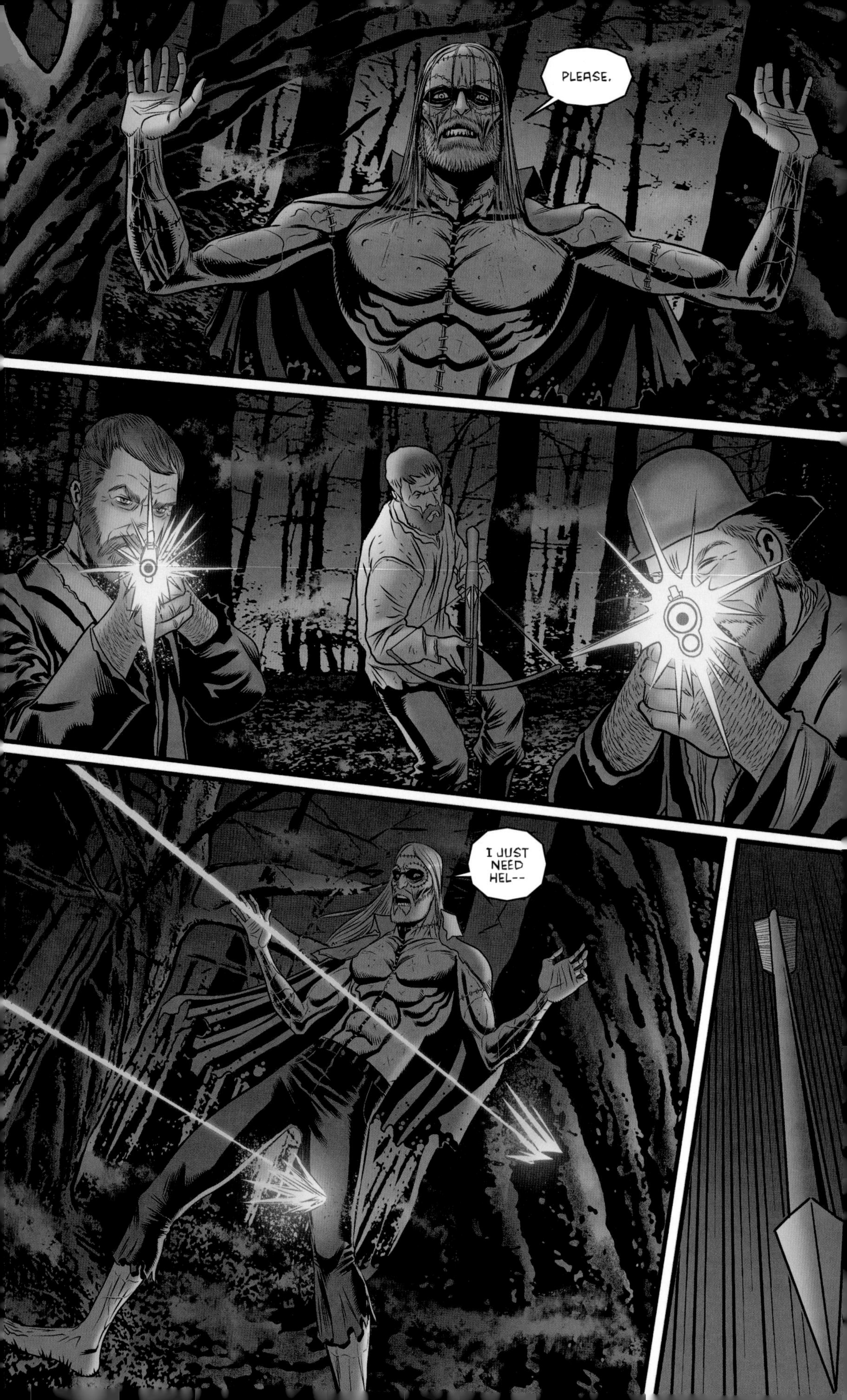
PLEASE.
I JUST NEED HEL--

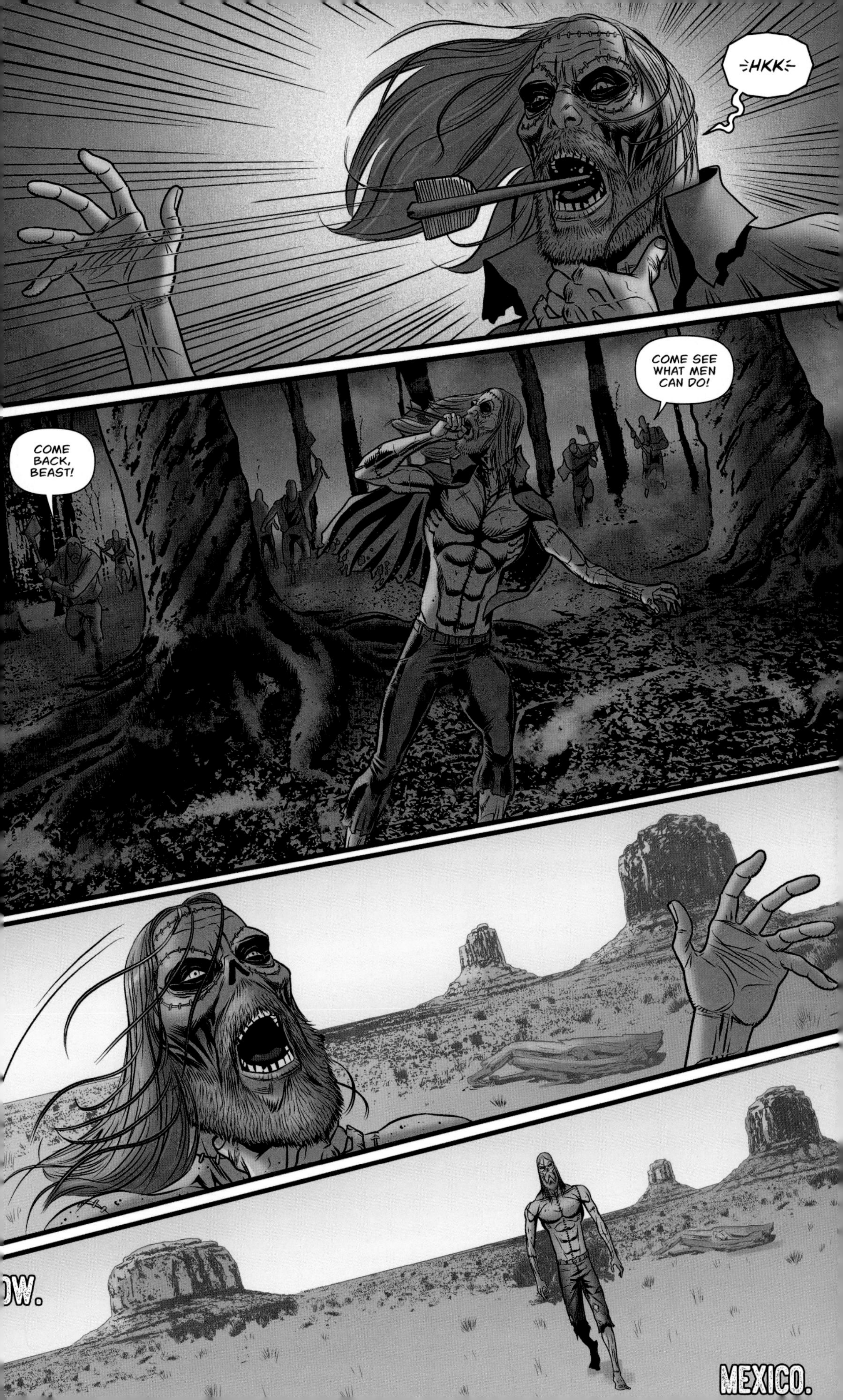
HKK
COME BACK, BEAST!
COME SEE WHAT MEN CAN DO!
...OW.
MEXICO.

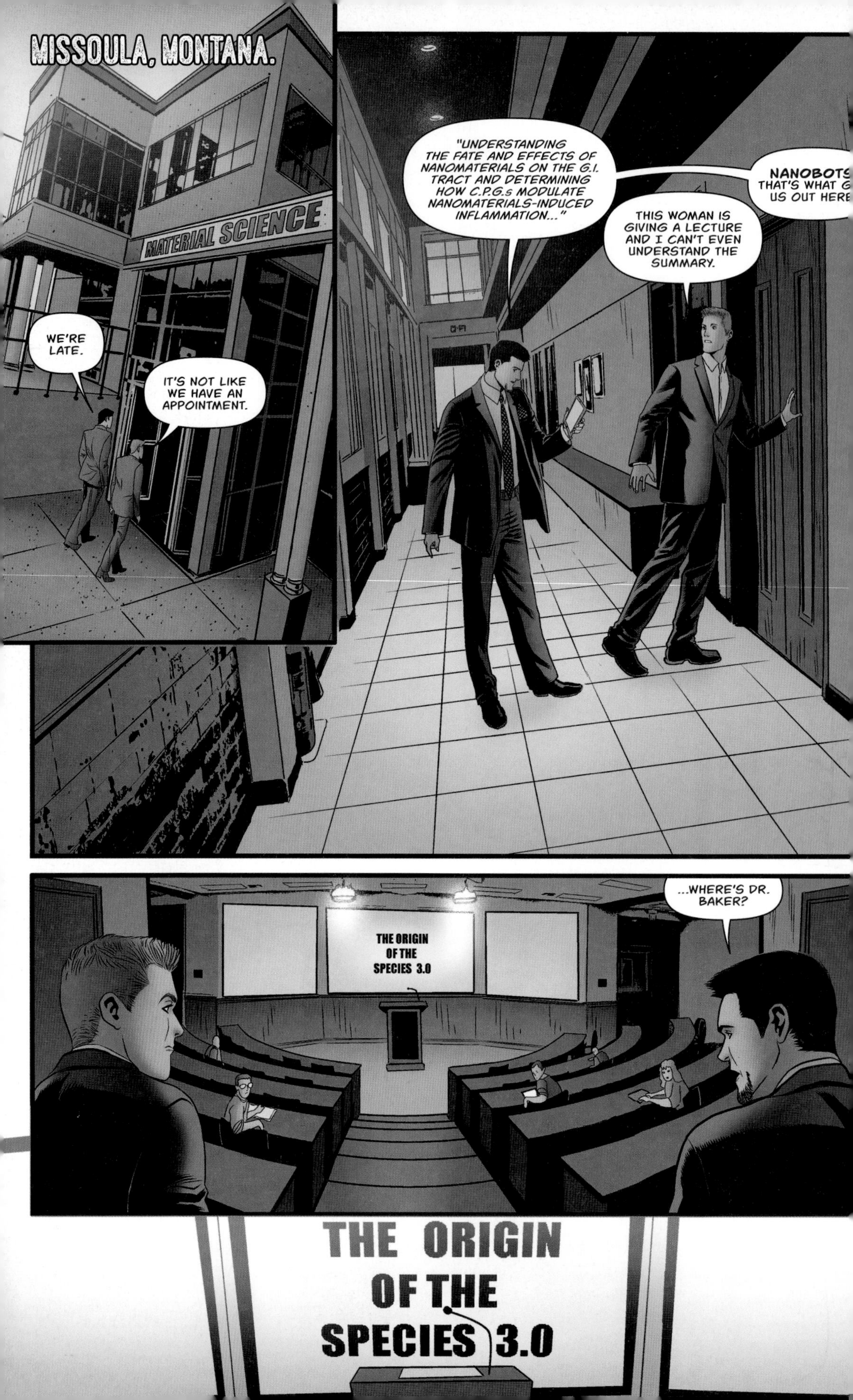
MISSOULA, MONTANA.
MATERIAL SCIENCE
WE'RE LATE.
IT'S NOT LIKE WE HAVE AN APPOINTMENT.
"UNDERSTANDING THE FATE AND EFFECTS OF NANOMATERIALS ON THE G.I. TRACT AND DETERMINING HOW C.P.G.s MODULATE NANOMATERIALS-INDUCED INFLAMMATION..."
THIS WOMAN IS GIVING A LECTURE AND I CAN'T EVEN UNDERSTAND THE SUMMARY.
THE ORIGIN OF THE SPECIES 3.0
...WHERE'S DR. BAKER?
THE ORIGIN OF THE SPECIES 3.0

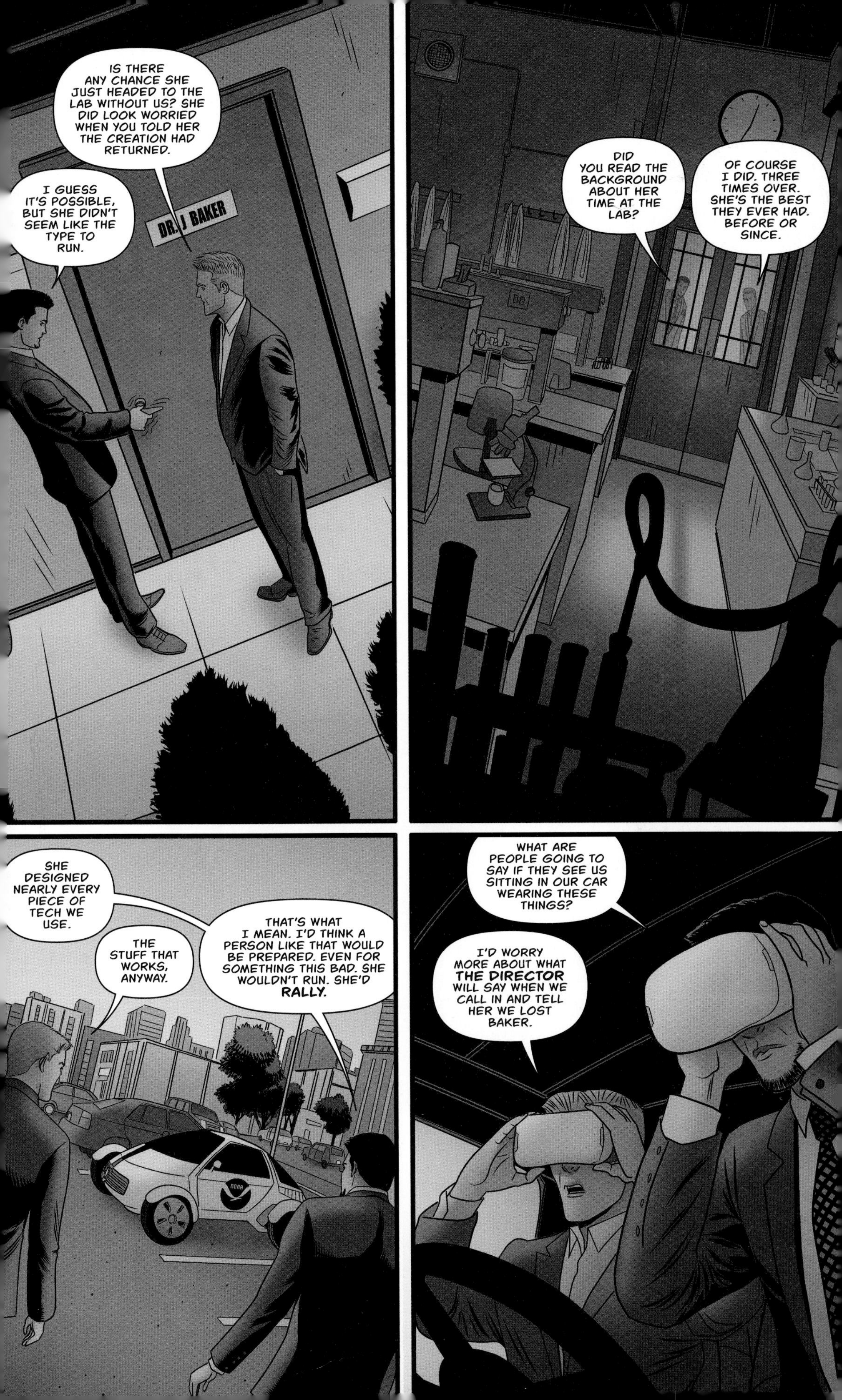
IS THERE ANY CHANCE SHE JUST HEADED TO THE LAB WITHOUT US? SHE DID LOOK WORRIED WHEN YOU TOLD HER THE CREATION HAD RETURNED.
I GUESS IT'S POSSIBLE, BUT SHE DIDN'T SEEM LIKE THE TYPE TO RUN.
DR. J BAKER
DID YOU READ THE BACKGROUND ABOUT HER TIME AT THE LAB?
OF COURSE I DID. THREE TIMES OVER. SHE'S THE BEST THEY EVER HAD. BEFORE OR SINCE.
SHE DESIGNED NEARLY EVERY PIECE OF TECH WE USE.
THE STUFF THAT WORKS, ANYWAY.
THAT'S WHAT I MEAN. I'D THINK A PERSON LIKE THAT WOULD BE PREPARED. EVEN FOR SOMETHING THIS BAD. SHE WOULDN'T RUN. SHE'D RALLY.
NOAA
WHAT ARE PEOPLE GOING TO SAY IF THEY SEE US SITTING IN OUR CAR WEARING THESE THINGS?
I'D WORRY MORE ABOUT WHAT THE DIRECTOR WILL SAY WHEN WE CALL IN AND TELL HER WE LOST BAKER.

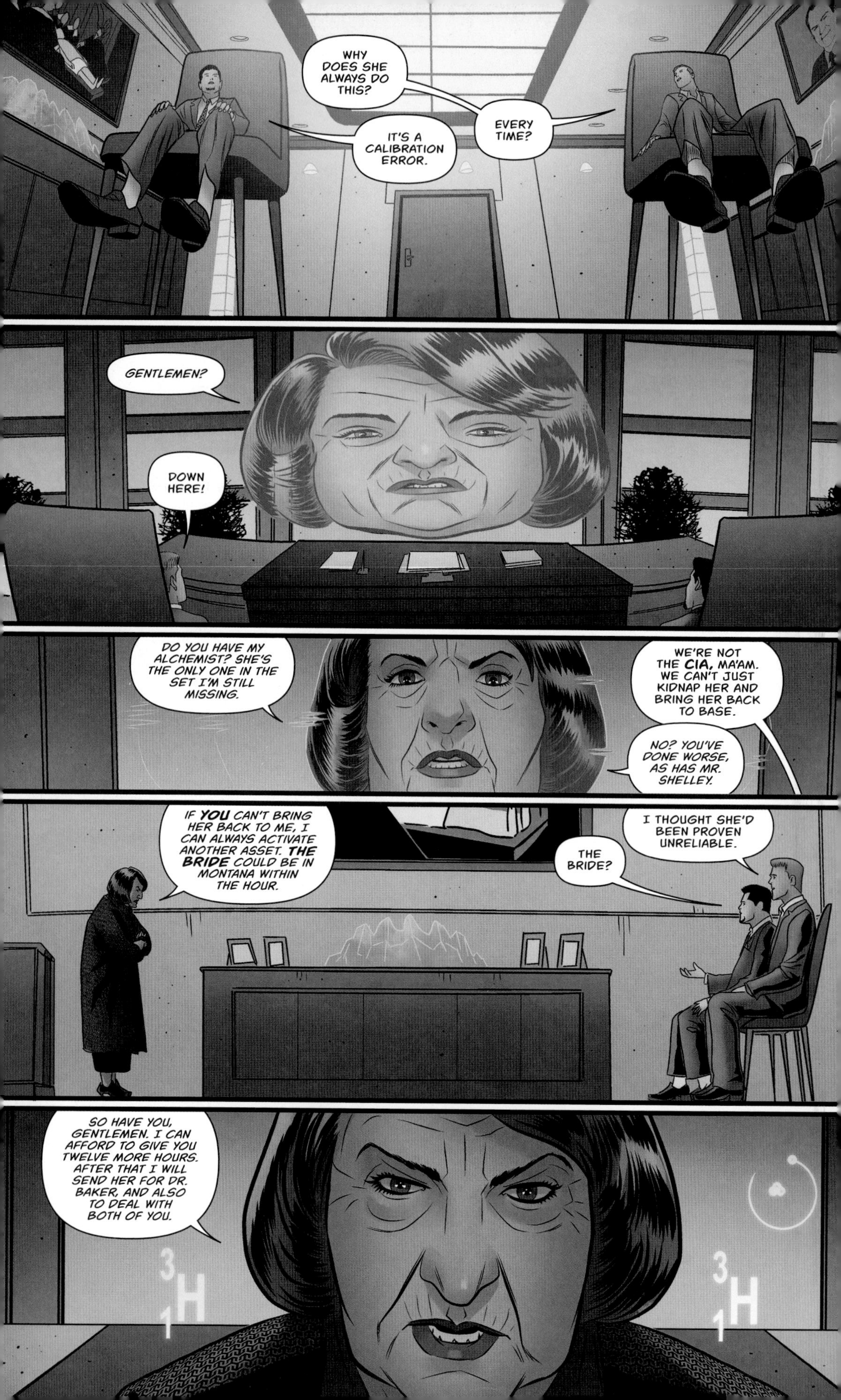
WHY DOES SHE ALWAYS DO THIS?
EVERY TIME?
IT'S A CALIBRATION ERROR.
GENTLEMEN?
DOWN HERE!
DO YOU HAVE MY ALCHEMIST? SHE'S THE ONLY ONE IN THE SET I'M STILL MISSING.
WE'RE NOT THE CIA, MA'AM. WE CAN'T JUST KIDNAP HER AND BRING HER BACK TO BASE.
NO? YOU'VE DONE WORSE, AS HAS MR. SHELLEY.
IF YOU CAN'T BRING HER BACK TO ME, I CAN ALWAYS ACTIVATE ANOTHER ASSET. THE BRIDE COULD BE IN MONTANA WITHIN THE HOUR.
THE BRIDE?
I THOUGHT SHE'D BEEN PROVEN UNRELIABLE.
SO HAVE YOU, GENTLEMEN. I CAN AFFORD TO GIVE YOU TWELVE MORE HOURS. AFTER THAT I WILL SEND HER FOR DR. BAKER, AND ALSO TO DEAL WITH BOTH OF YOU.
3 1 H
3 1 H

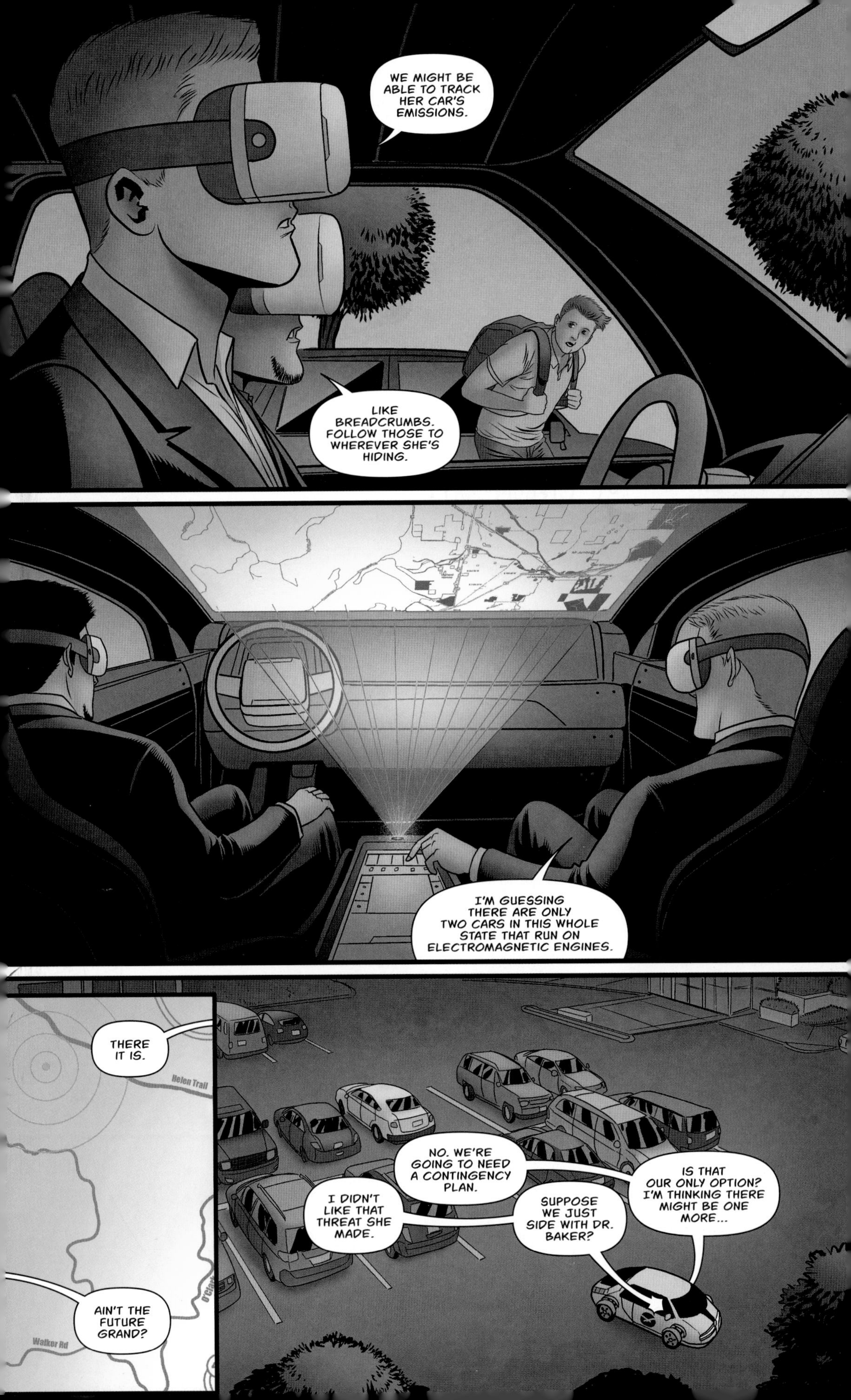
WE MIGHT BE ABLE TO TRACK HER CAR'S EMISSIONS.
LIKE BREADCRUMBS. FOLLOW THOSE TO WHEREVER SHE'S HIDING.
I'M GUESSING THERE ARE ONLY TWO CARS IN THIS WHOLE STATE THAT RUN ON ELECTROMAGNETIC ENGINES.
THERE IT IS.
Helen Trail
AIN'T THE FUTURE GRAND?
Walker Rd
I DIDN'T LIKE THAT THREAT SHE MADE.
NO. WE'RE GOING TO NEED A CONTINGENCY PLAN.
SUPPOSE WE JUST SIDE WITH DR. BAKER?
IS THAT OUR ONLY OPTION? I'M THINKING THERE MIGHT BE ONE MORE...

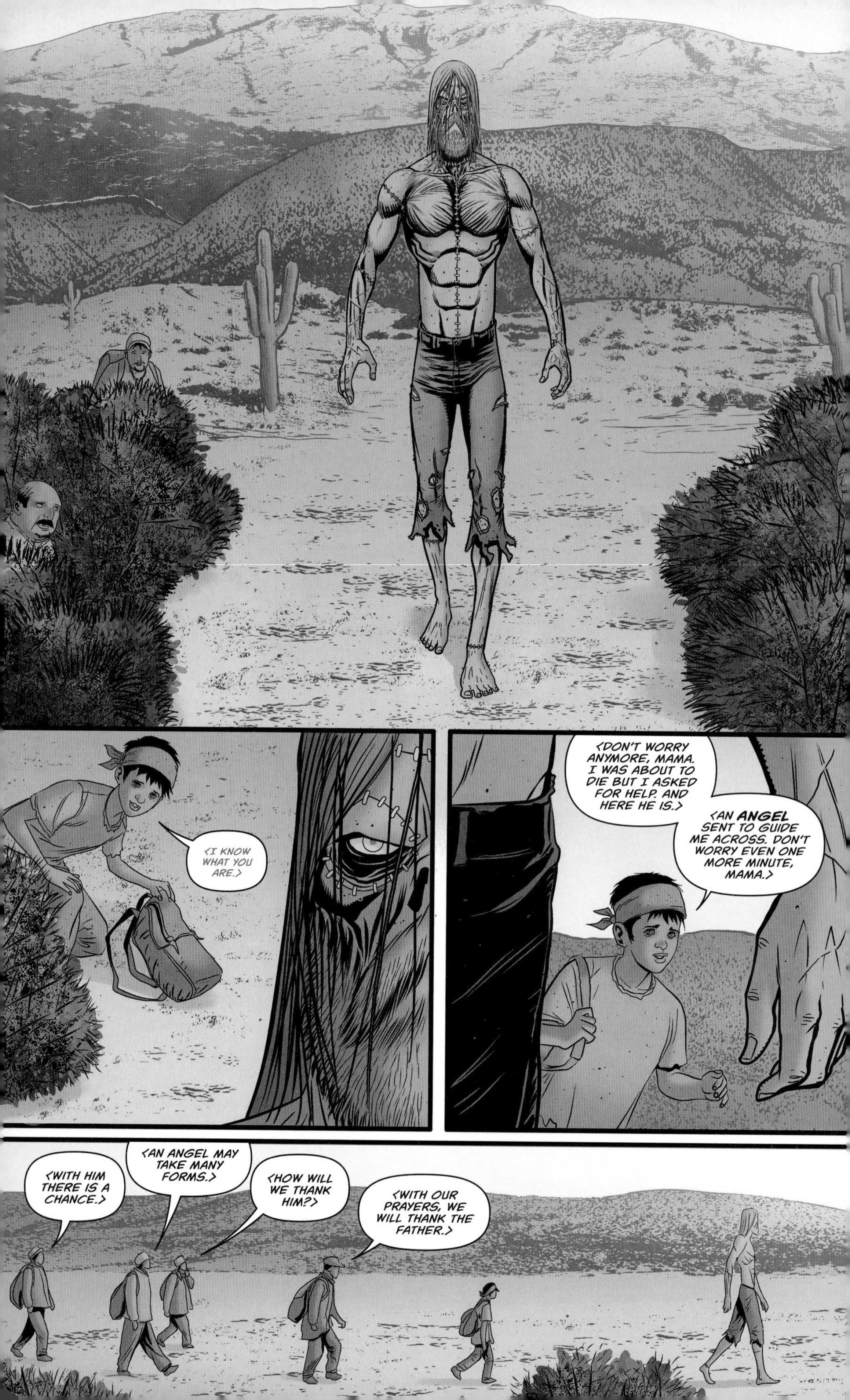
<I KNOW WHAT YOU ARE.>
<DON'T WORRY ANYMORE, MAMA. I WAS ABOUT TO DIE BUT I ASKED FOR HELP. AND HERE HE IS.>
<AN ANGEL SENT TO GUIDE ME ACROSS. DON'T WORRY EVEN ONE MORE MINUTE, MAMA.>
<WITH HIM THERE IS A CHANCE.>
<AN ANGEL MAY TAKE MANY FORMS.>
<HOW WILL WE THANK HIM?>
<WITH OUR PRAYERS, WE WILL THANK THE FATHER.>

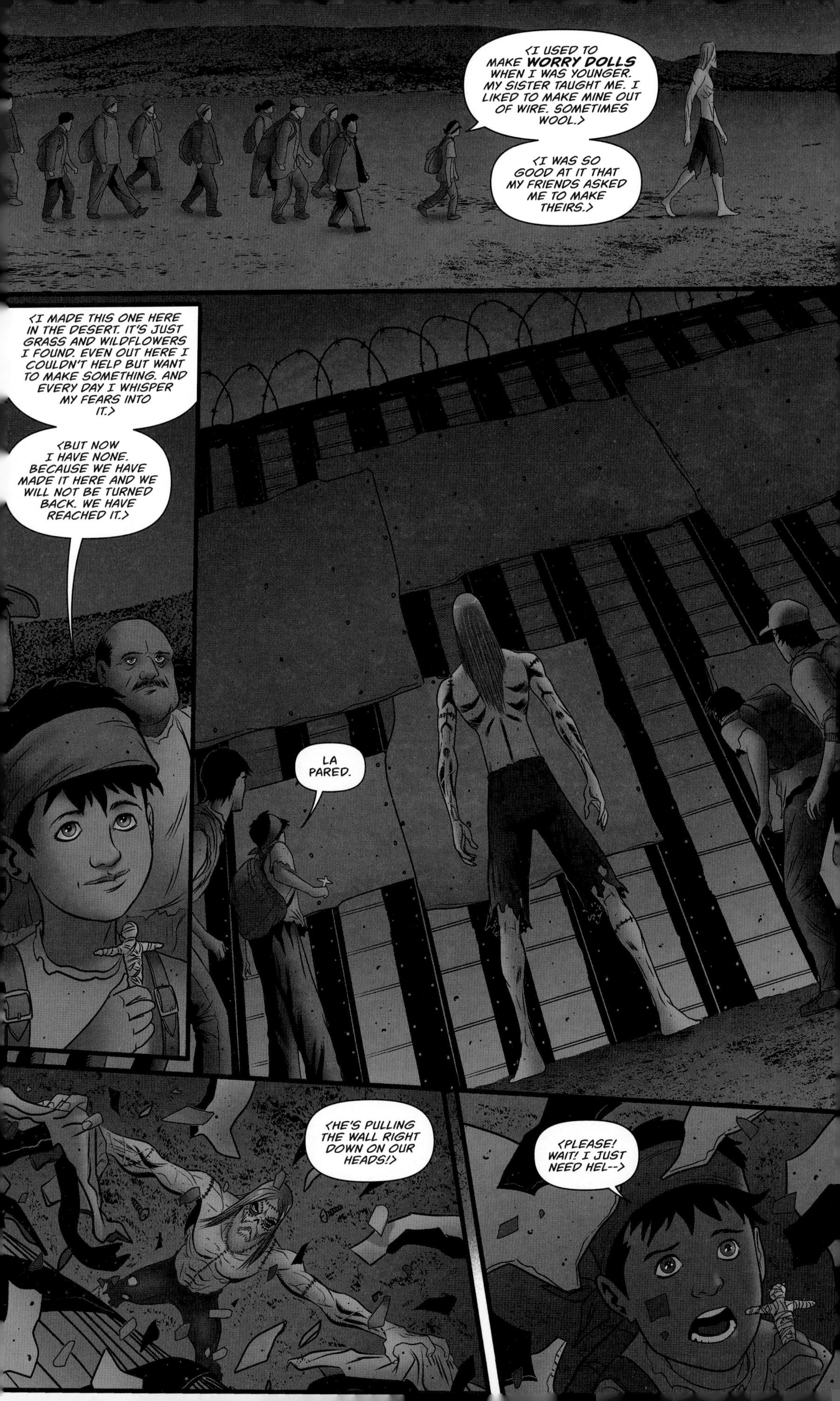

<I USED TO MAKE WORRY DOLLS WHEN I WAS YOUNGER. MY SISTER TAUGHT ME. I LIKED TO MAKE MINE OUT OF WIRE. SOMETIMES WOOL.>
<I WAS SO GOOD AT IT THAT MY FRIENDS ASKED ME TO MAKE THEIRS.>
<I MADE THIS ONE HERE IN THE DESERT. IT'S JUST GRASS AND WILDFLOWERS I FOUND. EVEN OUT HERE I COULDN'T HELP BUT WANT TO MAKE SOMETHING. AND EVERY DAY I WHISPER MY FEARS INTO IT.>
<BUT NOW I HAVE NONE. BECAUSE WE HAVE MADE IT HERE AND WE WILL NOT BE TURNED BACK. WE HAVE REACHED IT.>
LA PARED.
<HE'S PULLING THE WALL RIGHT DOWN ON OUR HEADS!>
<PLEASE! WAIT! I JUST NEED HEL-->

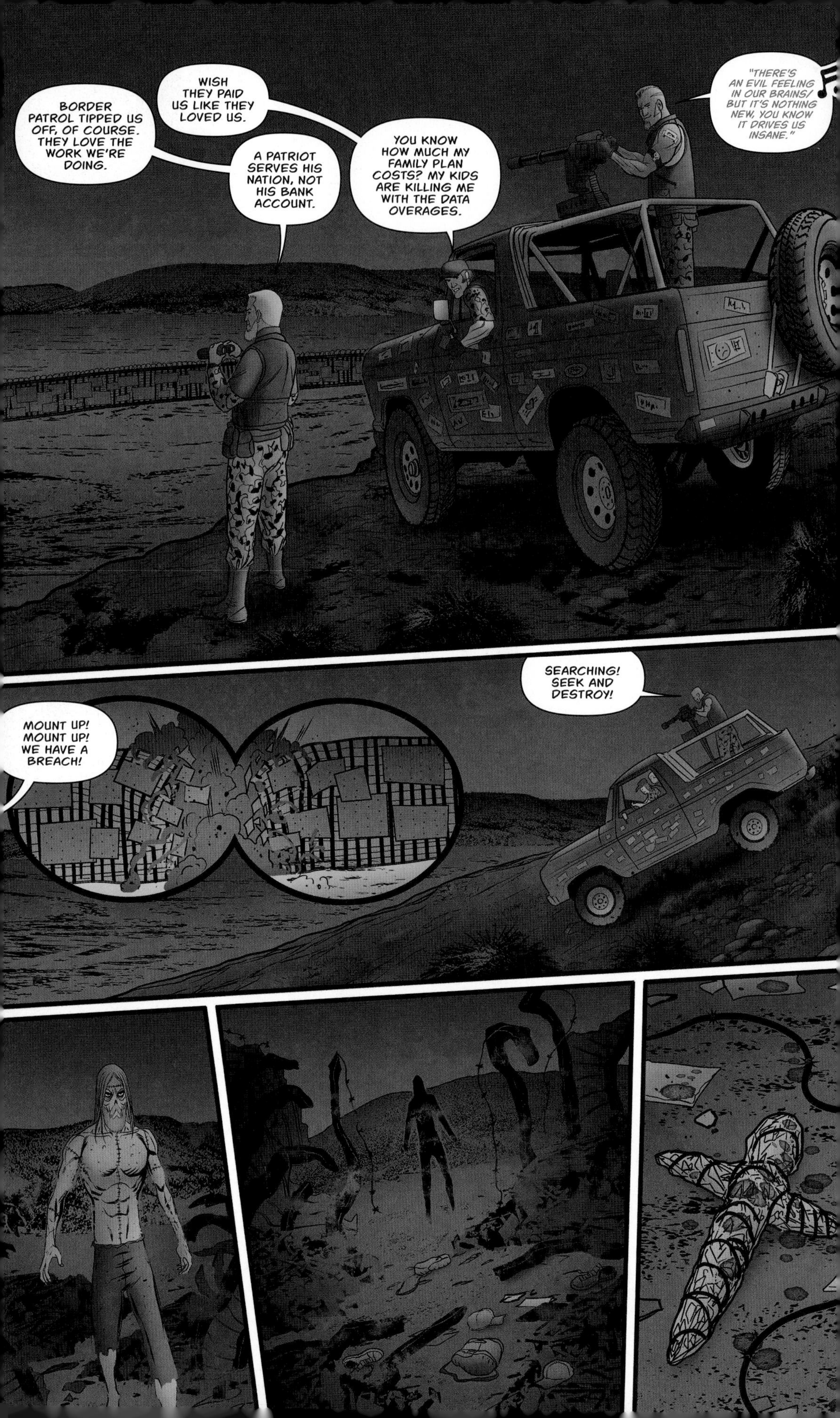
BORDER PATROL TIPPED US OFF, OF COURSE. THEY LOVE THE WORK WE'RE DOING.
WISH THEY PAID US LIKE THEY LOVED US.
A PATRIOT SERVES HIS NATION, NOT HIS BANK ACCOUNT.
YOU KNOW HOW MUCH MY FAMILY PLAN COSTS? MY KIDS ARE KILLING ME WITH THE DATA OVERAGES.
"THERE'S AN EVIL FEELING IN OUR BRAINS/ BUT IT'S NOTHING NEW, YOU KNOW IT DRIVES US INSANE."
MOUNT UP! MOUNT UP! WE HAVE A BREACH!
SEARCHING! SEEK AND DESTROY!

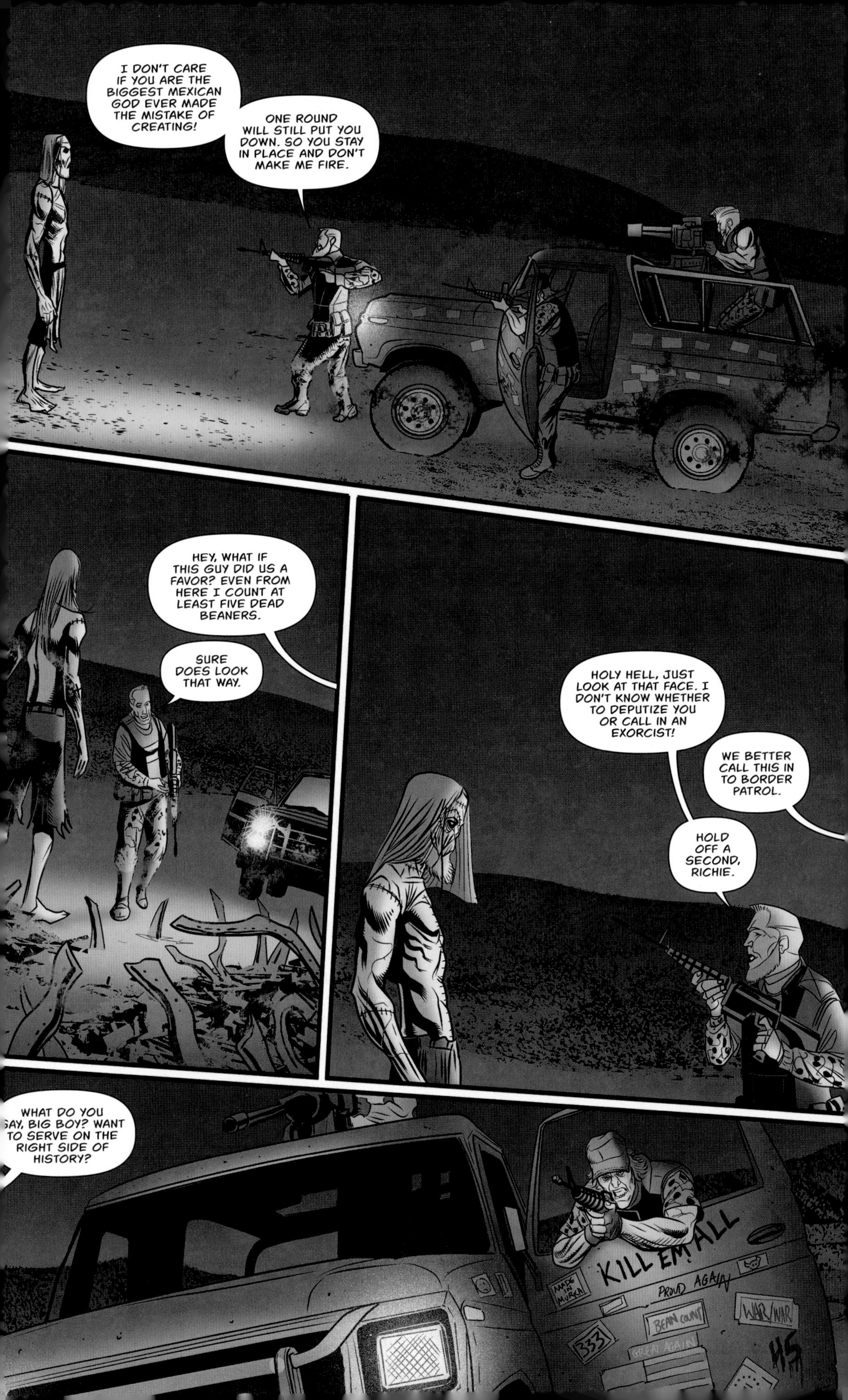

I DON'T CARE IF YOU ARE THE BIGGEST MEXICAN GOD EVER MADE THE MISTAKE OF CREATING!
ONE ROUND WILL STILL PUT YOU DOWN. SO YOU STAY IN PLACE AND DON'T MAKE ME FIRE.
HEY, WHAT IF THIS GUY DID US A FAVOR? EVEN FROM HERE I COUNT AT LEAST FIVE DEAD BEANERS.
SURE DOES LOOK THAT WAY.
HOLY HELL, JUST LOOK AT THAT FACE. I DON'T KNOW WHETHER TO DEPUTIZE YOU OR CALL IN AN EXORCIST!
WE BETTER CALL THIS IN TO BORDER PATROL.
HOLD OFF A SECOND, RICHIE.
WHAT DO YOU SAY, BIG BOY? WANT TO SERVE ON THE RIGHT SIDE OF HISTORY?
KILL EM ALL
MADE IN MURICA
PROUD AGAIN
WAR/WAR
BEAN COUNT
333
GREAT AGAIN

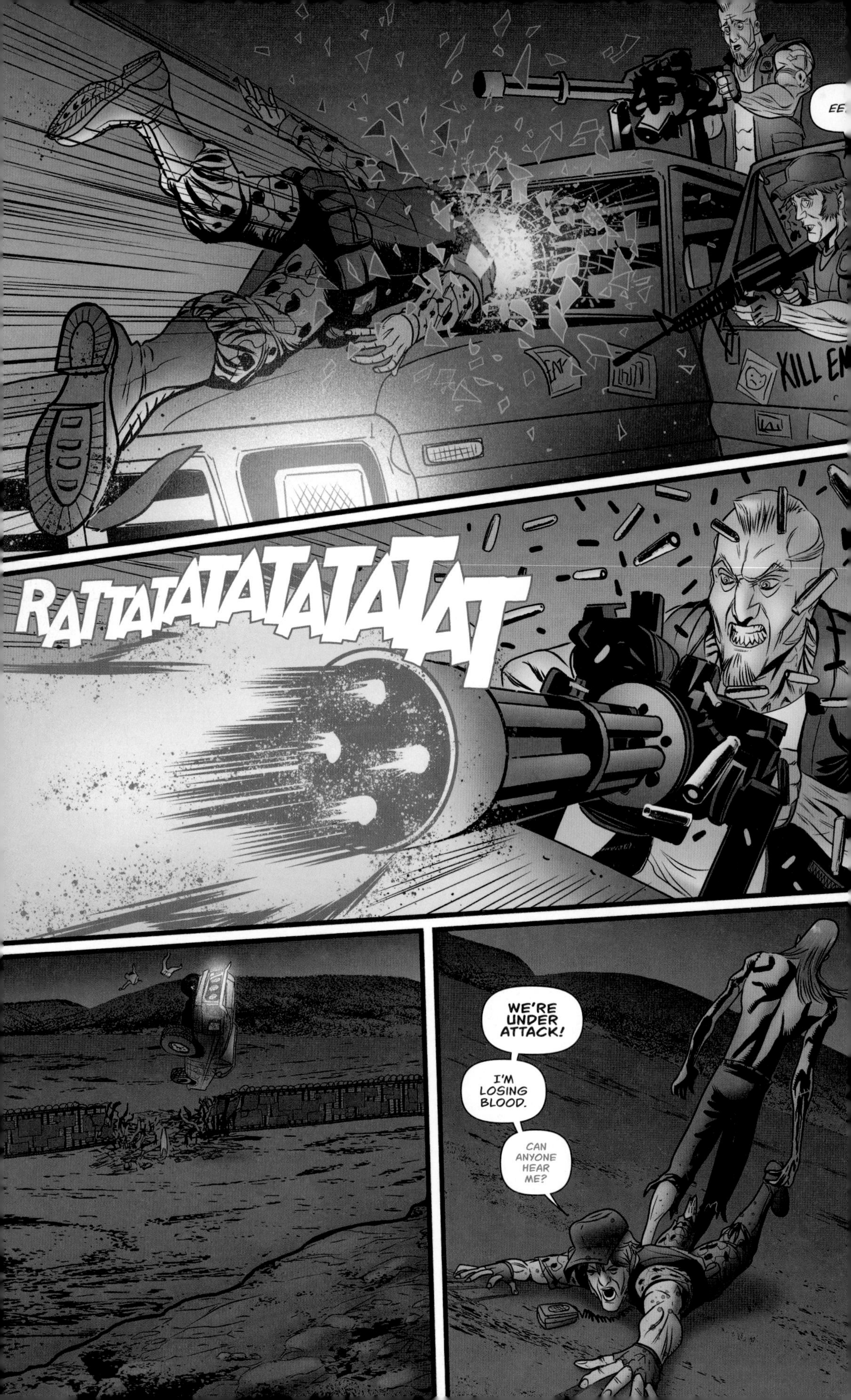
EE
KILL EM
RATTATATATATATAT
WE'RE UNDER ATTACK!
I'M LOSING BLOOD.
CAN ANYONE HEAR ME?

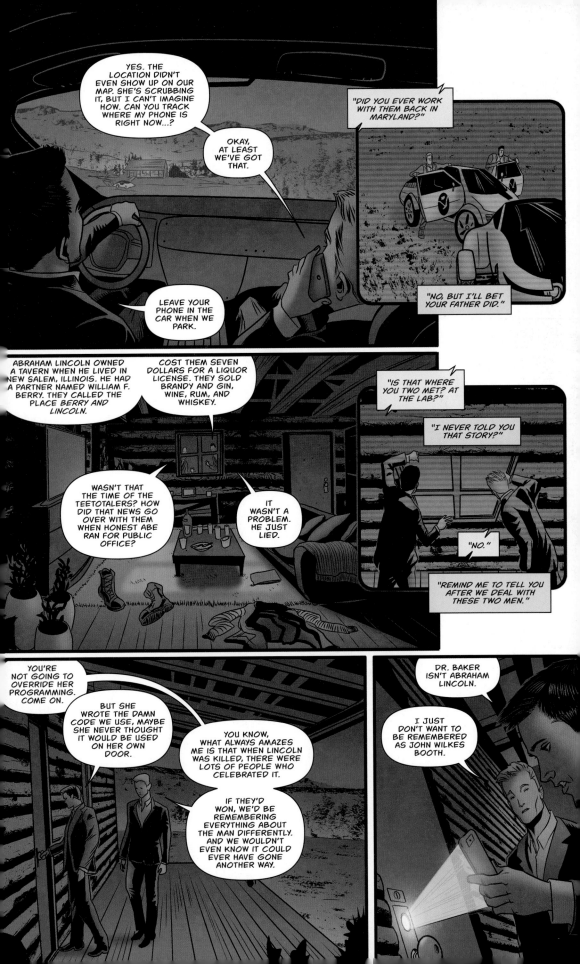

YES. THE LOCATION DIDN'T EVEN SHOW UP ON OUR MAP. SHE'S SCRUBBING IT, BUT I CAN'T IMAGINE HOW. CAN YOU TRACK WHERE MY PHONE IS RIGHT NOW...?

OKAY, AT LEAST WE'VE GOT THAT.

LEAVE YOUR PHONE IN THE CAR WHEN WE PARK.

"DID YOU EVER WORK WITH THEM BACK IN MARYLAND?"

"NO, BUT I'LL BET YOUR FATHER DID."

ABRAHAM LINCOLN OWNED A TAVERN WHEN HE LIVED IN NEW SALEM, ILLINOIS. HE HAD A PARTNER NAMED WILLIAM F. BERRY. THEY CALLED THE PLACE *BERRY AND LINCOLN.*

COST THEM SEVEN DOLLARS FOR A LIQUOR LICENSE. THEY SOLD BRANDY AND GIN, WINE, RUM, AND WHISKEY.

WASN'T THAT THE TIME OF THE TEETOTALERS? HOW DID THAT NEWS GO OVER WITH THEM WHEN HONEST ABE RAN FOR PUBLIC OFFICE?

IT WASN'T A PROBLEM. HE JUST LIED.

"IS THAT WHERE YOU TWO MET? AT THE LAB?"

"I NEVER TOLD YOU THAT STORY?"

"NO."

"REMIND ME TO TELL YOU AFTER WE DEAL WITH THESE TWO MEN."

YOU'RE NOT GOING TO OVERRIDE HER PROGRAMMING. COME ON.

BUT SHE WROTE THE DAMN CODE WE USE, MAYBE SHE NEVER THOUGHT IT WOULD BE USED ON HER OWN DOOR.

YOU KNOW, WHAT ALWAYS AMAZES ME IS THAT WHEN LINCOLN WAS KILLED, THERE WERE LOTS OF PEOPLE WHO CELEBRATED IT.

IF THEY'D WON, WE'D BE REMEMBERING EVERYTHING ABOUT THE MAN DIFFERENTLY. AND WE WOULDN'T EVEN KNOW IT COULD EVER HAVE GONE ANOTHER WAY.

DR. BAKER ISN'T ABRAHAM LINCOLN.

I JUST DON'T WANT TO BE REMEMBERED AS JOHN WILKES BOOTH.

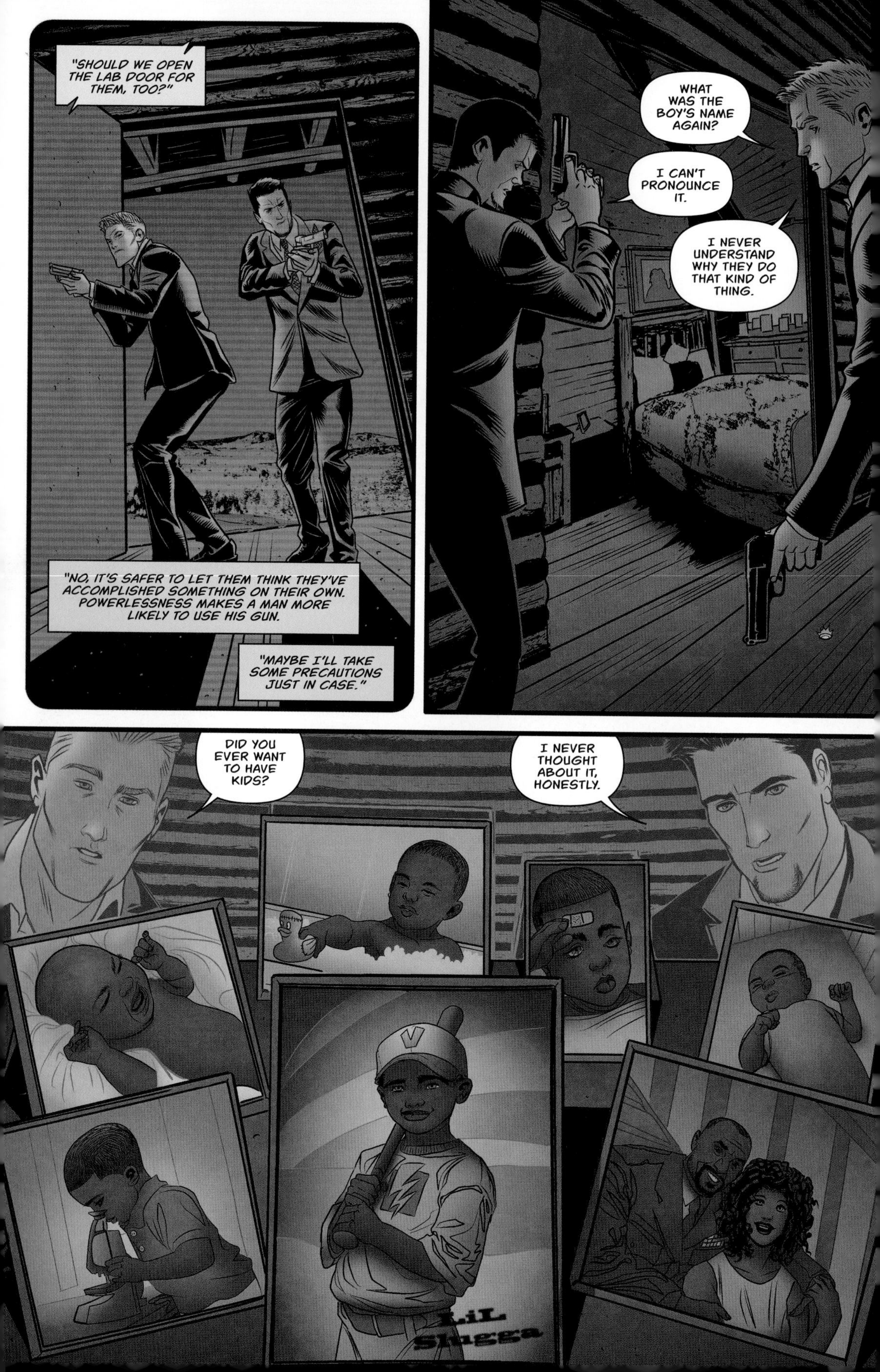
"SHOULD WE OPEN THE LAB DOOR FOR THEM, TOO?"
"NO, IT'S SAFER TO LET THEM THINK THEY'VE ACCOMPLISHED SOMETHING ON THEIR OWN. POWERLESSNESS MAKES A MAN MORE LIKELY TO USE HIS GUN.
"MAYBE I'LL TAKE SOME PRECAUTIONS JUST IN CASE."
WHAT WAS THE BOY'S NAME AGAIN?
I CAN'T PRONOUNCE IT.
I NEVER UNDERSTAND WHY THEY DO THAT KIND OF THING.
DID YOU EVER WANT TO HAVE KIDS?
I NEVER THOUGHT ABOUT IT, HONESTLY.
LiL Slugga

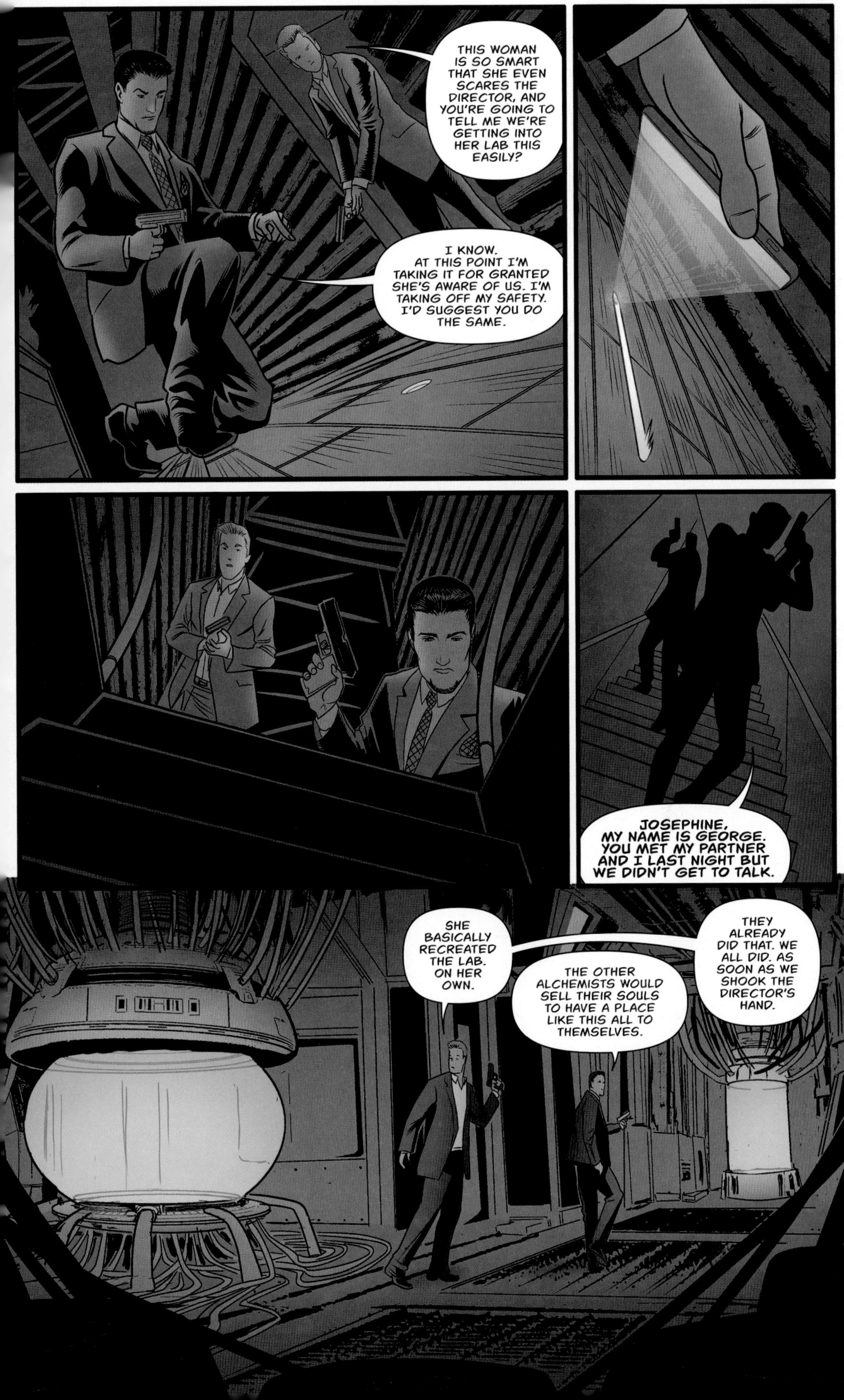
THIS WOMAN IS SO SMART THAT SHE EVEN SCARES THE DIRECTOR, AND YOU'RE GOING TO TELL ME WE'RE GETTING INTO HER LAB THIS EASILY?
I KNOW. AT THIS POINT I'M TAKING IT FOR GRANTED SHE'S AWARE OF US. I'M TAKING OFF MY SAFETY. I'D SUGGEST YOU DO THE SAME.
JOSEPHINE, MY NAME IS GEORGE. YOU MET MY PARTNER AND I LAST NIGHT BUT WE DIDN'T GET TO TALK.
SHE BASICALLY RECREATED THE LAB. ON HER OWN.
THE OTHER ALCHEMISTS WOULD SELL THEIR SOULS TO HAVE A PLACE LIKE THIS ALL TO THEMSELVES.
THEY ALREADY DID THAT. WE ALL DID. AS SOON AS WE SHOOK THE DIRECTOR'S HAND.

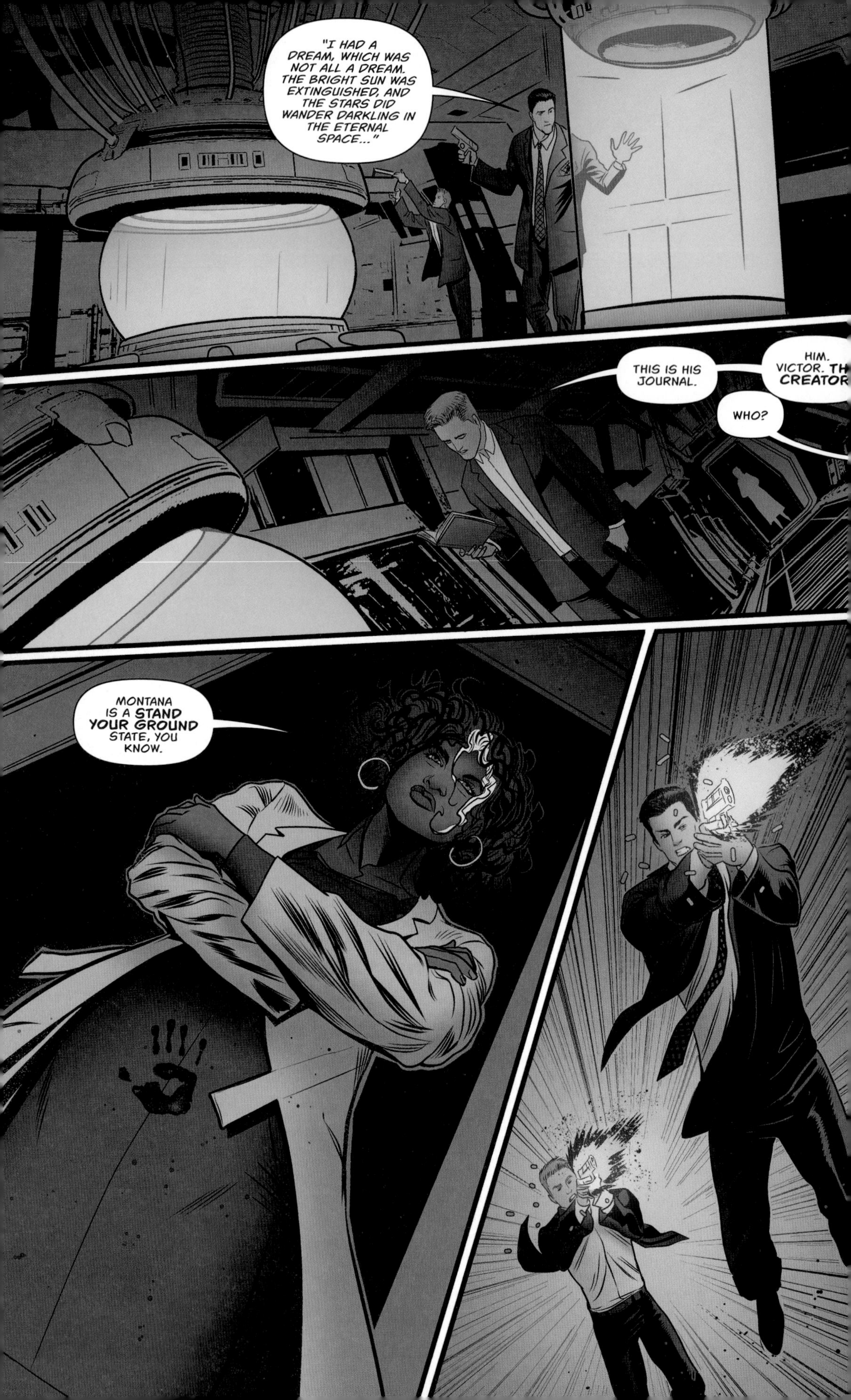
"I HAD A DREAM, WHICH WAS NOT ALL A DREAM. THE BRIGHT SUN WAS EXTINGUISHED, AND THE STARS DID WANDER DARKLING IN THE ETERNAL SPACE..."
THIS IS HIS JOURNAL.
WHO?
HIM. VICTOR. THE CREATOR
MONTANA IS A STAND YOUR GROUND STATE, YOU KNOW.

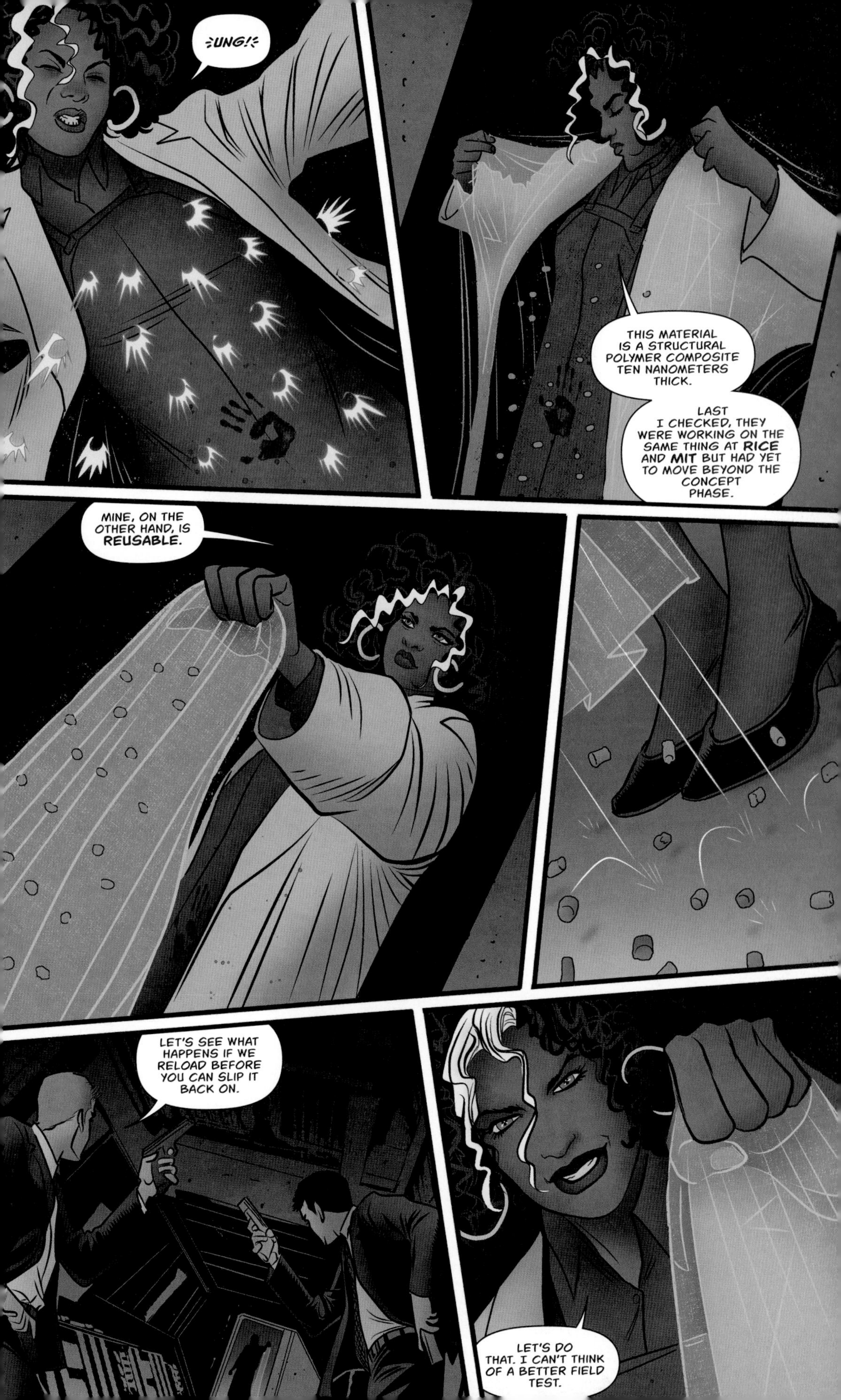
UNG!
THIS MATERIAL IS A STRUCTURAL POLYMER COMPOSITE TEN NANOMETERS THICK.
LAST I CHECKED, THEY WERE WORKING ON THE SAME THING AT RICE AND MIT BUT HAD YET TO MOVE BEYOND THE CONCEPT PHASE.
MINE, ON THE OTHER HAND, IS REUSABLE.
LET'S SEE WHAT HAPPENS IF WE RELOAD BEFORE YOU CAN SLIP IT BACK ON.
LET'S DO THAT. I CAN'T THINK OF A BETTER FIELD TEST.

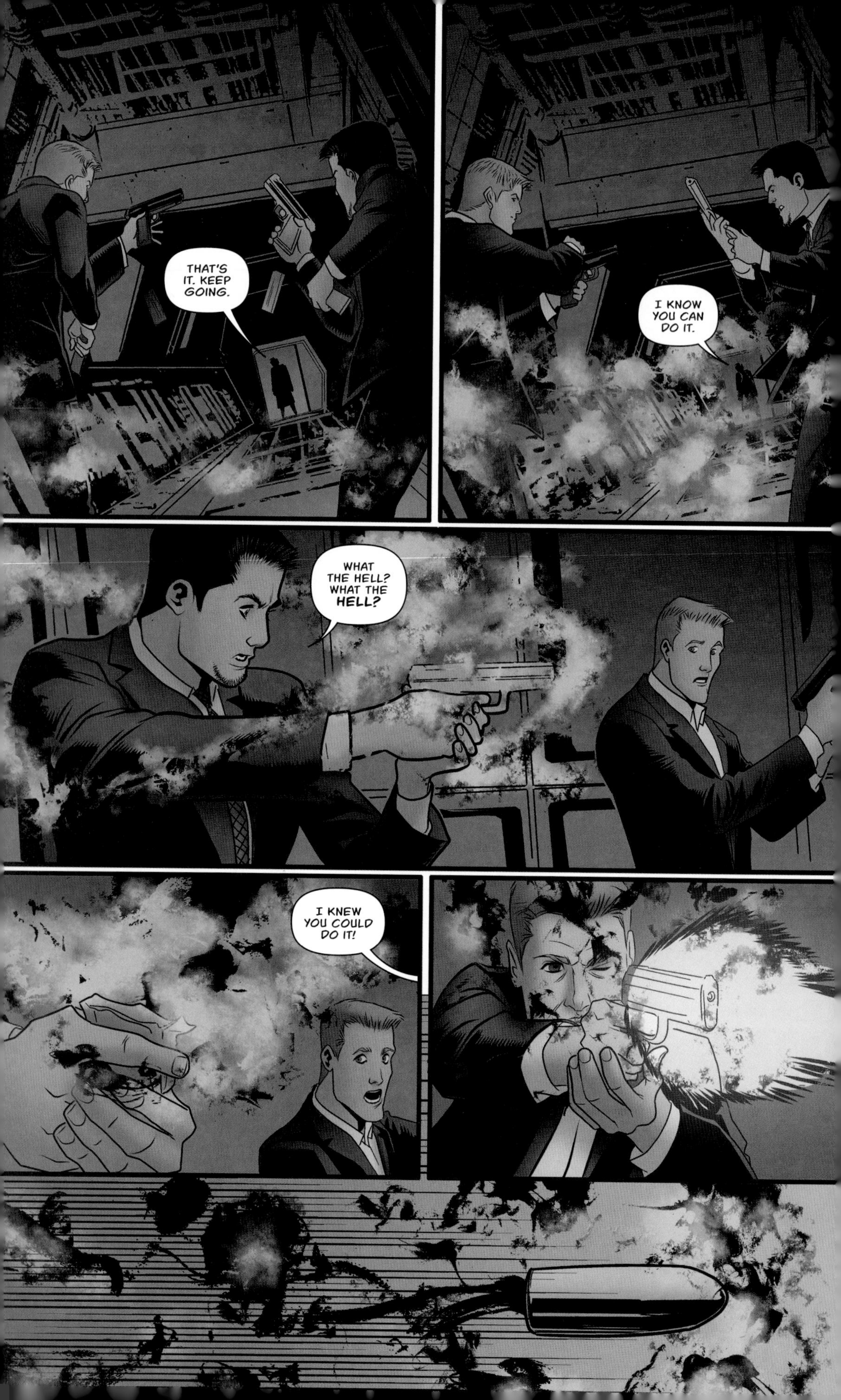
THAT'S IT. KEEP GOING.
I KNOW YOU CAN DO IT.
WHAT THE HELL? WHAT THE **HELL?**
I KNEW YOU COULD DO IT!

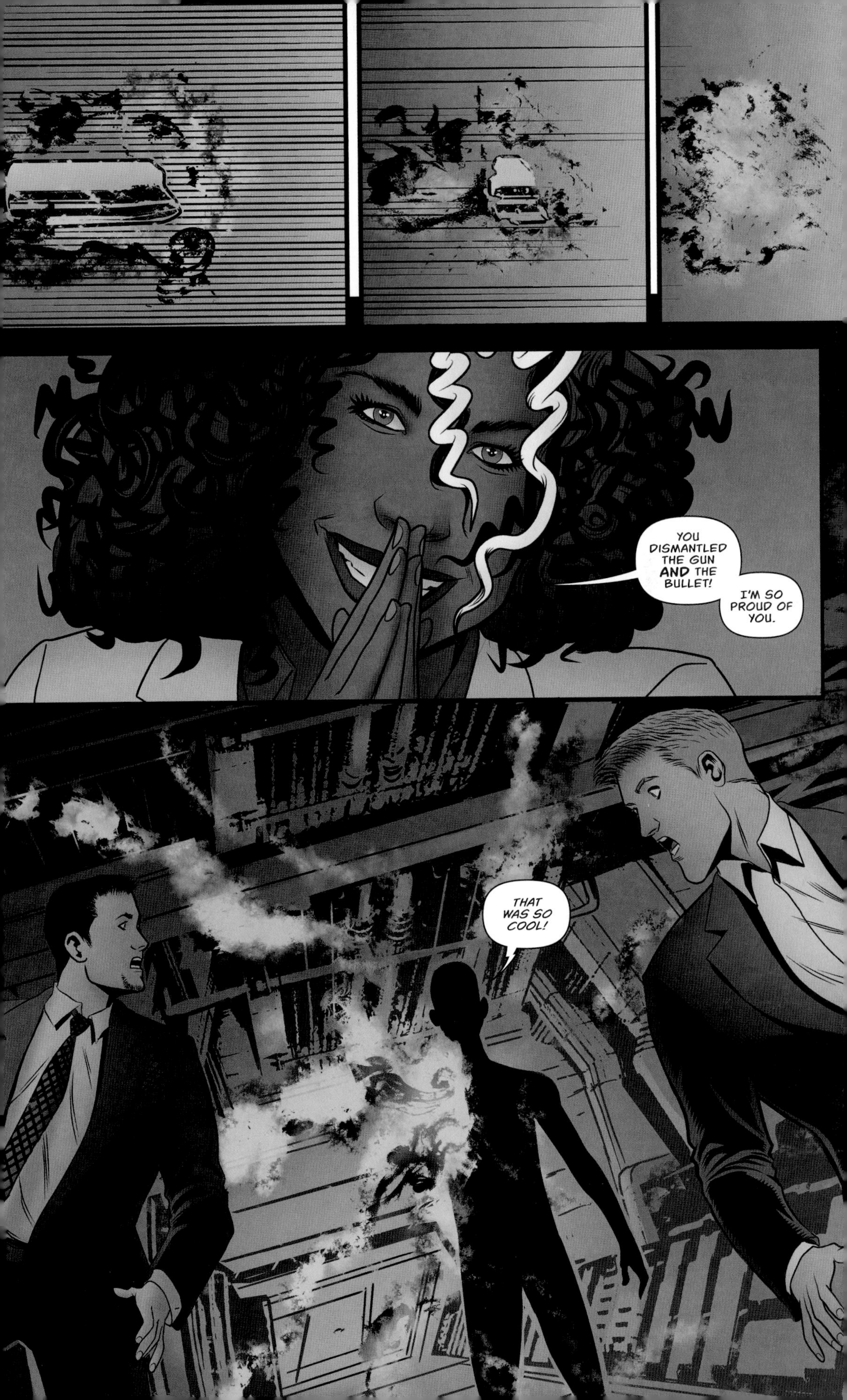
YOU DISMANTLED THE GUN **AND** THE BULLET!
I'M SO PROUD OF YOU.
THAT WAS SO COOL!

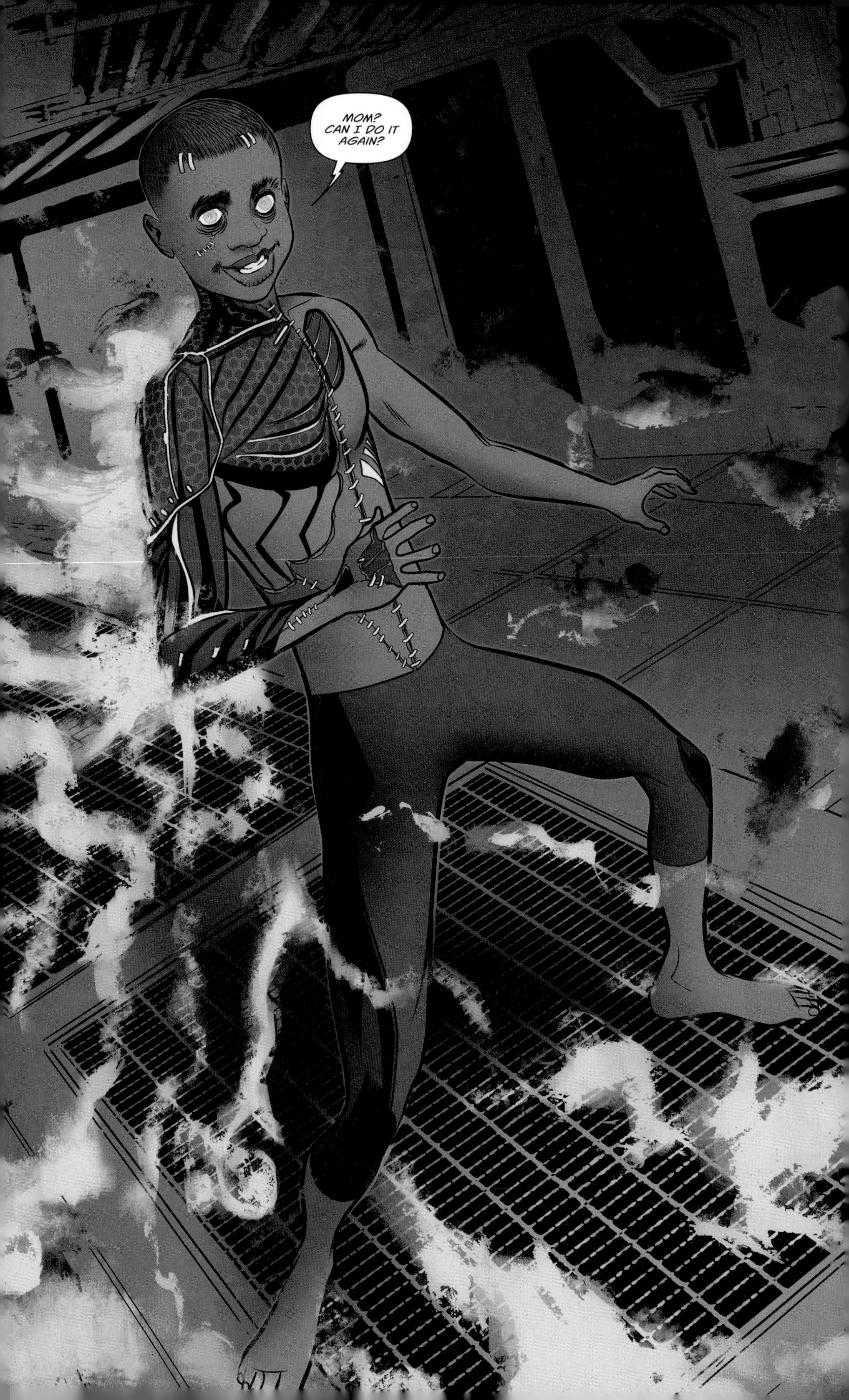
MOM? CAN I DO IT AGAIN?

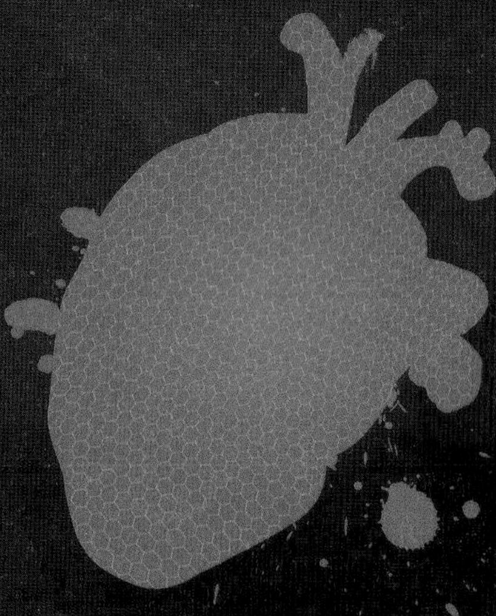

CHAPTER
THREE

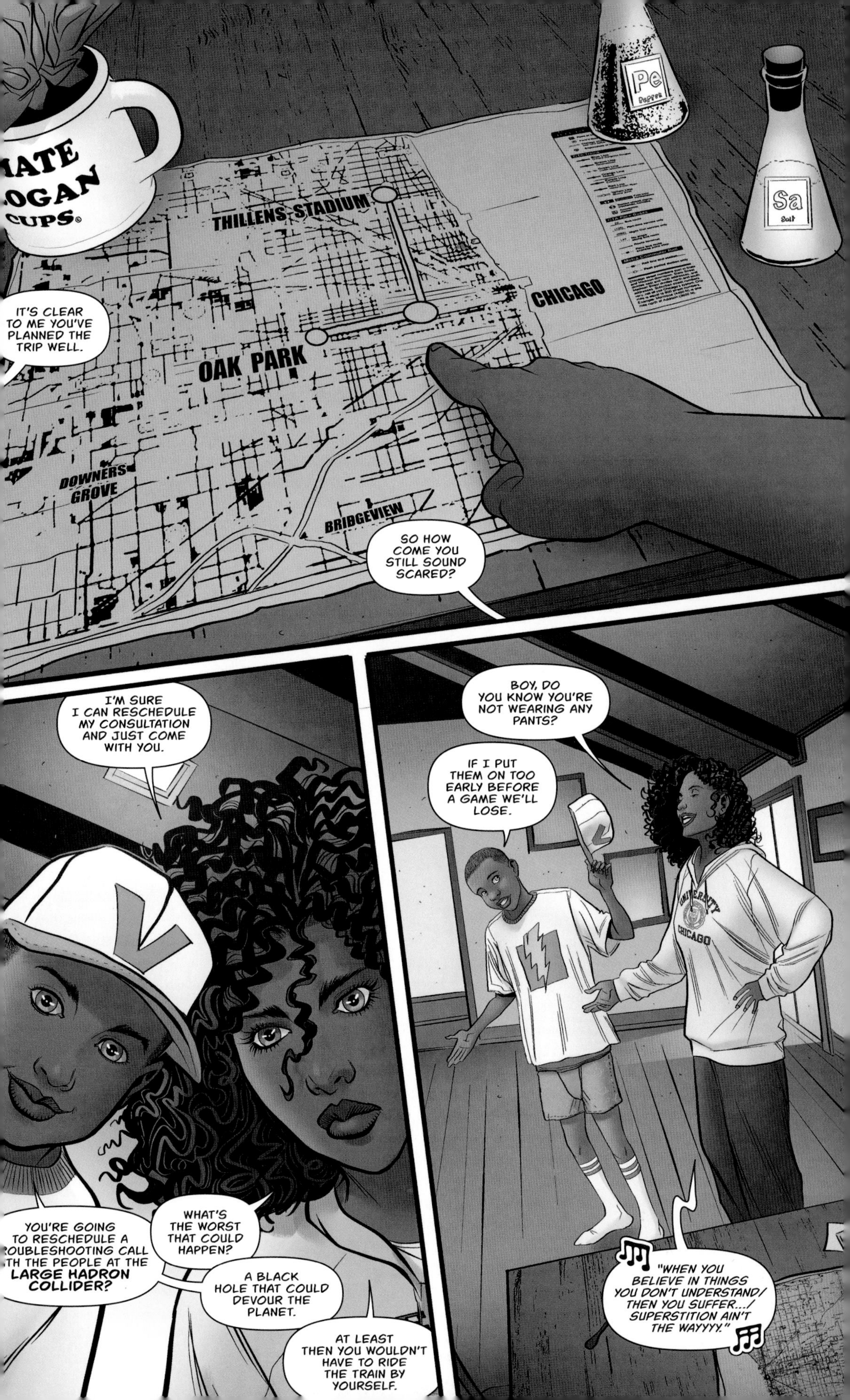

Pe
Sa
THILLENS STADIUM
CHICAGO
OAK PARK
DOWNERS GROVE
BRIDGEVIEW
IT'S CLEAR TO ME YOU'VE PLANNED THE TRIP WELL.
SO HOW COME YOU STILL SOUND SCARED?
I'M SURE I CAN RESCHEDULE MY CONSULTATION AND JUST COME WITH YOU.
YOU'RE GOING TO RESCHEDULE A ROUBLESHOOTING CALL TH THE PEOPLE AT THE **LARGE HADRON COLLIDER?**
WHAT'S THE WORST THAT COULD HAPPEN?
A BLACK HOLE THAT COULD DEVOUR THE PLANET.
AT LEAST THEN YOU WOULDN'T HAVE TO RIDE THE TRAIN BY YOURSELF.
BOY, DO YOU KNOW YOU'RE NOT WEARING ANY PANTS?
IF I PUT THEM ON TOO EARLY BEFORE A GAME WE'LL LOSE.
UNIVERSITY CHICAGO
"WHEN YOU BELIEVE IN THINGS YOU DON'T UNDERSTAND/ THEN YOU SUFFER.../ SUPERSTITION AIN'T THE WAYYYY."

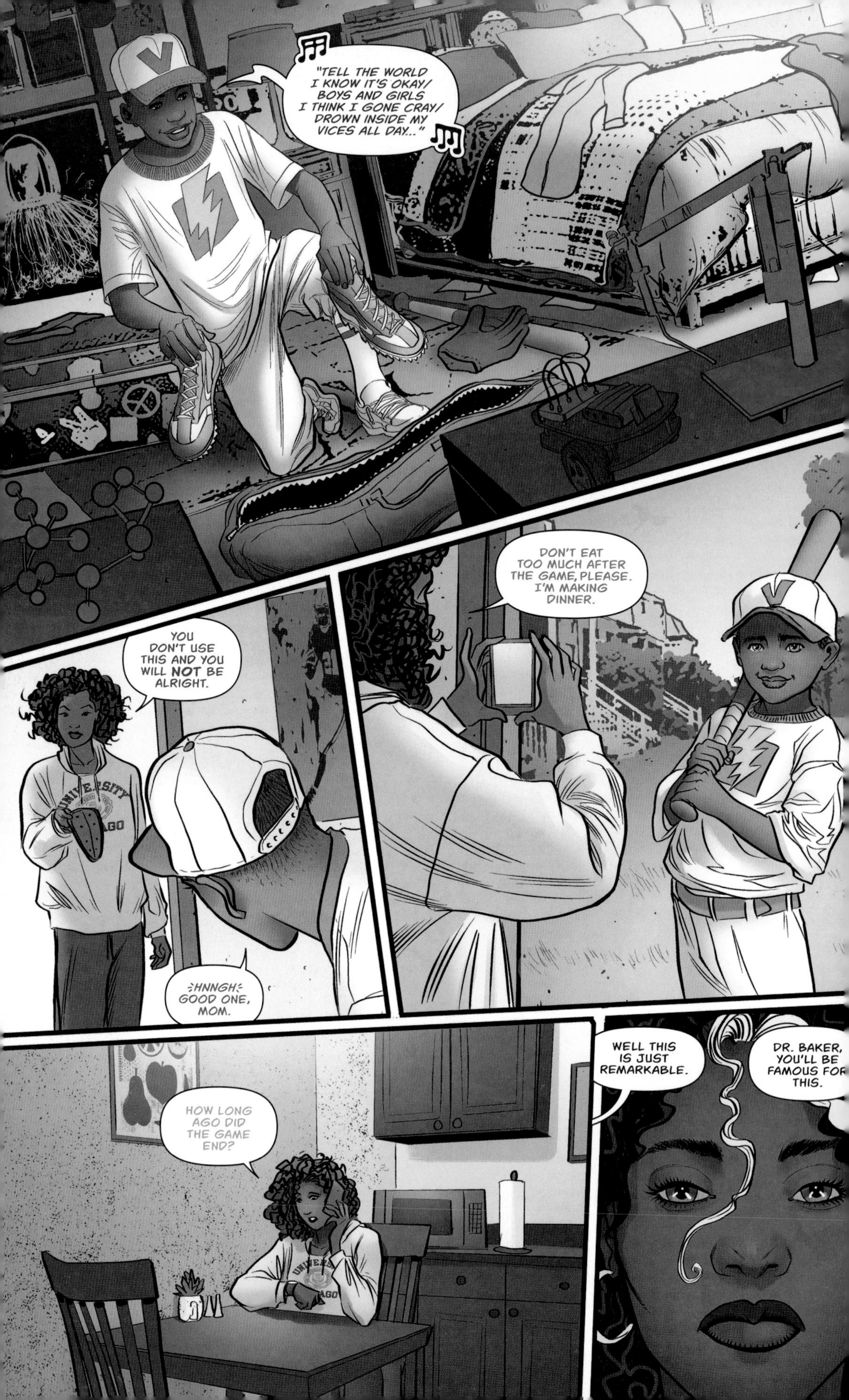
"TELL THE WORLD I KNOW IT'S OKAY/ BOYS AND GIRLS I THINK I GONE CRAY/ DROWN INSIDE MY VICES ALL DAY..."
DON'T EAT TOO MUCH AFTER THE GAME, PLEASE. I'M MAKING DINNER.
YOU DON'T USE THIS AND YOU WILL **NOT** BE ALRIGHT.
HNNGH GOOD ONE, MOM.
HOW LONG AGO DID THE GAME END?
WELL THIS IS JUST REMARKABLE.
DR. BAKER, YOU'LL BE FAMOUS FOR THIS.

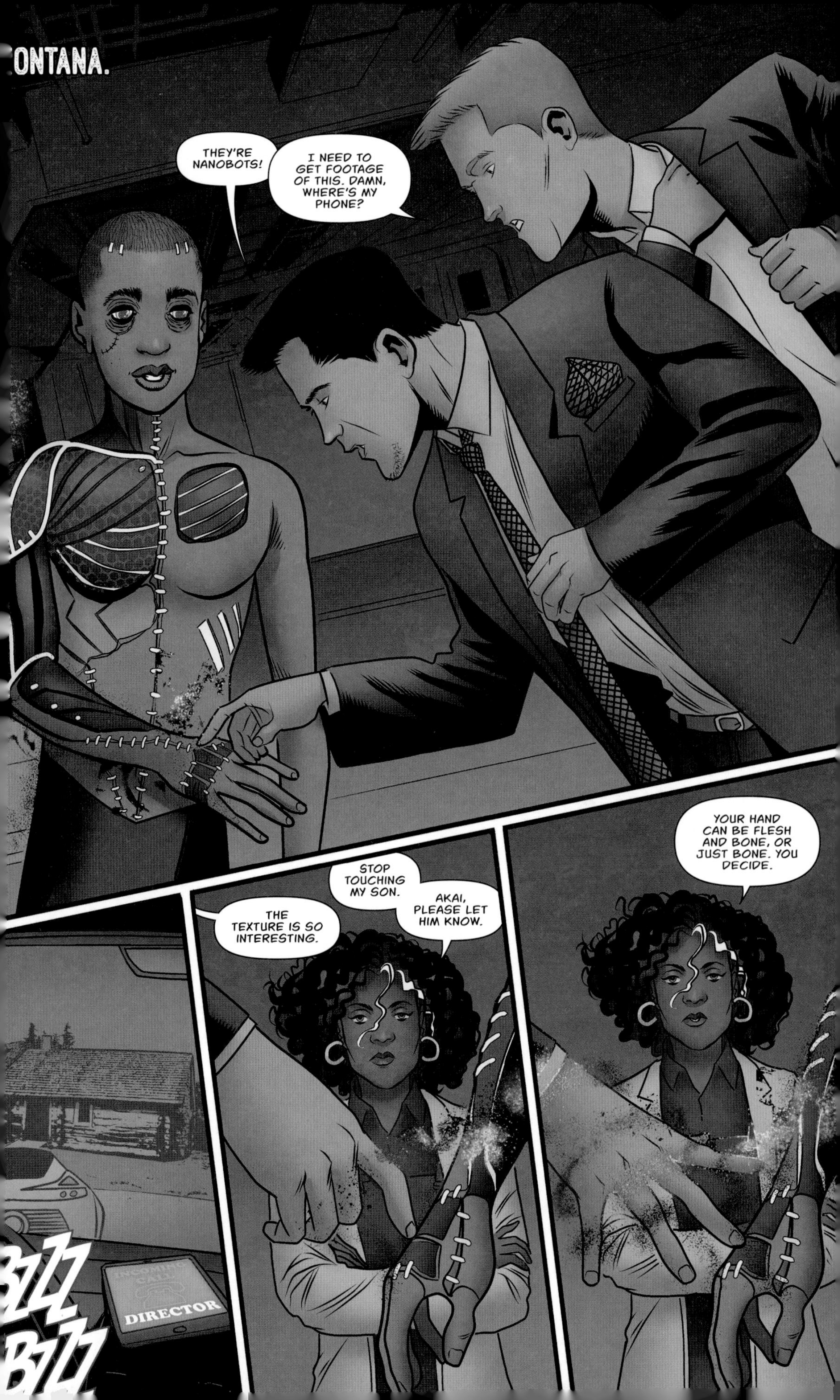

ONTANA.
THEY'RE NANOBOTS!
I NEED TO GET FOOTAGE OF THIS. DAMN, WHERE'S MY PHONE?
INCOMING CALL
DIRECTOR
BZZZ BZZZ
THE TEXTURE IS SO INTERESTING.
STOP TOUCHING MY SON.
AKAI, PLEASE LET HIM KNOW.
YOUR HAND CAN BE FLESH AND BONE, OR JUST BONE. YOU DECIDE.

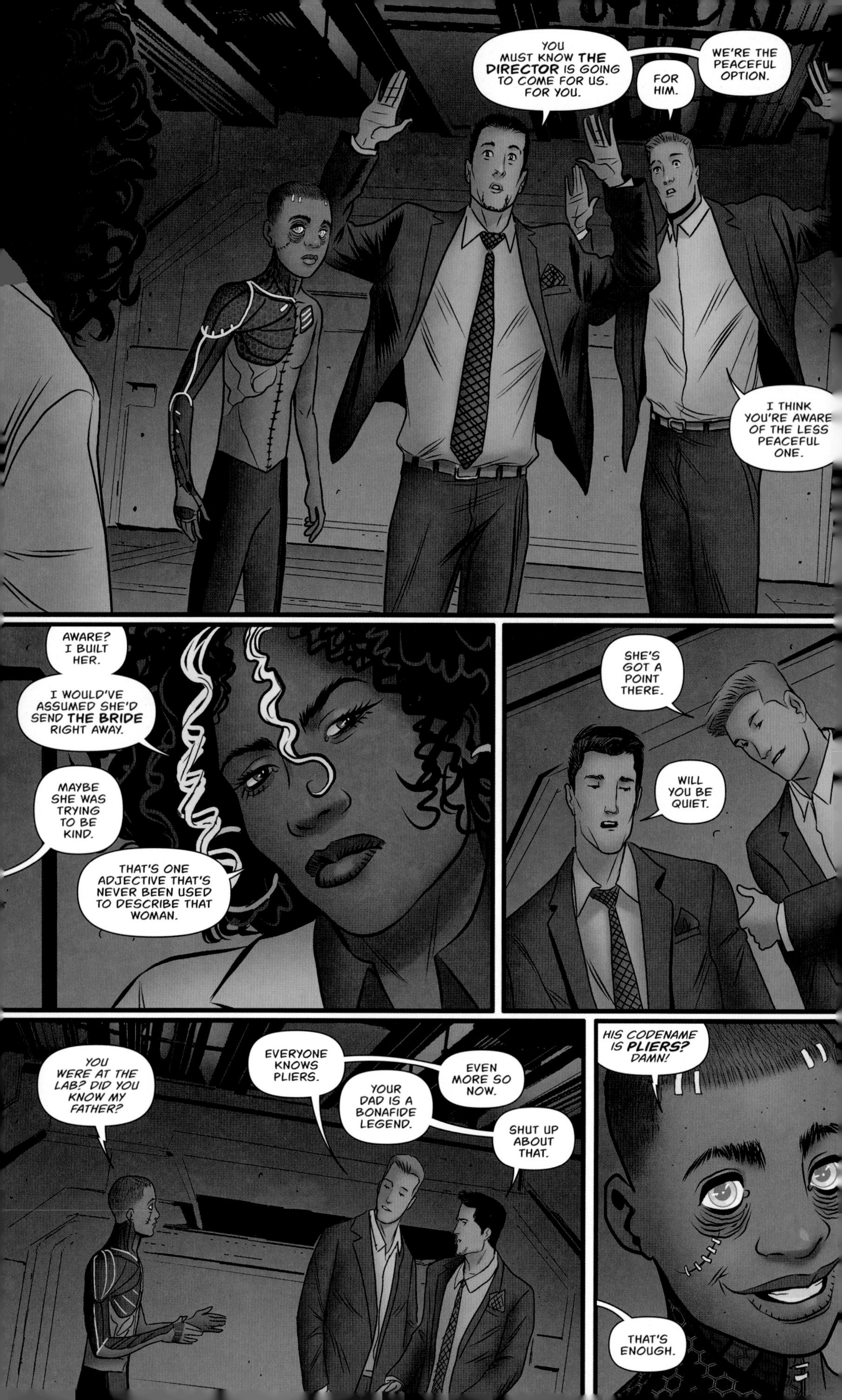

YOU MUST KNOW **THE DIRECTOR** IS GOING TO COME FOR US. FOR YOU.
FOR HIM.
WE'RE THE PEACEFUL OPTION.
I THINK YOU'RE AWARE OF THE LESS PEACEFUL ONE.
AWARE? I BUILT HER.
I WOULD'VE ASSUMED SHE'D SEND **THE BRIDE** RIGHT AWAY.
MAYBE SHE WAS TRYING TO BE KIND.
THAT'S ONE ADJECTIVE THAT'S NEVER BEEN USED TO DESCRIBE THAT WOMAN.
SHE'S GOT A POINT THERE.
WILL YOU BE QUIET.
YOU WERE AT THE LAB? DID YOU KNOW MY FATHER?
EVERYONE KNOWS PLIERS.
EVEN MORE SO NOW.
YOUR DAD IS A BONAFIDE LEGEND.
SHUT UP ABOUT THAT.
*HIS CODENAME IS **PLIERS?** DAMN!*
THAT'S ENOUGH.

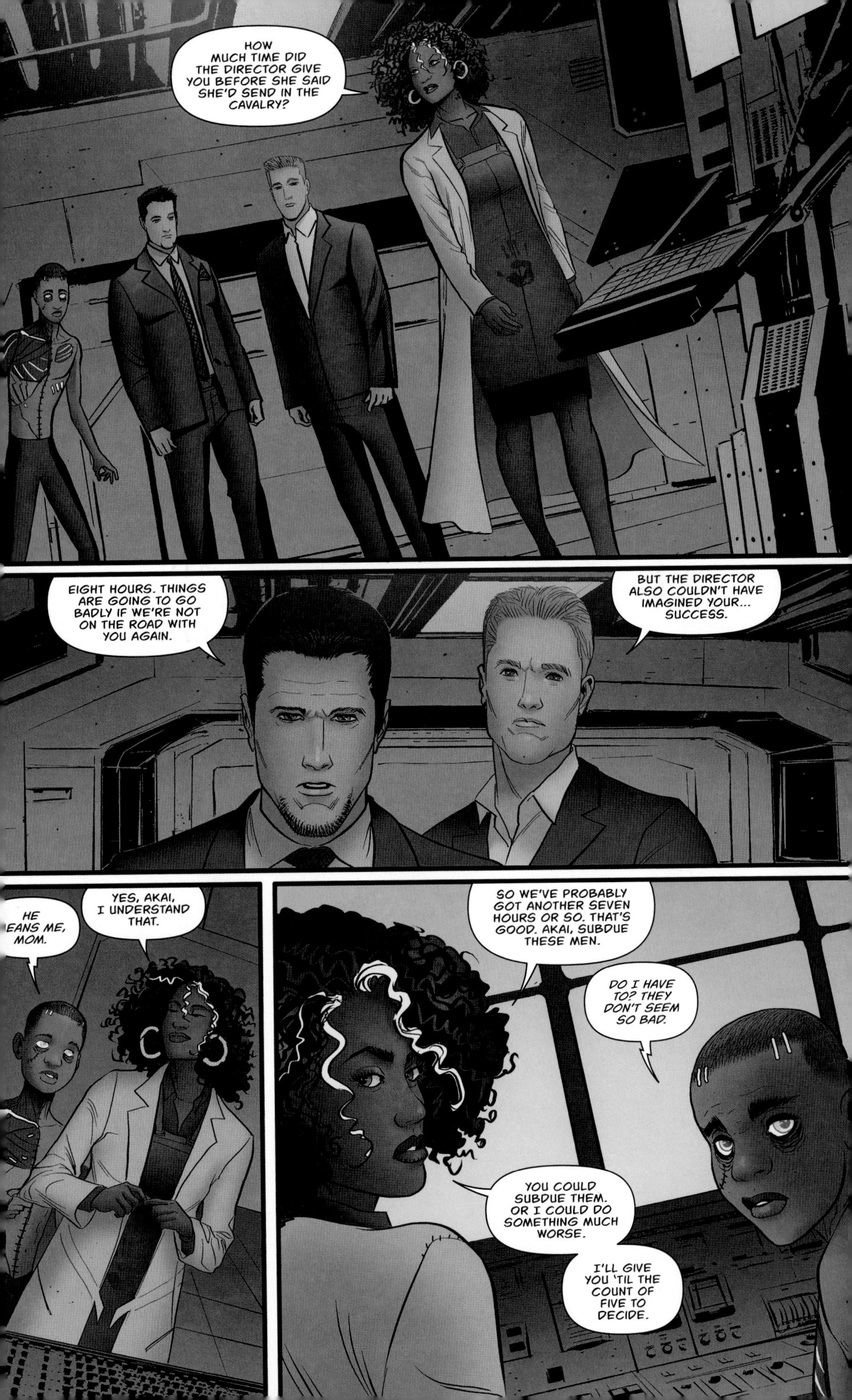
HOW MUCH TIME DID THE DIRECTOR GIVE YOU BEFORE SHE SAID SHE'D SEND IN THE CAVALRY?
EIGHT HOURS. THINGS ARE GOING TO GO BADLY IF WE'RE NOT ON THE ROAD WITH YOU AGAIN.
BUT THE DIRECTOR ALSO COULDN'T HAVE IMAGINED YOUR... SUCCESS.
HE EANS ME, MOM.
YES, AKAI, I UNDERSTAND THAT.
SO WE'VE PROBABLY GOT ANOTHER SEVEN HOURS OR SO. THAT'S GOOD. AKAI, SUBDUE THESE MEN.
DO I HAVE TO? THEY DON'T SEEM SO BAD.
YOU COULD SUBDUE THEM. OR I COULD DO SOMETHING MUCH WORSE.
I'LL GIVE YOU 'TIL THE COUNT OF FIVE TO DECIDE.

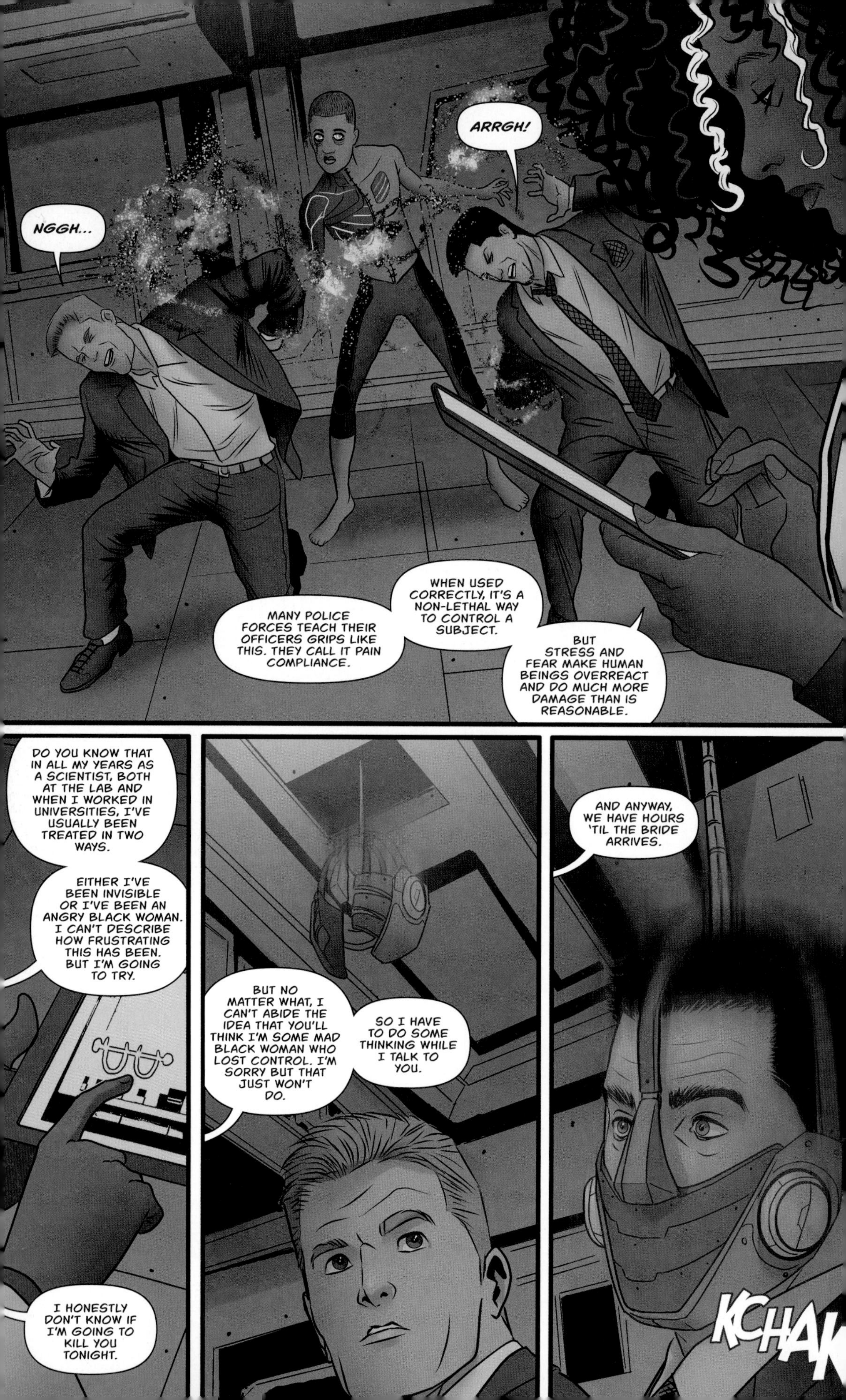
NGGH...
ARRGH!
MANY POLICE FORCES TEACH THEIR OFFICERS GRIPS LIKE THIS. THEY CALL IT PAIN COMPLIANCE.
WHEN USED CORRECTLY, IT'S A NON-LETHAL WAY TO CONTROL A SUBJECT.
BUT STRESS AND FEAR MAKE HUMAN BEINGS OVERREACT AND DO MUCH MORE DAMAGE THAN IS REASONABLE.
DO YOU KNOW THAT IN ALL MY YEARS AS A SCIENTIST, BOTH AT THE LAB AND WHEN I WORKED IN UNIVERSITIES, I'VE USUALLY BEEN TREATED IN TWO WAYS.
EITHER I'VE BEEN INVISIBLE OR I'VE BEEN AN ANGRY BLACK WOMAN. I CAN'T DESCRIBE HOW FRUSTRATING THIS HAS BEEN. BUT I'M GOING TO TRY.
I HONESTLY DON'T KNOW IF I'M GOING TO KILL YOU TONIGHT.
BUT NO MATTER WHAT, I CAN'T ABIDE THE IDEA THAT YOU'LL THINK I'M SOME MAD BLACK WOMAN WHO LOST CONTROL. I'M SORRY BUT THAT JUST WON'T DO.
SO I HAVE TO DO SOME THINKING WHILE I TALK TO YOU.
AND ANYWAY, WE HAVE HOURS 'TIL THE BRIDE ARRIVES.
KCHAK

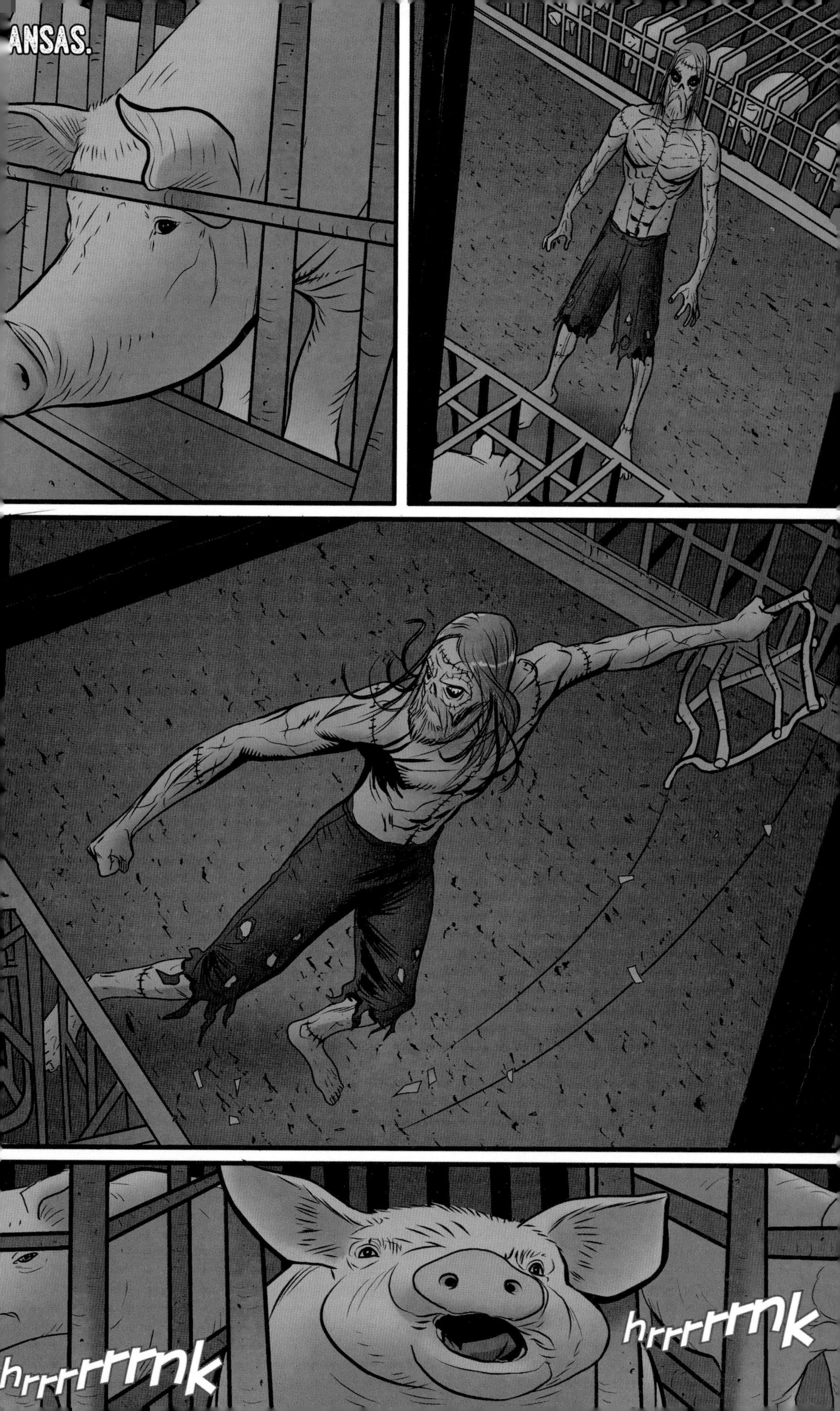
ANSAS.
hrrrrrrnk
hrrrrrnk

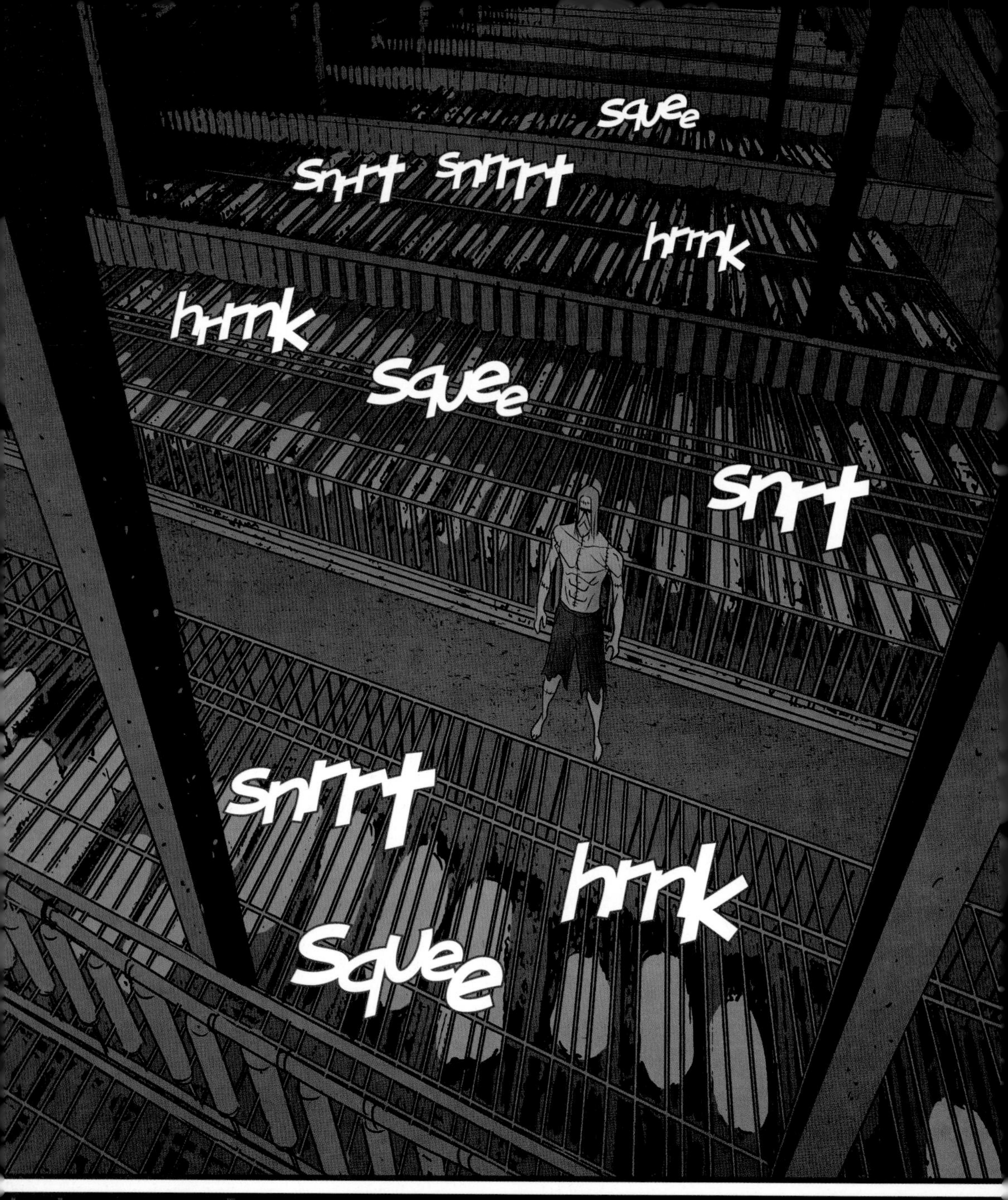
squee
snrrt snrrrt
hrrnk
hrrnk
squee
snrrt
snrrrt
hrrnk
squee

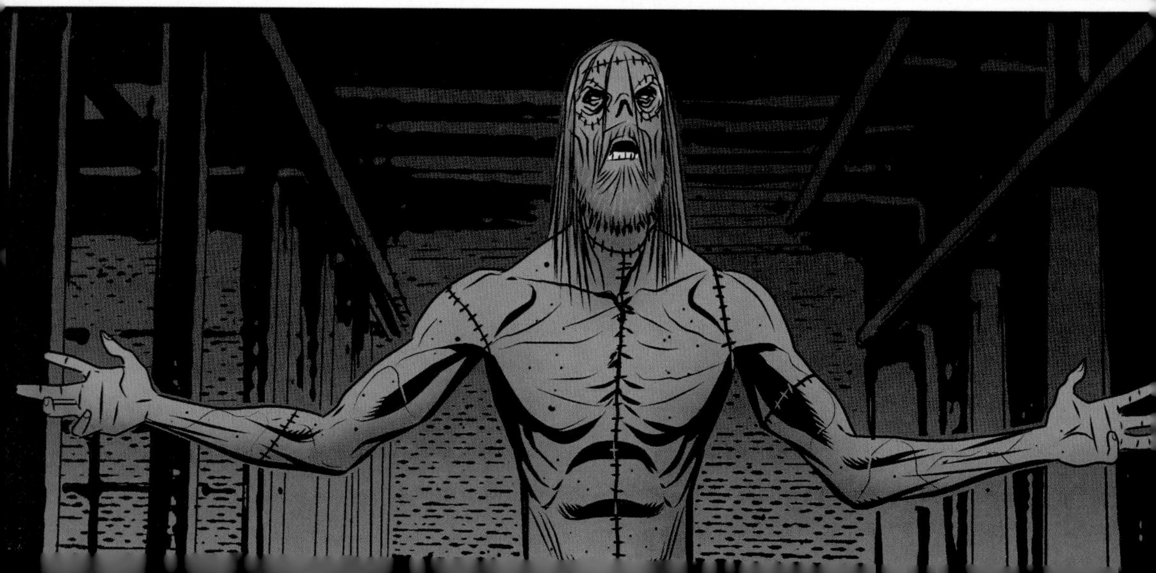

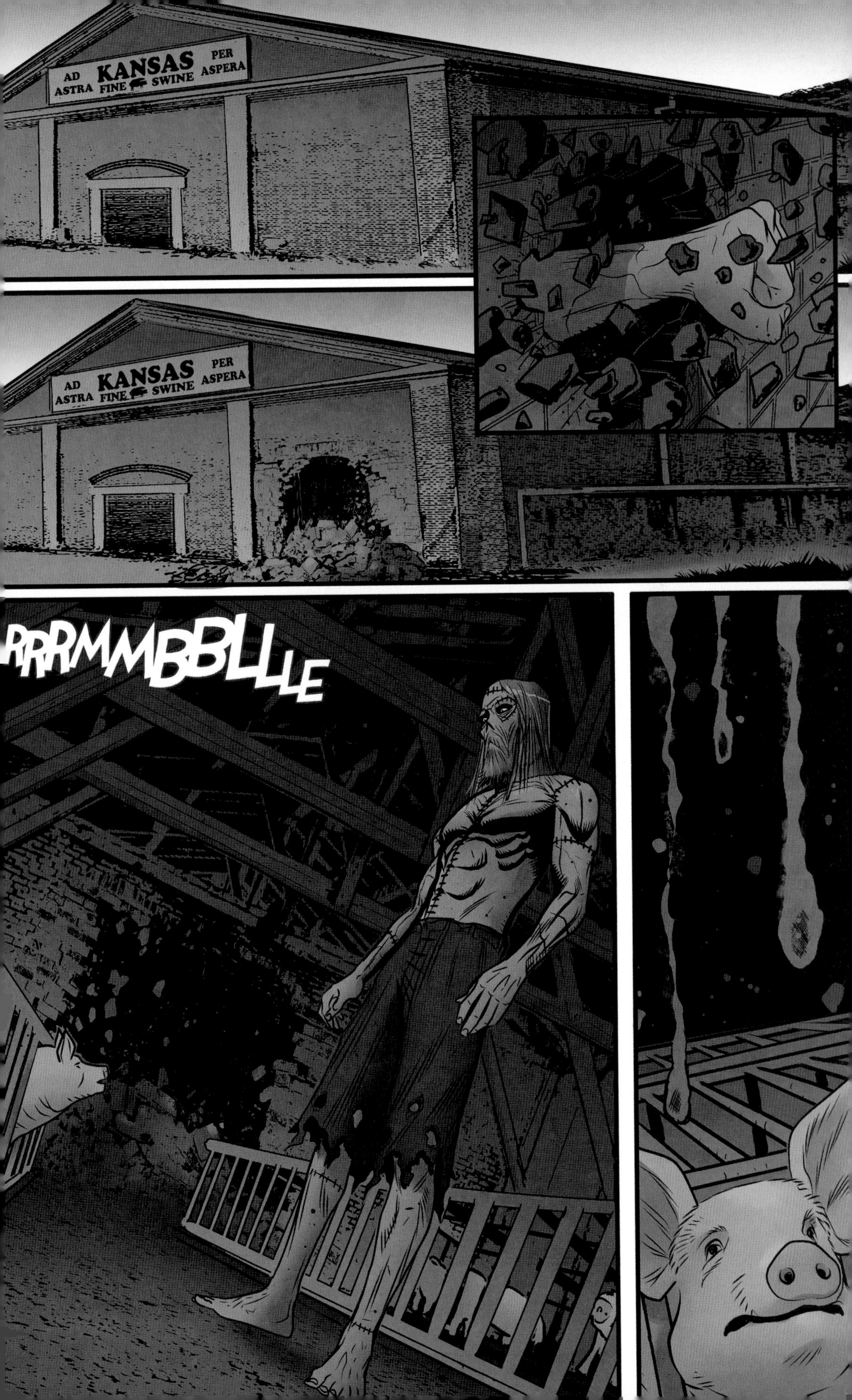
AD KANSAS PER
ASTRA FINE SWINE ASPERA
AD KANSAS PER
ASTRA FINE SWINE ASPERA
RRRMMBBLLLE

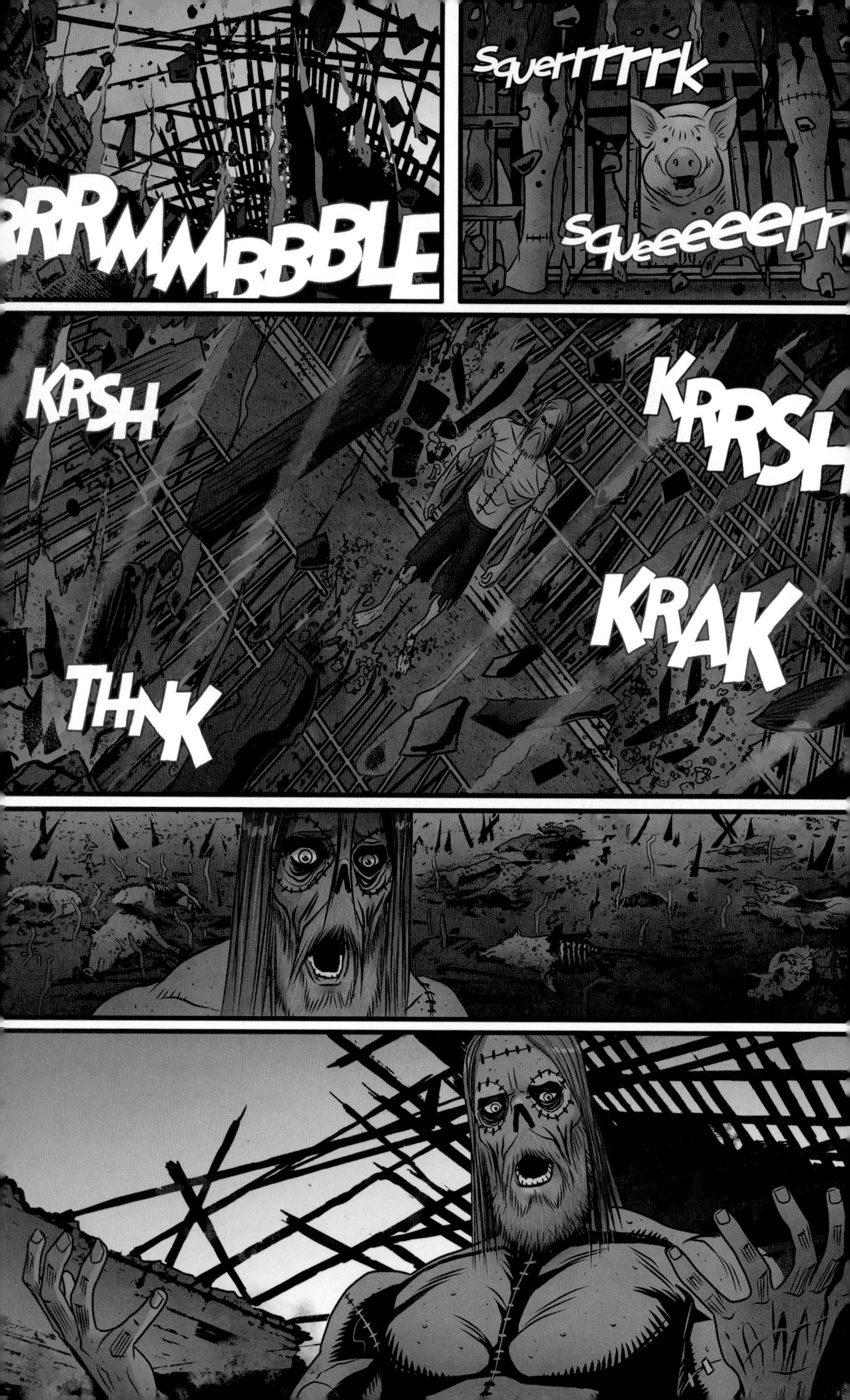
RRRMMBBBLE
Squerrrrrrk
Squeeeeeerrr
KRSH
KRRSH
KRAK
THNK

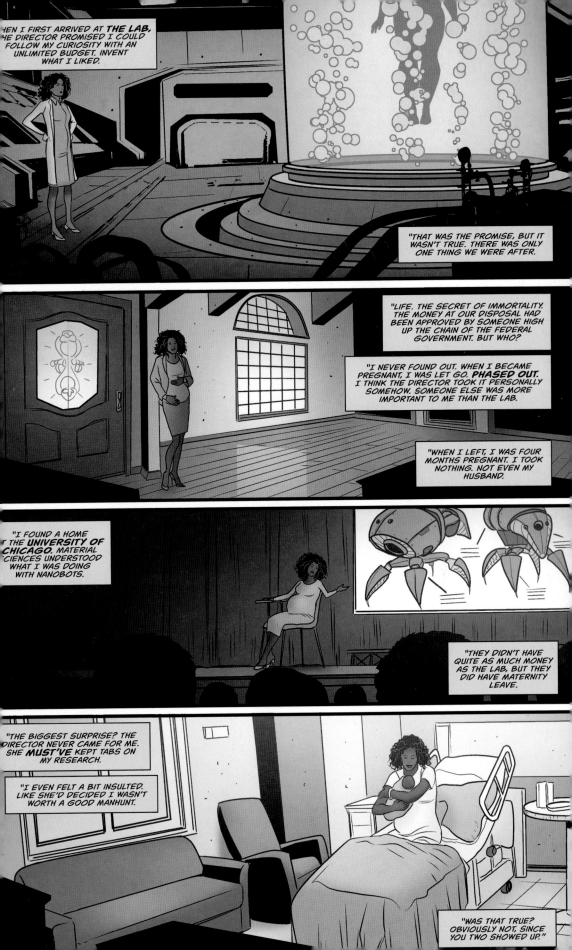

"HEN I FIRST ARRIVED AT **THE LAB**, 'HE DIRECTOR PROMISED I COULD FOLLOW MY CURIOSITY WITH AN UNLIMITED BUDGET. INVENT WHAT I LIKED.

"THAT WAS THE PROMISE, BUT IT WASN'T TRUE. THERE WAS ONLY ONE THING WE WERE AFTER.

"LIFE. THE SECRET OF IMMORTALITY. THE MONEY AT OUR DISPOSAL HAD BEEN APPROVED BY SOMEONE HIGH UP THE CHAIN OF THE FEDERAL GOVERNMENT. BUT WHO?

"I NEVER FOUND OUT. WHEN I BECAME PREGNANT, I WAS LET GO. **PHASED OUT.** I THINK THE DIRECTOR TOOK IT PERSONALLY SOMEHOW. SOMEONE ELSE WAS MORE IMPORTANT TO ME THAN THE LAB.

"WHEN I LEFT, I WAS FOUR MONTHS PREGNANT. I TOOK NOTHING. NOT EVEN MY HUSBAND.

"I FOUND A HOME 'T THE **UNIVERSITY OF CHICAGO.** MATERIAL 'CIENCES UNDERSTOOD WHAT I WAS DOING WITH NANOBOTS.

"THEY DIDN'T HAVE QUITE AS MUCH MONEY AS THE LAB, BUT THEY DID HAVE MATERNITY LEAVE.

"THE BIGGEST SURPRISE? THE 'IRECTOR NEVER CAME FOR ME. SHE **MUST'VE** KEPT TABS ON MY RESEARCH.

"I EVEN FELT A BIT INSULTED. LIKE SHE'D DECIDED I WASN'T WORTH A GOOD MANHUNT.

"WAS THAT TRUE? OBVIOUSLY NOT, SINCE YOU TWO SHOWED UP."

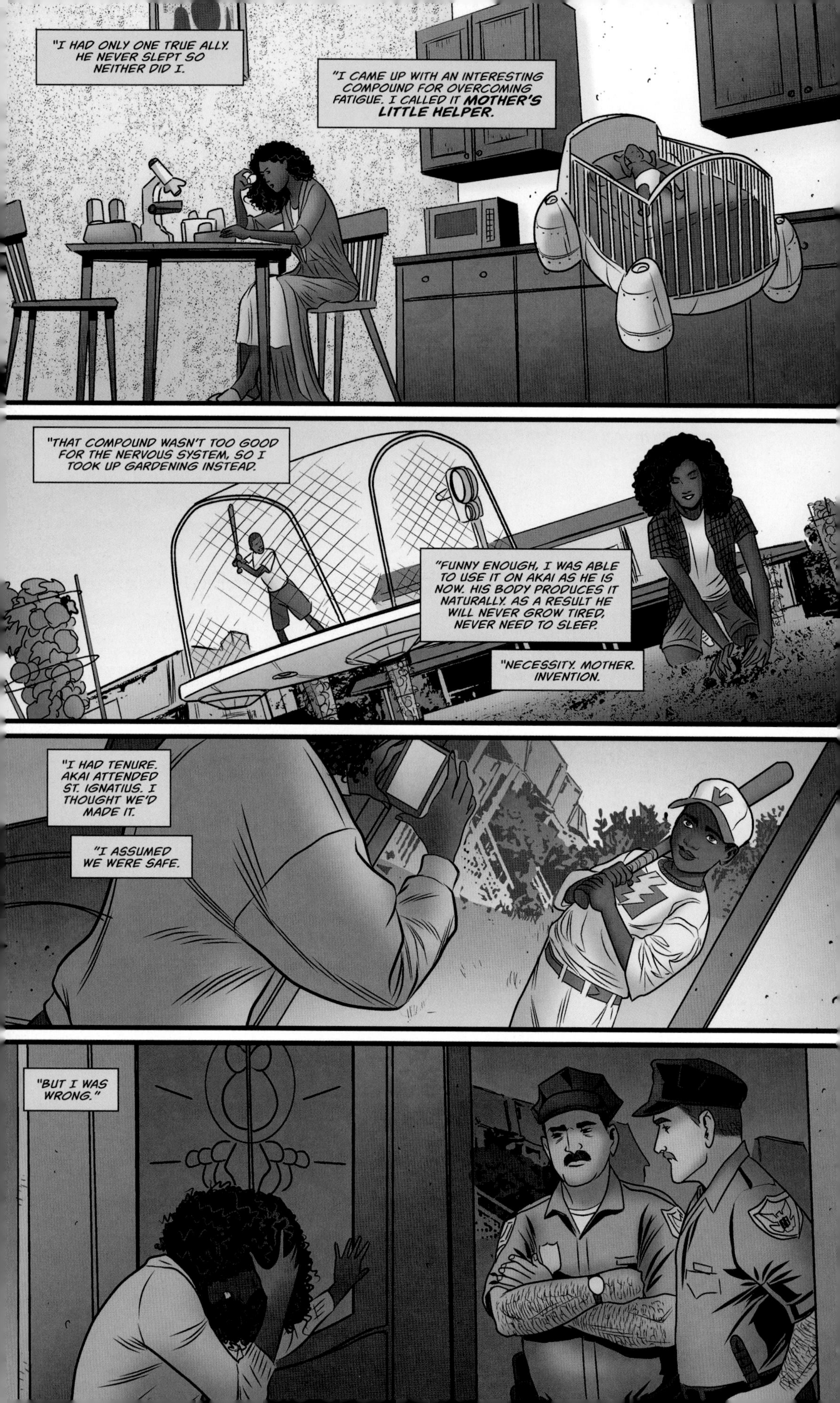
"I HAD ONLY ONE TRUE ALLY. HE NEVER SLEPT SO NEITHER DID I.
"I CAME UP WITH AN INTERESTING COMPOUND FOR OVERCOMING FATIGUE. I CALLED IT **MOTHER'S LITTLE HELPER.**
"THAT COMPOUND WASN'T TOO GOOD FOR THE NERVOUS SYSTEM, SO I TOOK UP GARDENING INSTEAD.
"FUNNY ENOUGH, I WAS ABLE TO USE IT ON AKAI AS HE IS NOW. HIS BODY PRODUCES IT NATURALLY. AS A RESULT HE WILL NEVER GROW TIRED, NEVER NEED TO SLEEP.
"NECESSITY. MOTHER. INVENTION.
"I HAD TENURE. AKAI ATTENDED ST. IGNATIUS. I THOUGHT WE'D MADE IT.
"I ASSUMED WE WERE SAFE.
"BUT I WAS WRONG."

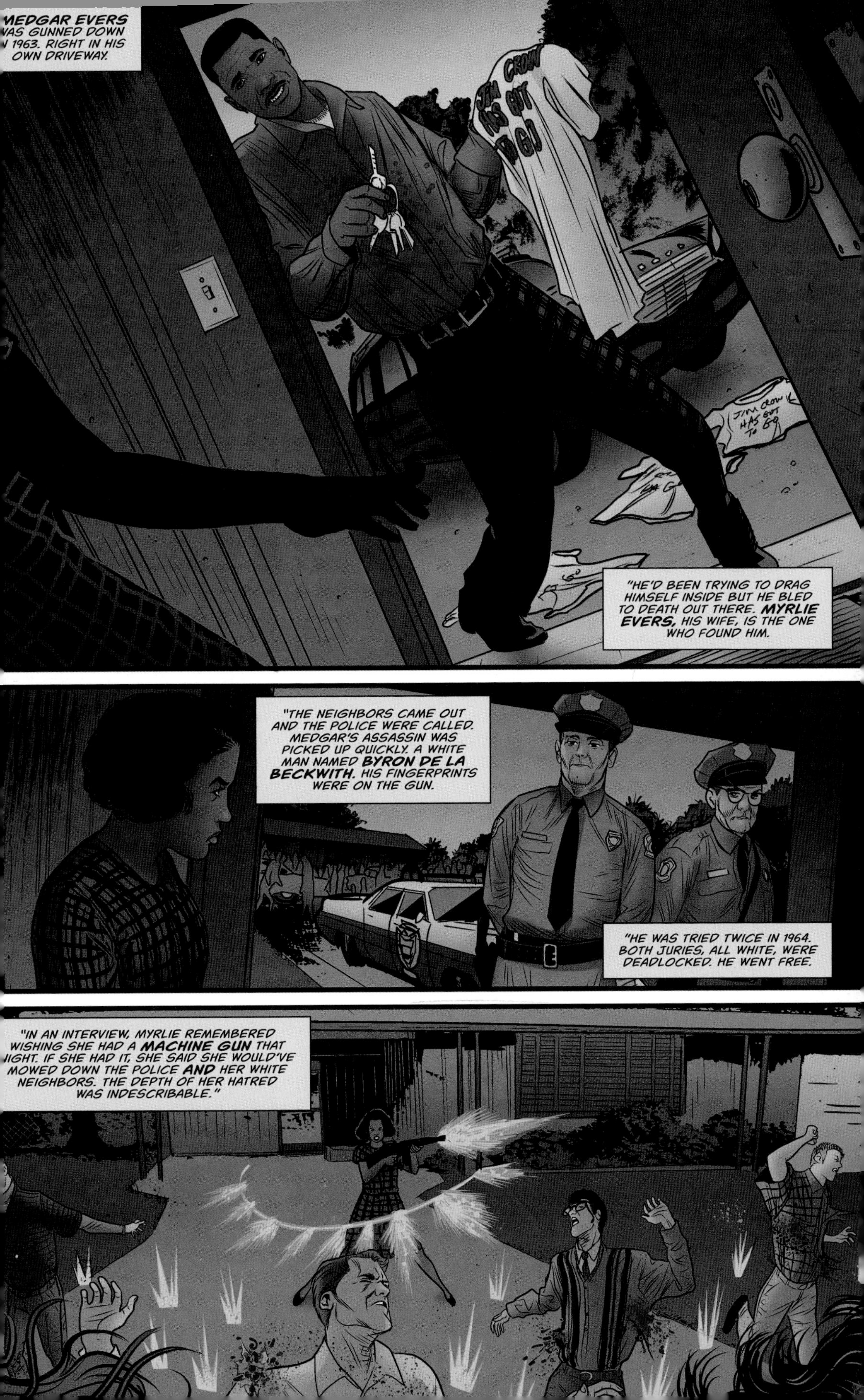

MEDGAR EVERS WAS GUNNED DOWN IN 1963. RIGHT IN HIS OWN DRIVEWAY.
JIM CROW HAS GOT TO GO
JIM CROW HAS GOT TO GO
"HE'D BEEN TRYING TO DRAG HIMSELF INSIDE BUT HE BLED TO DEATH OUT THERE. MYRLIE EVERS, HIS WIFE, IS THE ONE WHO FOUND HIM.
"THE NEIGHBORS CAME OUT AND THE POLICE WERE CALLED. MEDGAR'S ASSASSIN WAS PICKED UP QUICKLY. A WHITE MAN NAMED BYRON DE LA BECKWITH. HIS FINGERPRINTS WERE ON THE GUN.
"HE WAS TRIED TWICE IN 1964. BOTH JURIES, ALL WHITE, WERE DEADLOCKED. HE WENT FREE.
"IN AN INTERVIEW, MYRLIE REMEMBERED WISHING SHE HAD A MACHINE GUN THAT NIGHT. IF SHE HAD IT, SHE SAID SHE WOULD'VE MOWED DOWN THE POLICE AND HER WHITE NEIGHBORS. THE DEPTH OF HER HATRED WAS INDESCRIBABLE."

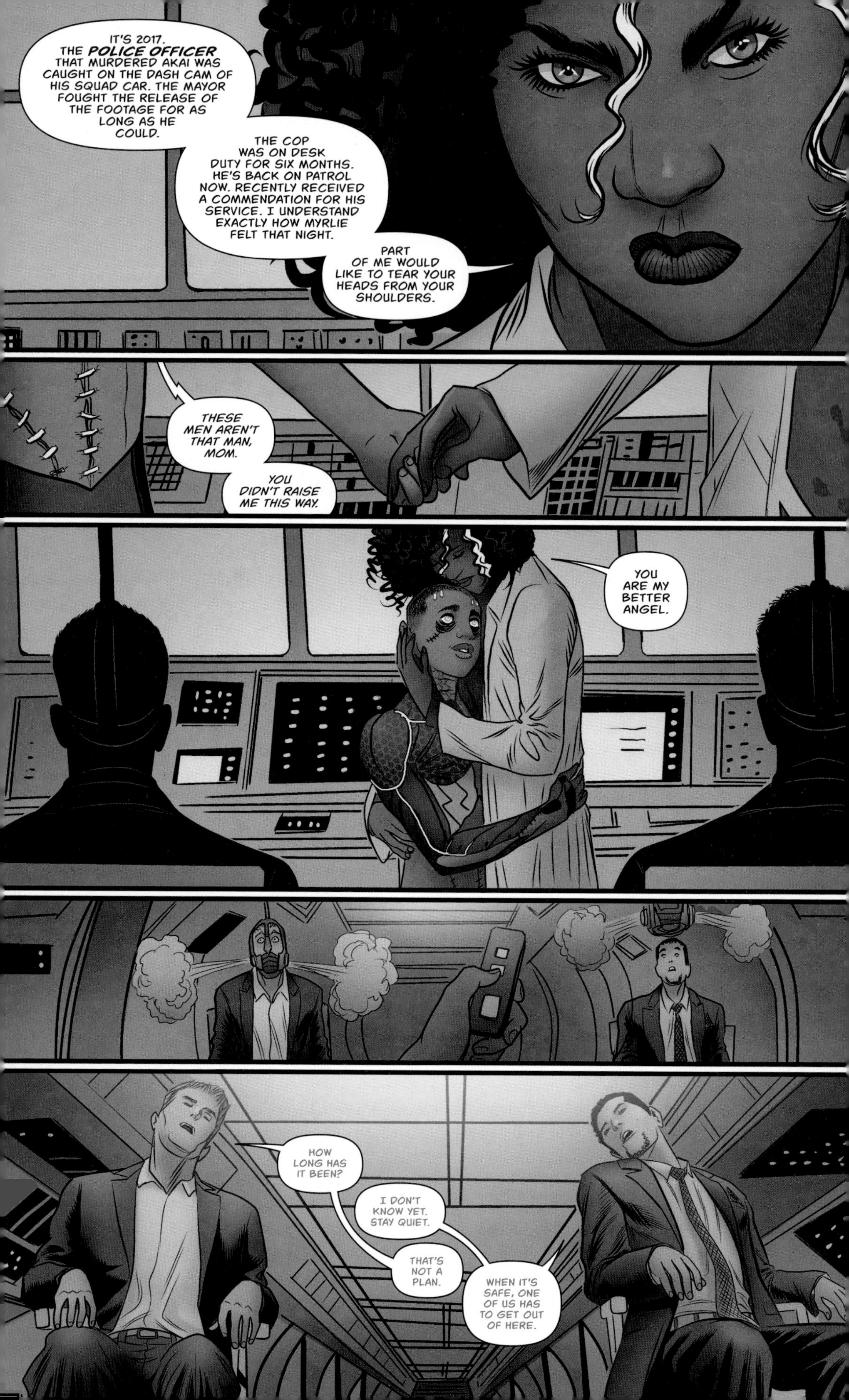
IT'S 2017. THE POLICE OFFICER THAT MURDERED AKAI WAS CAUGHT ON THE DASH CAM OF HIS SQUAD CAR. THE MAYOR FOUGHT THE RELEASE OF THE FOOTAGE FOR AS LONG AS HE COULD.
THE COP WAS ON DESK DUTY FOR SIX MONTHS. HE'S BACK ON PATROL NOW. RECENTLY RECEIVED A COMMENDATION FOR HIS SERVICE. I UNDERSTAND EXACTLY HOW MYRLIE FELT THAT NIGHT.
PART OF ME WOULD LIKE TO TEAR YOUR HEADS FROM YOUR SHOULDERS.
THESE MEN AREN'T THAT MAN, MOM.
YOU DIDN'T RAISE ME THIS WAY.
YOU ARE MY BETTER ANGEL.
HOW LONG HAS IT BEEN?
I DON'T KNOW YET. STAY QUIET.
THAT'S NOT A PLAN.
WHEN IT'S SAFE, ONE OF US HAS TO GET OUT OF HERE.

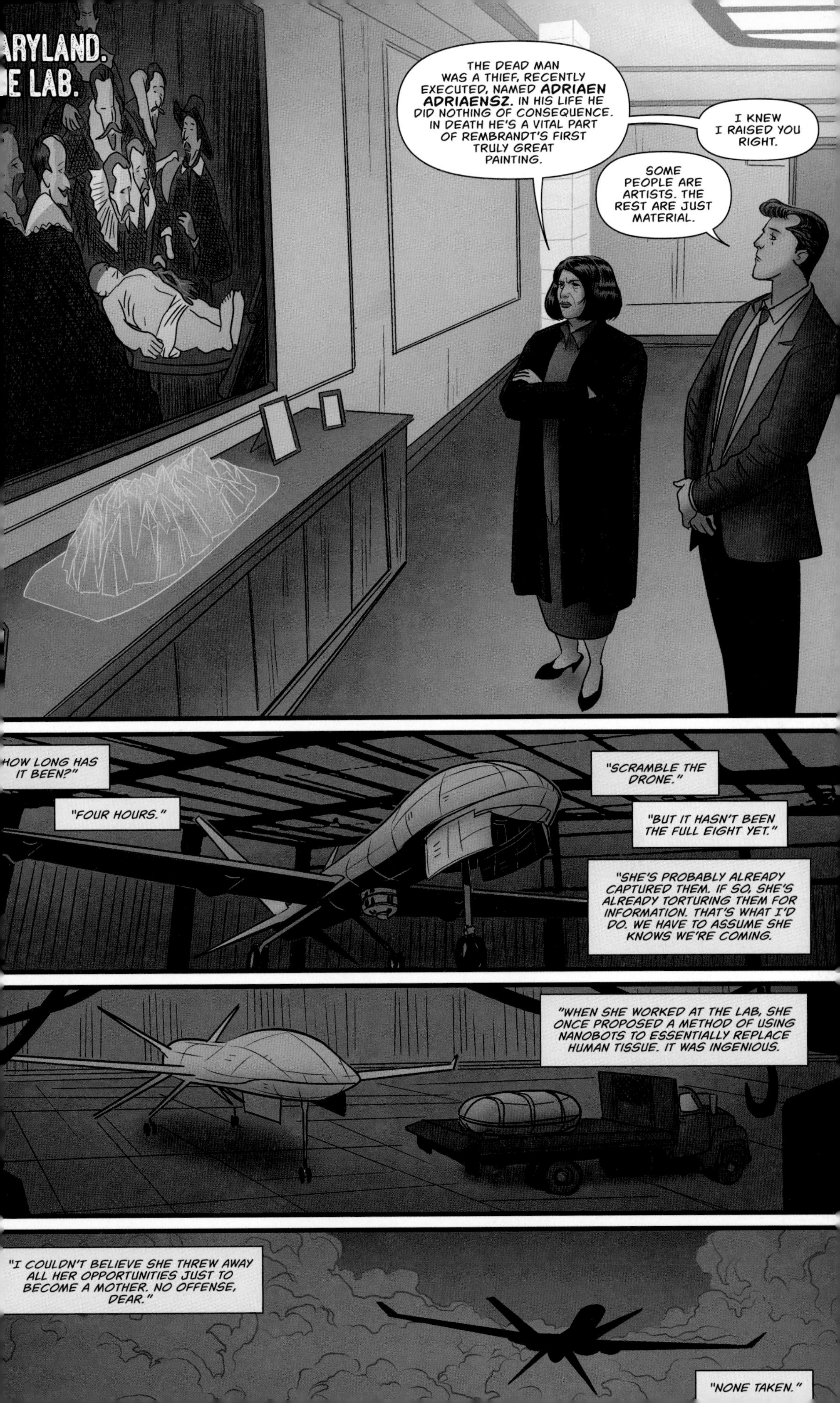
ARYLAND.
E LAB.
THE DEAD MAN WAS A THIEF, RECENTLY EXECUTED, NAMED ADRIAEN ADRIAENSZ. IN HIS LIFE HE DID NOTHING OF CONSEQUENCE. IN DEATH HE'S A VITAL PART OF REMBRANDT'S FIRST TRULY GREAT PAINTING.
I KNEW I RAISED YOU RIGHT.
SOME PEOPLE ARE ARTISTS. THE REST ARE JUST MATERIAL.
HOW LONG HAS IT BEEN?"
"FOUR HOURS."
"SCRAMBLE THE DRONE."
"BUT IT HASN'T BEEN THE FULL EIGHT YET."
"SHE'S PROBABLY ALREADY CAPTURED THEM. IF SO, SHE'S ALREADY TORTURING THEM FOR INFORMATION. THAT'S WHAT I'D DO. WE HAVE TO ASSUME SHE KNOWS WE'RE COMING.
"WHEN SHE WORKED AT THE LAB, SHE ONCE PROPOSED A METHOD OF USING NANOBOTS TO ESSENTIALLY REPLACE HUMAN TISSUE. IT WAS INGENIOUS.
"I COULDN'T BELIEVE SHE THREW AWAY ALL HER OPPORTUNITIES JUST TO BECOME A MOTHER. NO OFFENSE, DEAR."
"NONE TAKEN."

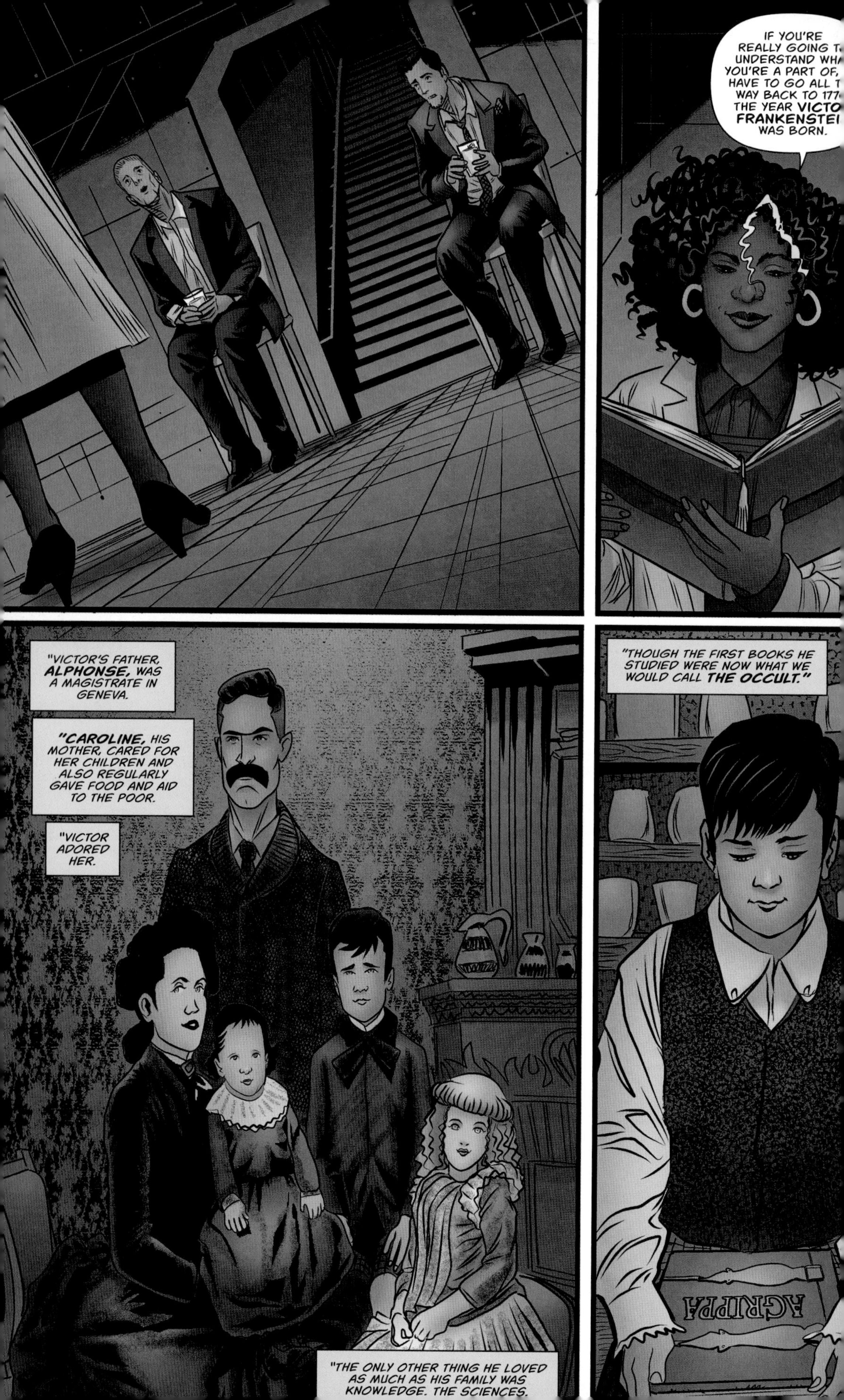
IF YOU'RE REALLY GOING T UNDERSTAND WH YOU'RE A PART OF, HAVE TO GO ALL T WAY BACK TO 177 THE YEAR VICTO FRANKENSTEI WAS BORN.
"VICTOR'S FATHER, ALPHONSE, WAS A MAGISTRATE IN GENEVA.
"CAROLINE, HIS MOTHER, CARED FOR HER CHILDREN AND ALSO REGULARLY GAVE FOOD AND AID TO THE POOR.
"VICTOR ADORED HER.
"THE ONLY OTHER THING HE LOVED AS MUCH AS HIS FAMILY WAS KNOWLEDGE. THE SCIENCES.
"THOUGH THE FIRST BOOKS HE STUDIED WERE NOW WHAT WE WOULD CALL THE OCCULT."
AGRIPPA

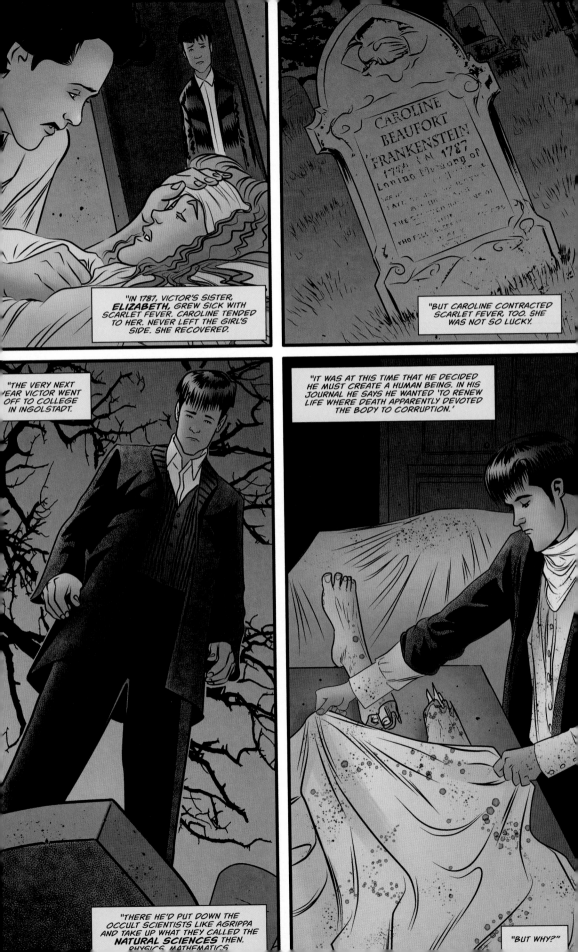

"IN 1787, VICTOR'S SISTER, **ELIZABETH,** GREW SICK WITH SCARLET FEVER. CAROLINE TENDED TO HER. NEVER LEFT THE GIRL'S SIDE. SHE RECOVERED.

"BUT CAROLINE CONTRACTED SCARLET FEVER, TOO. SHE WAS NOT SO LUCKY."

CAROLINE
BEAUFORT
FRANKENSTEIN

"THE VERY NEXT YEAR VICTOR WENT OFF TO COLLEGE IN INGOLSTADT.

"IT WAS AT THIS TIME THAT HE DECIDED HE MUST CREATE A HUMAN BEING. IN HIS JOURNAL HE SAYS HE WANTED 'TO RENEW LIFE WHERE DEATH APPARENTLY DEVOTED THE BODY TO CORRUPTION.'

"THERE HE'D PUT DOWN THE OCCULT SCIENTISTS LIKE AGRIPPA AND TAKE UP WHAT THEY CALLED THE **NATURAL SCIENCES** THEN.

"BUT WHY?"

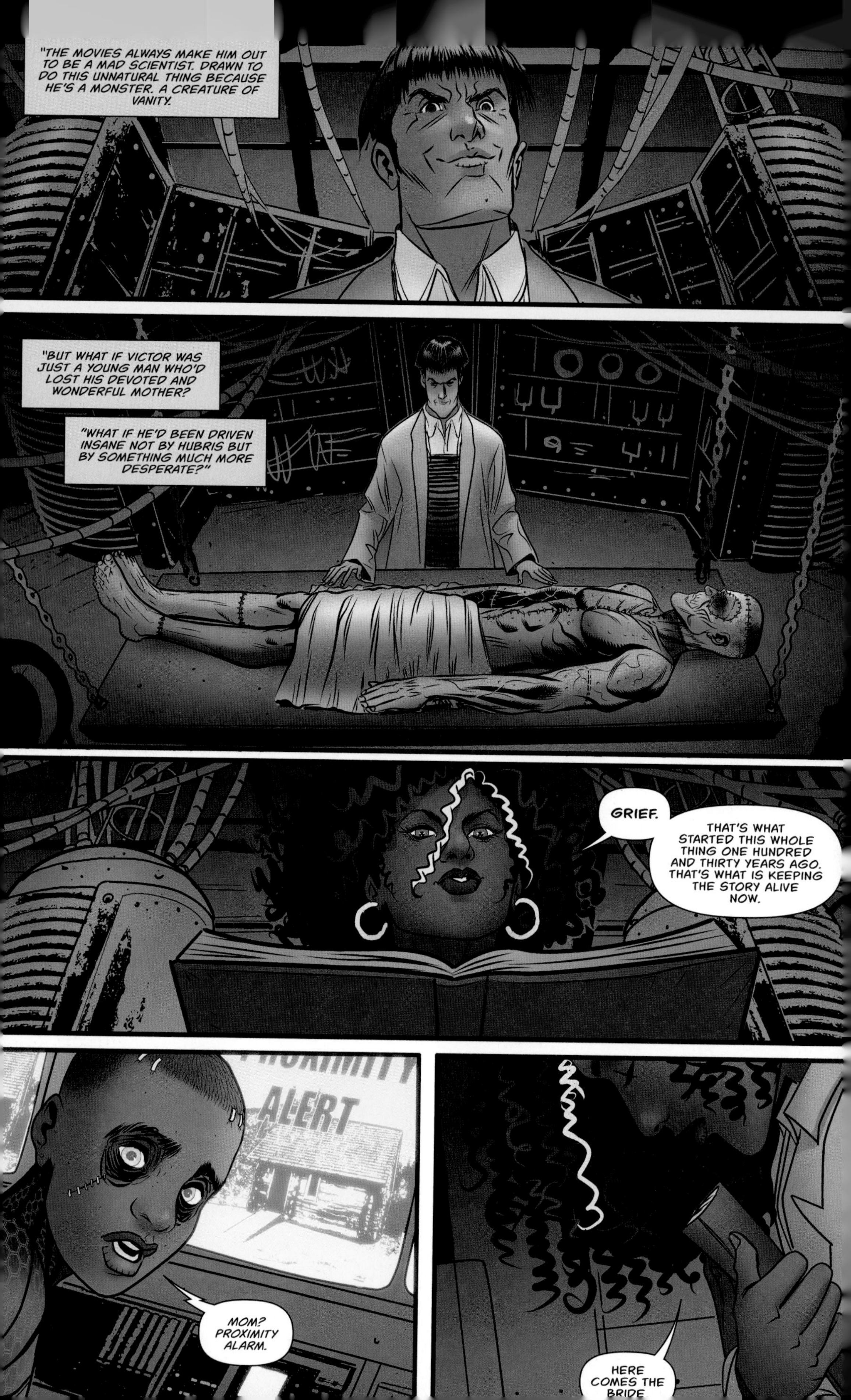
"THE MOVIES ALWAYS MAKE HIM OUT TO BE A MAD SCIENTIST. DRAWN TO DO THIS UNNATURAL THING BECAUSE HE'S A MONSTER. A CREATURE OF VANITY.
"BUT WHAT IF VICTOR WAS JUST A YOUNG MAN WHO'D LOST HIS DEVOTED AND WONDERFUL MOTHER?
"WHAT IF HE'D BEEN DRIVEN INSANE NOT BY HUBRIS BUT BY SOMETHING MUCH MORE DESPERATE?"
GRIEF.
THAT'S WHAT STARTED THIS WHOLE THING ONE HUNDRED AND THIRTY YEARS AGO. THAT'S WHAT IS KEEPING THE STORY ALIVE NOW.
ALERT
MOM? PROXIMITY ALARM.
HERE COMES THE BRIDE

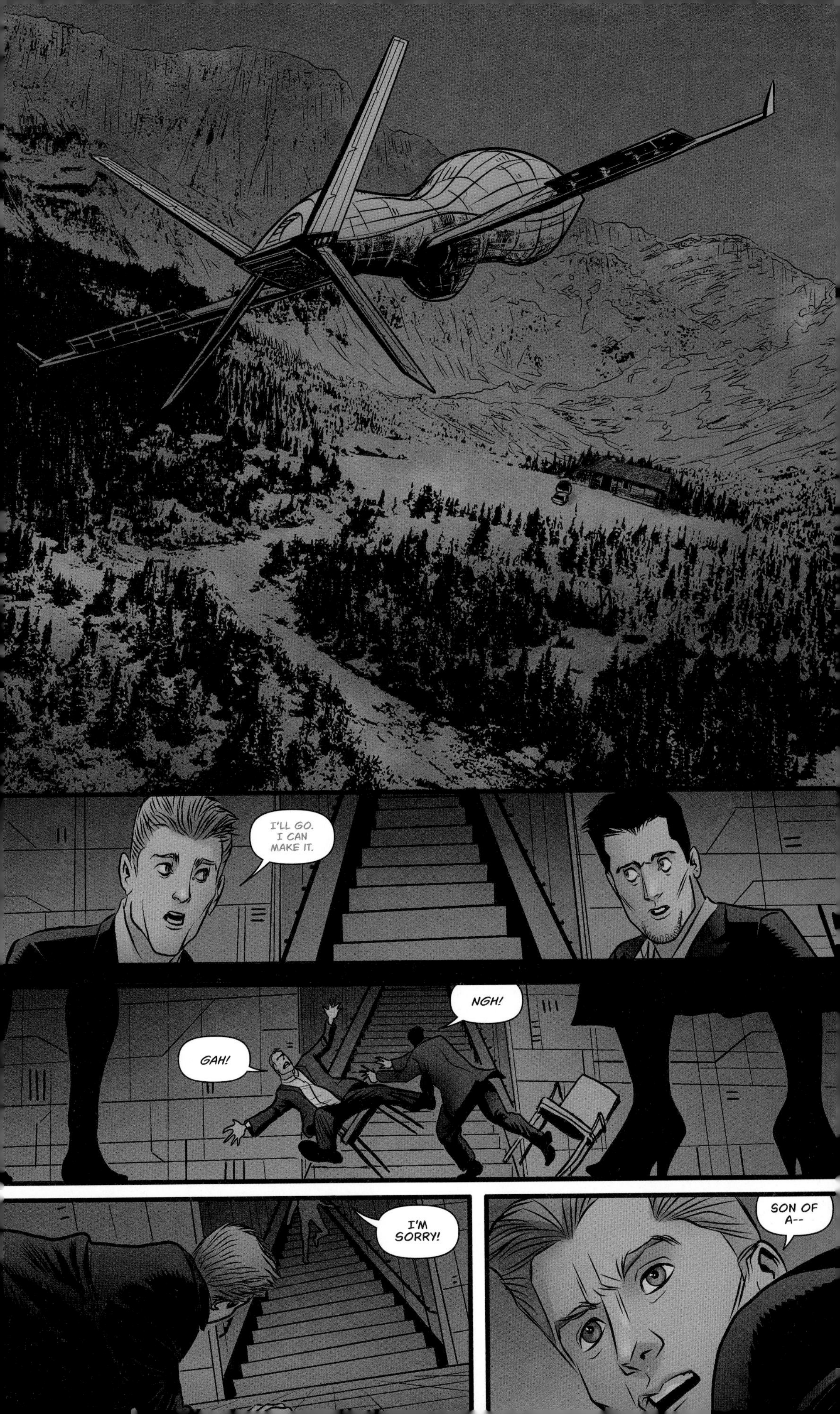
I'LL GO. I CAN MAKE IT.
NGH!
GAH!
I'M SORRY!
SON OF A--

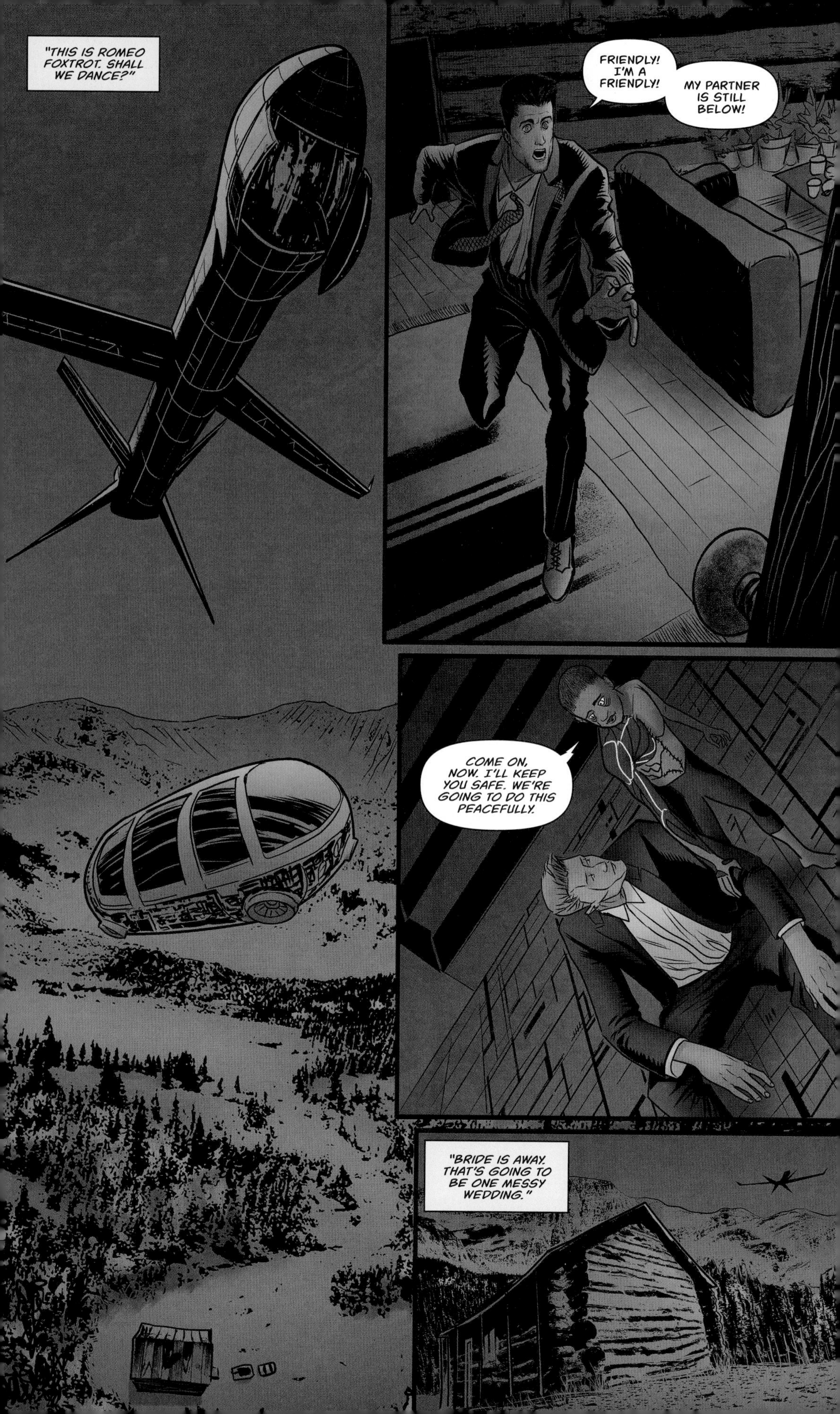
"THIS IS ROMEO FOXTROT. SHALL WE DANCE?"
FRIENDLY! I'M A FRIENDLY!
MY PARTNER IS STILL BELOW!
COME ON, NOW. I'LL KEEP YOU SAFE. WE'RE GOING TO DO THIS PEACEFULLY.
"BRIDE IS AWAY. THAT'S GOING TO BE ONE MESSY WEDDING."

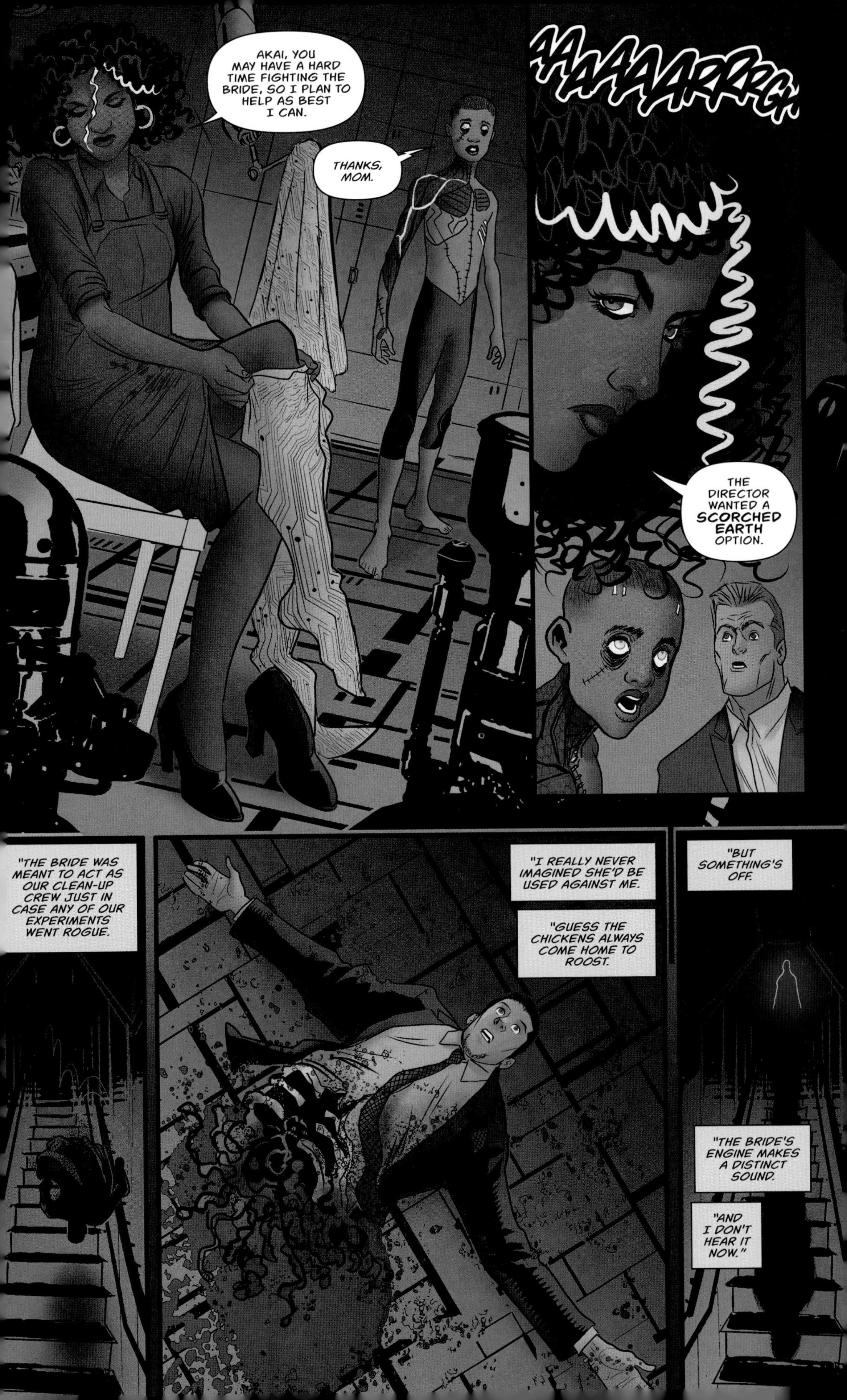
AKAI, YOU MAY HAVE A HARD TIME FIGHTING THE BRIDE, SO I PLAN TO HELP AS BEST I CAN.
THANKS, MOM.
AAAAAARRRGH
THE DIRECTOR WANTED A **SCORCHED EARTH** OPTION.
"THE BRIDE WAS MEANT TO ACT AS OUR CLEAN-UP CREW JUST IN CASE ANY OF OUR EXPERIMENTS WENT ROGUE.
"I REALLY NEVER IMAGINED SHE'D BE USED AGAINST ME.
"GUESS THE CHICKENS ALWAYS COME HOME TO ROOST.
"BUT SOMETHING'S OFF.
"THE BRIDE'S ENGINE MAKES A DISTINCT SOUND.
"AND I DON'T HEAR IT NOW."

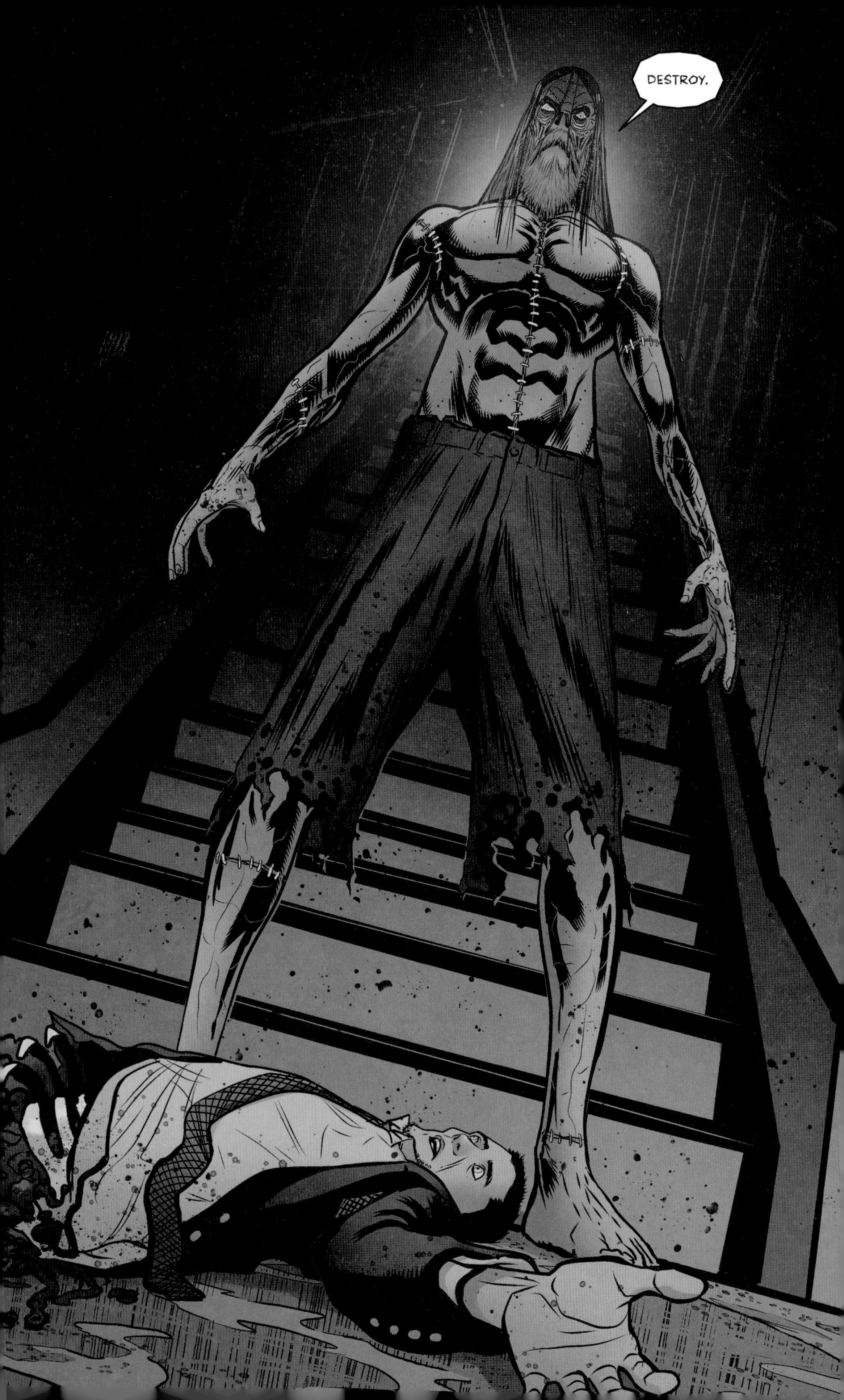
DESTROY.

CHAPTER
FOUR

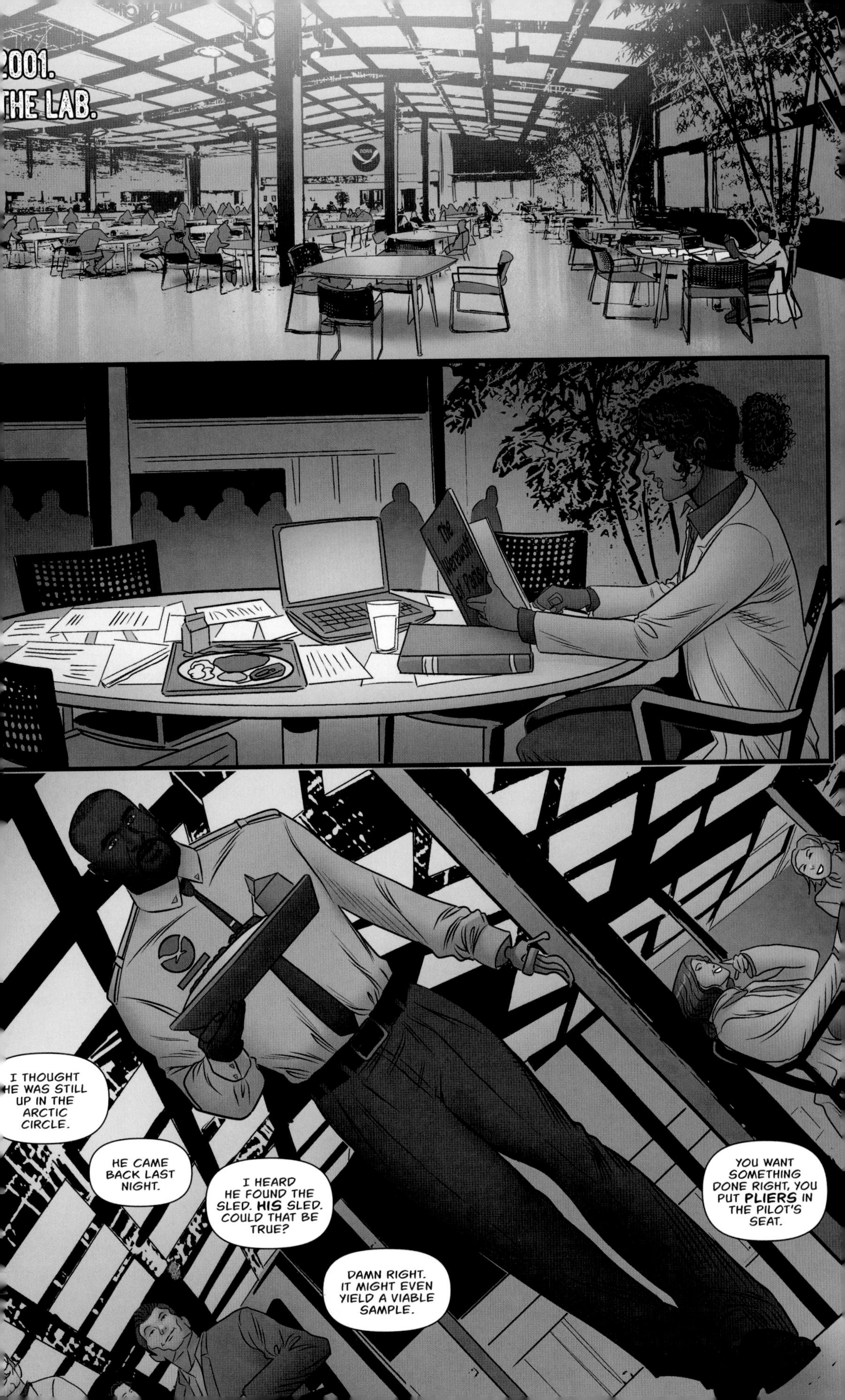
2001.
THE LAB.
I THOUGHT HE WAS STILL UP IN THE ARCTIC CIRCLE.
HE CAME BACK LAST NIGHT.
I HEARD HE FOUND THE SLED. HIS SLED. COULD THAT BE TRUE?
DAMN RIGHT. IT MIGHT EVEN YIELD A VIABLE SAMPLE.
YOU WANT SOMETHING DONE RIGHT, YOU PUT PLIERS IN THE PILOT'S SEAT.

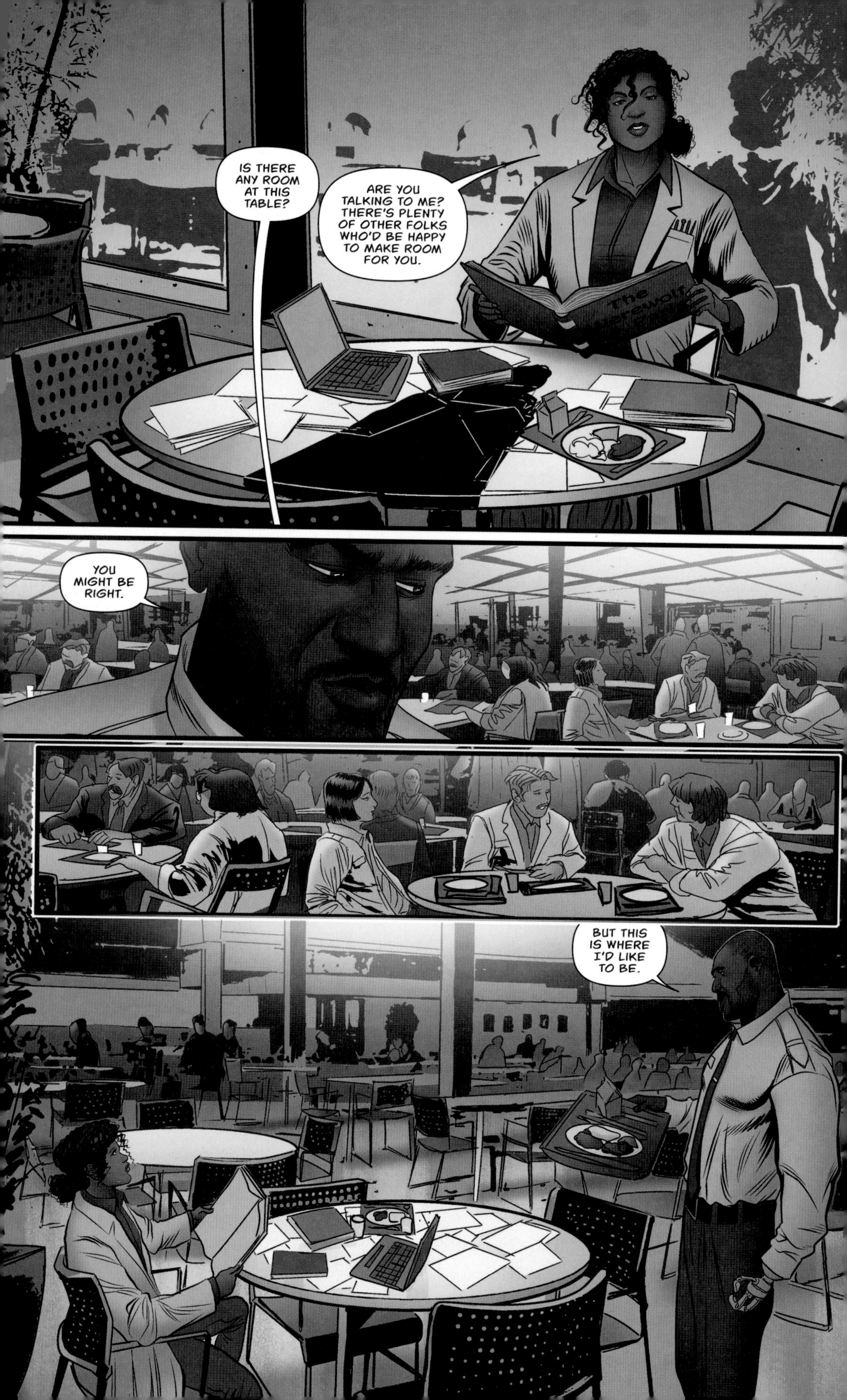
IS THERE ANY ROOM AT THIS TABLE?
ARE YOU TALKING TO ME? THERE'S PLENTY OF OTHER FOLKS WHO'D BE HAPPY TO MAKE ROOM FOR YOU.
YOU MIGHT BE RIGHT.
BUT THIS IS WHERE I'D LIKE TO BE.

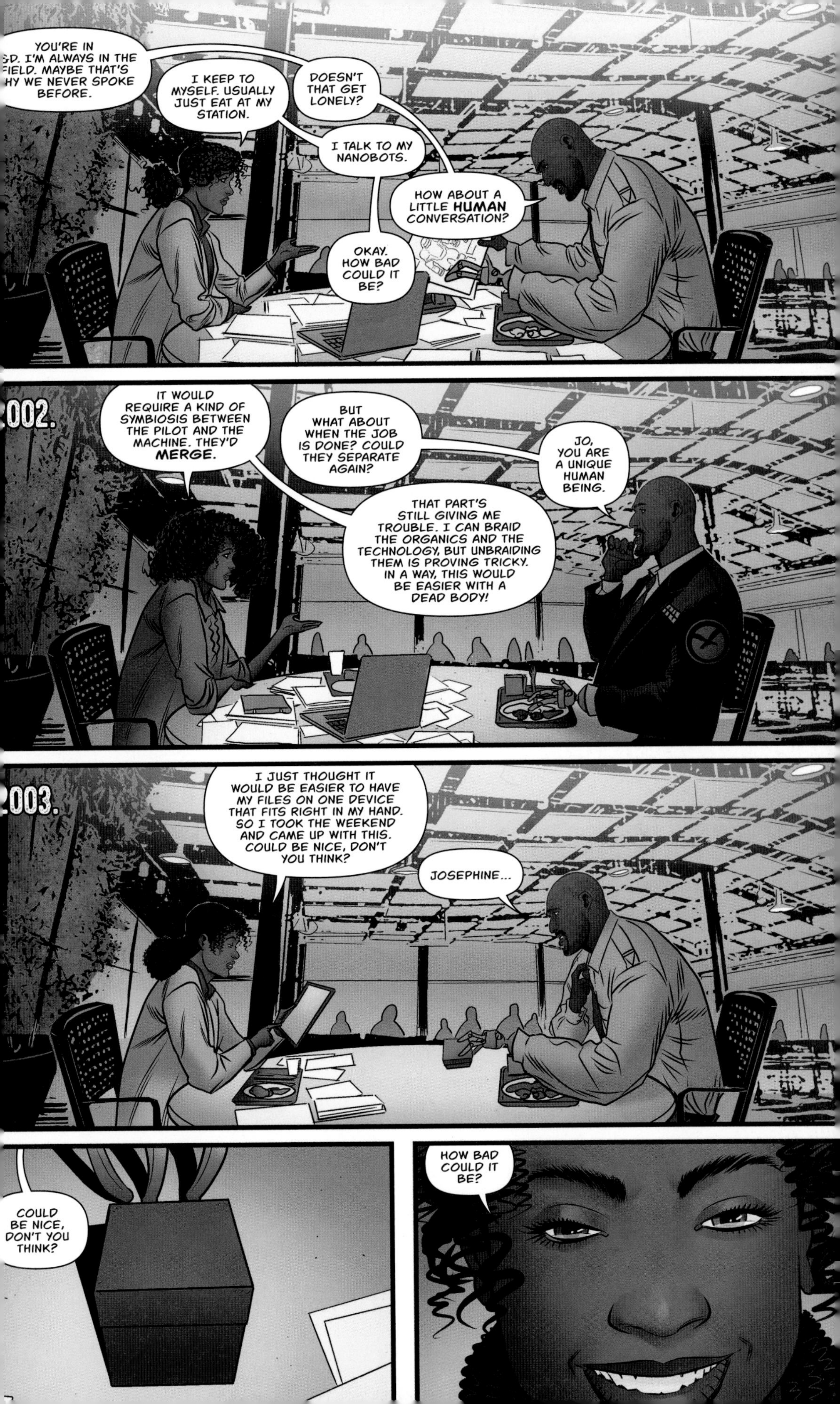

YOU'RE IN GD. I'M ALWAYS IN THE FIELD. MAYBE THAT'S WHY WE NEVER SPOKE BEFORE.
I KEEP TO MYSELF. USUALLY JUST EAT AT MY STATION.
DOESN'T THAT GET LONELY?
I TALK TO MY NANOBOTS.
HOW ABOUT A LITTLE **HUMAN** CONVERSATION?
OKAY. HOW BAD COULD IT BE?
002.
IT WOULD REQUIRE A KIND OF SYMBIOSIS BETWEEN THE PILOT AND THE MACHINE. THEY'D **MERGE.**
BUT WHAT ABOUT WHEN THE JOB IS DONE? COULD THEY SEPARATE AGAIN?
THAT PART'S STILL GIVING ME TROUBLE. I CAN BRAID THE ORGANICS AND THE TECHNOLOGY, BUT UNBRAIDING THEM IS PROVING TRICKY. IN A WAY, THIS WOULD BE EASIER WITH A DEAD BODY!
JO, YOU ARE A UNIQUE HUMAN BEING.
003.
I JUST THOUGHT IT WOULD BE EASIER TO HAVE MY FILES ON ONE DEVICE THAT FITS RIGHT IN MY HAND. SO I TOOK THE WEEKEND AND CAME UP WITH THIS. COULD BE NICE, DON'T YOU THINK?
JOSEPHINE...
COULD BE NICE, DON'T YOU THINK?
HOW BAD COULD IT BE?

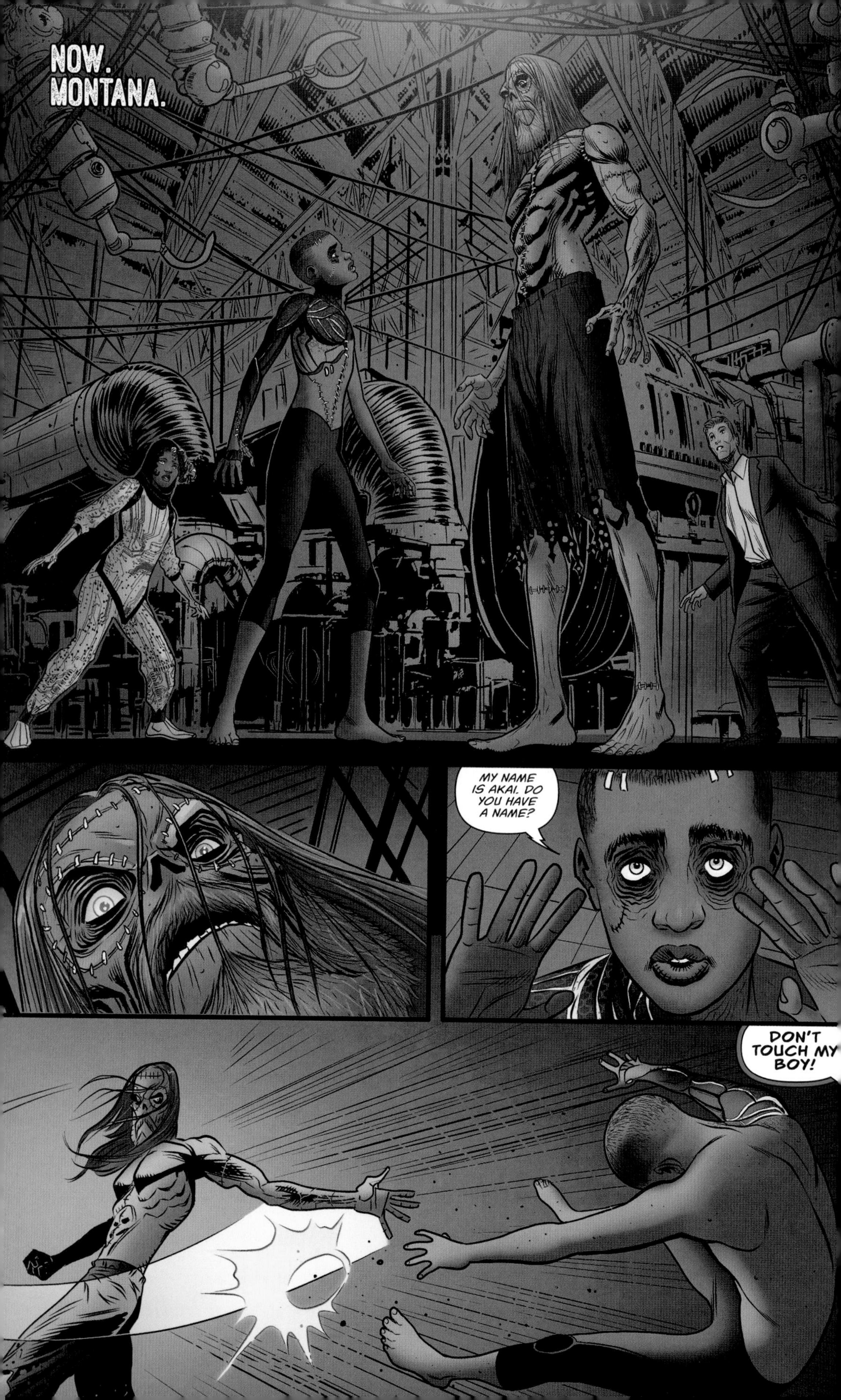
NOW.
MONTANA.
MY NAME IS AKAI. DO YOU HAVE A NAME?
DON'T TOUCH MY BOY!

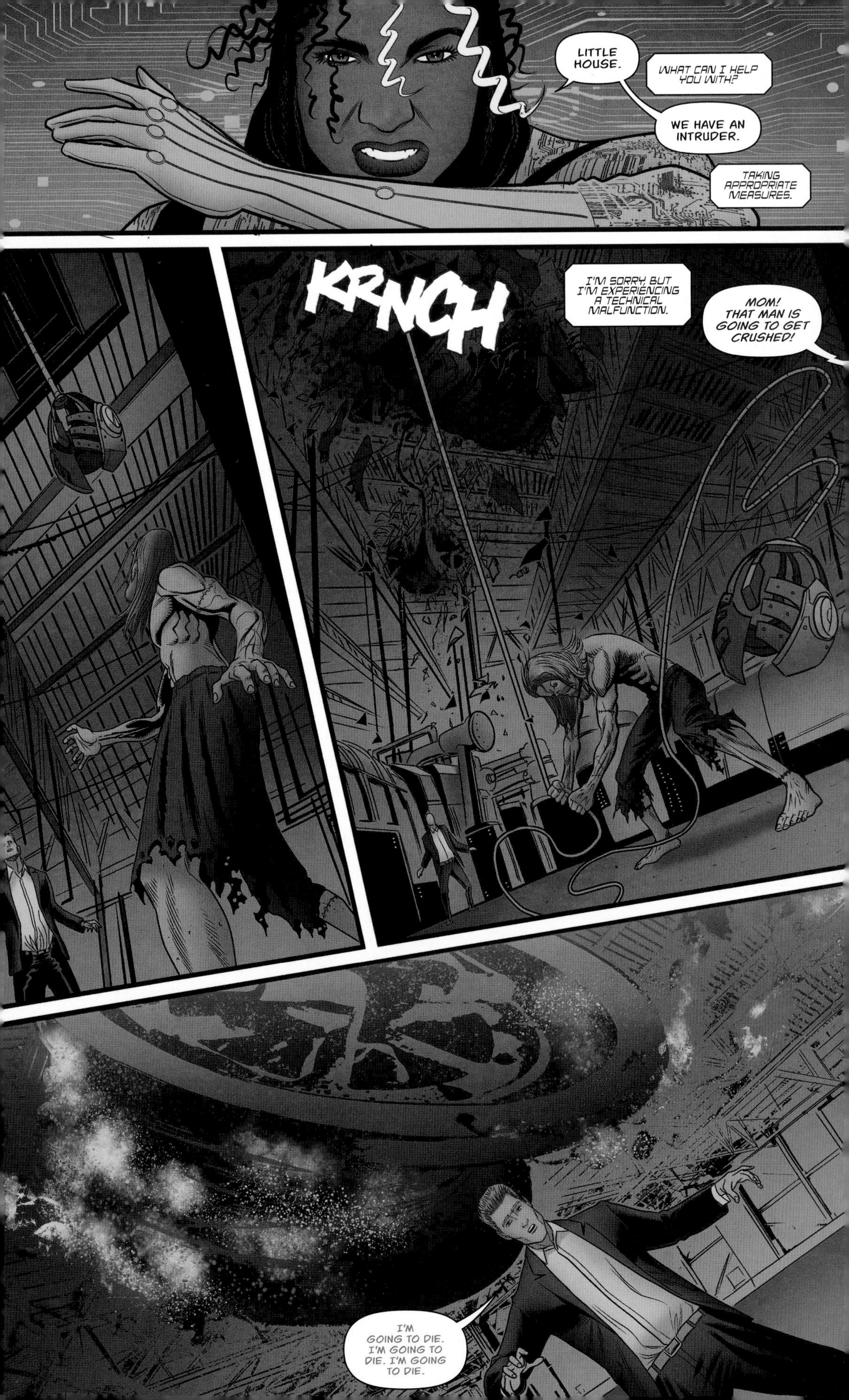
LITTLE HOUSE.
WHAT CAN I HELP YOU WITH?
WE HAVE AN INTRUDER.
TAKING APPROPRIATE MEASURES.
KRNCH
I'M SORRY, BUT I'M EXPERIENCING A TECHNICAL MALFUNCTION.
MOM! THAT MAN IS GOING TO GET CRUSHED!
I'M GOING TO DIE. I'M GOING TO DIE. I'M GOING TO DIE.

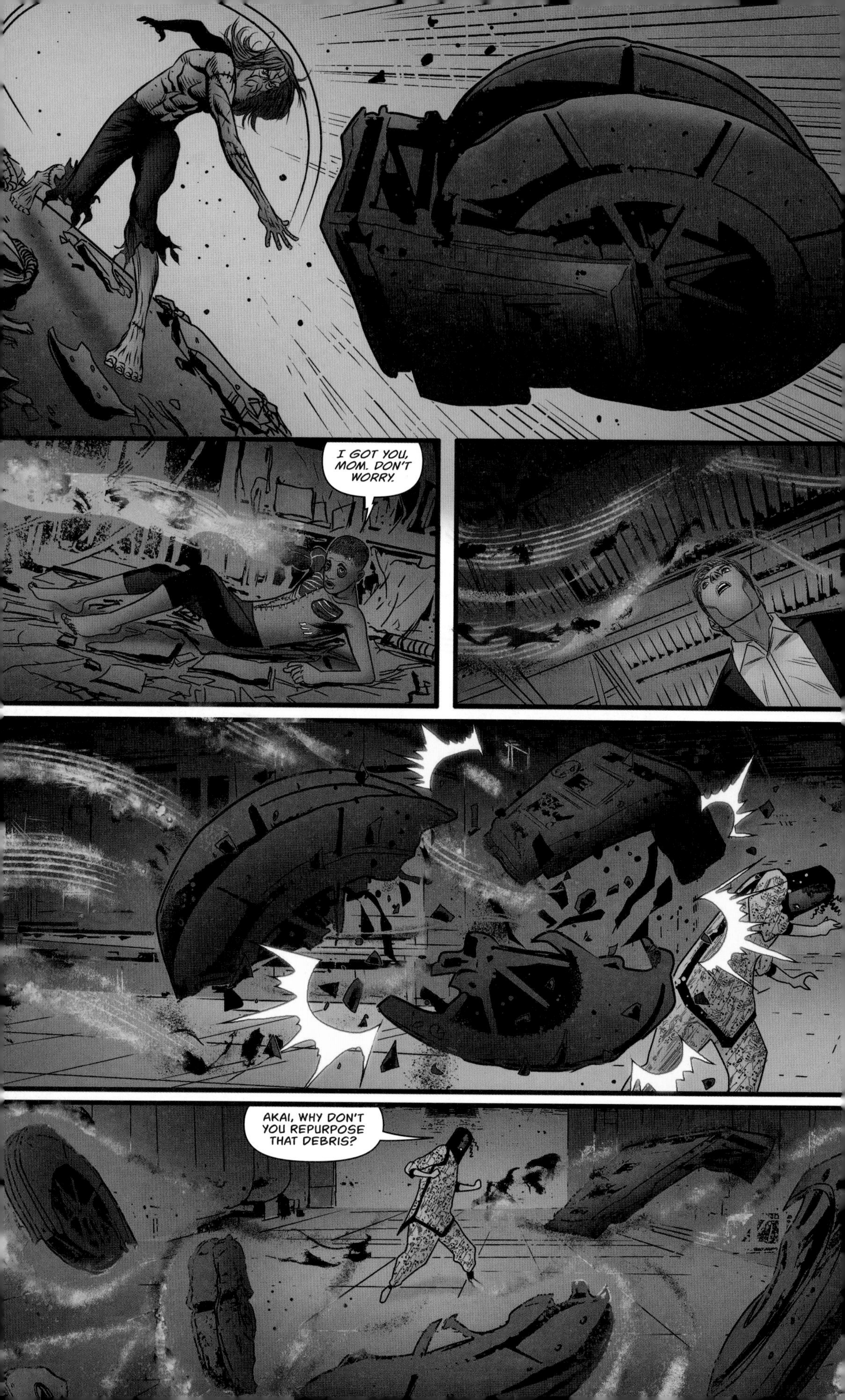
I GOT YOU, MOM. DON'T WORRY.
AKAI, WHY DON'T YOU REPURPOSE THAT DEBRIS?

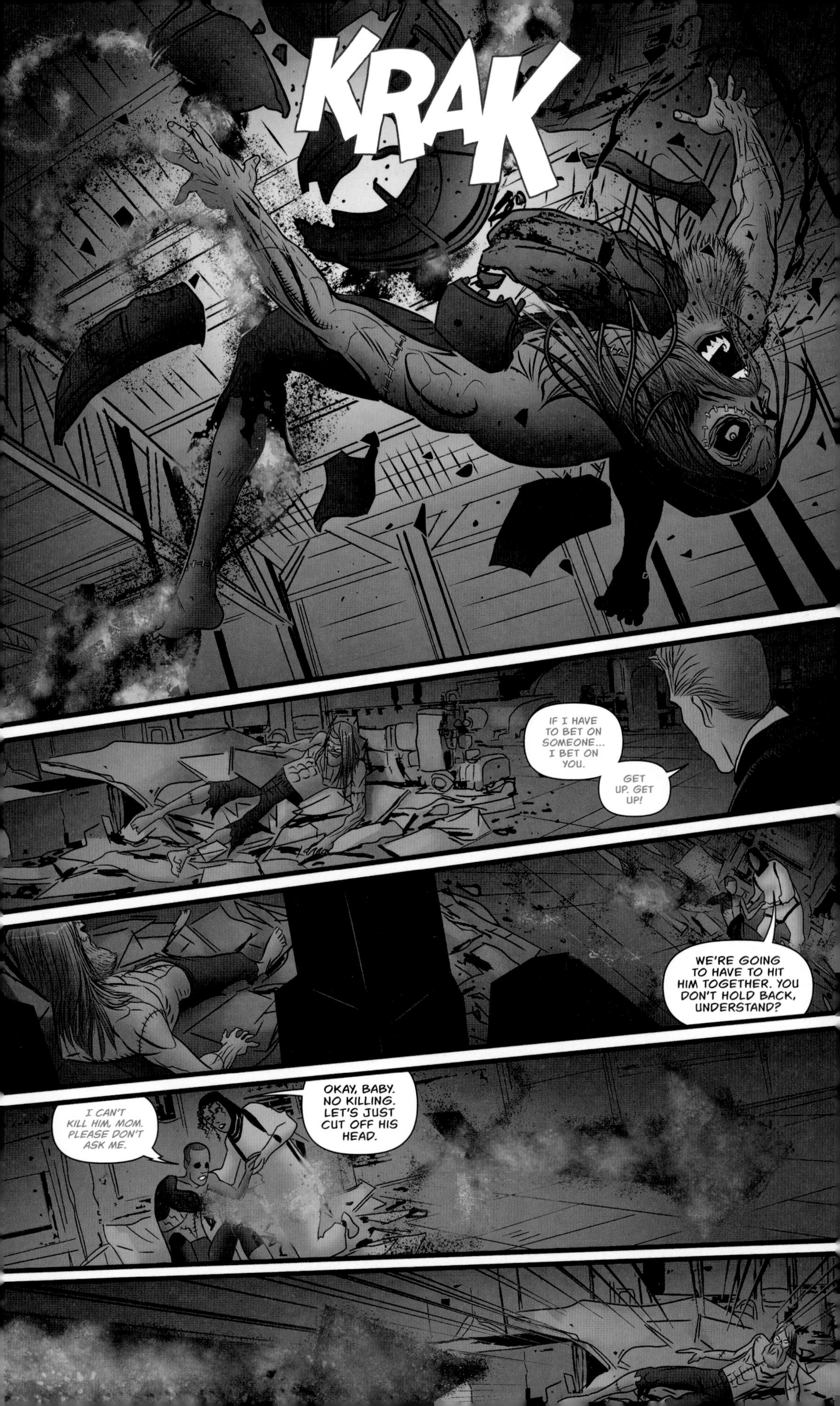
KRAK
IF I HAVE TO BET ON SOMEONE... I BET ON YOU.
GET UP. GET UP!
WE'RE GOING TO HAVE TO HIT HIM TOGETHER. YOU DON'T HOLD BACK, UNDERSTAND?
I CAN'T KILL HIM, MOM. PLEASE DON'T ASK ME.
OKAY, BABY. NO KILLING. LET'S JUST CUT OFF HIS HEAD.

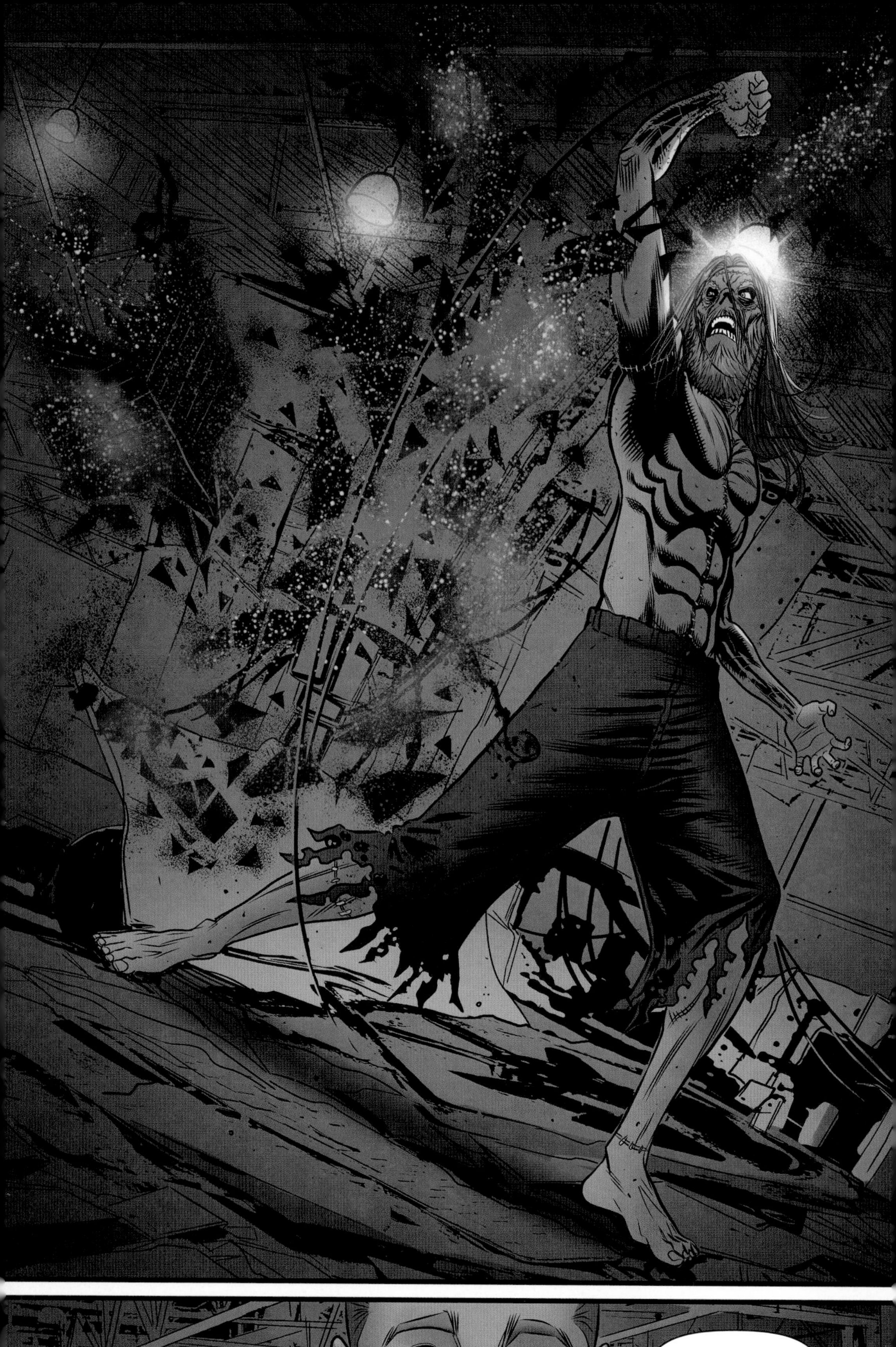
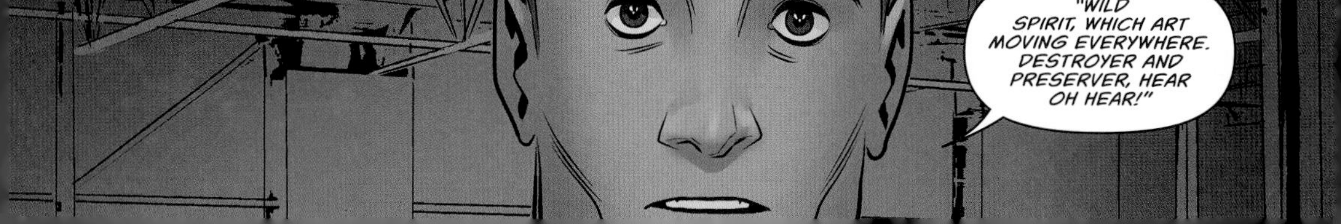
"WILD SPIRIT, WHICH ART MOVING EVERYWHERE. DESTROYER AND PRESERVER, HEAR OH HEAR!"

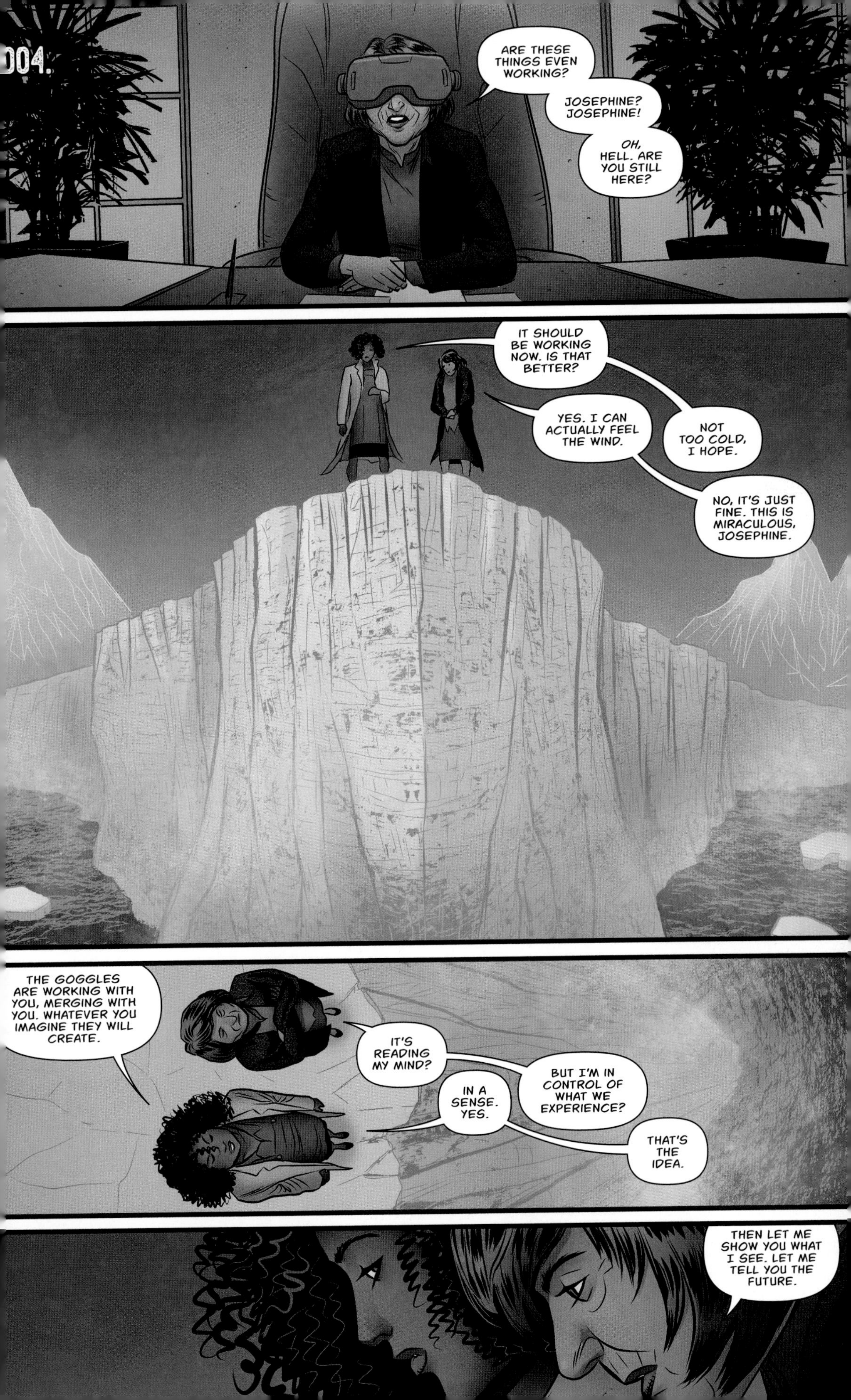
004.
ARE THESE THINGS EVEN WORKING?
JOSEPHINE? JOSEPHINE!
OH, HELL. ARE YOU STILL HERE?
IT SHOULD BE WORKING NOW. IS THAT BETTER?
YES. I CAN ACTUALLY FEEL THE WIND.
NOT TOO COLD, I HOPE.
NO, IT'S JUST FINE. THIS IS MIRACULOUS, JOSEPHINE.
THE GOGGLES ARE WORKING WITH YOU, MERGING WITH YOU. WHATEVER YOU IMAGINE THEY WILL CREATE.
IT'S READING MY MIND?
IN A SENSE. YES.
BUT I'M IN CONTROL OF WHAT WE EXPERIENCE?
THAT'S THE IDEA.
THEN LET ME SHOW YOU WHAT I SEE. LET ME TELL YOU THE FUTURE.

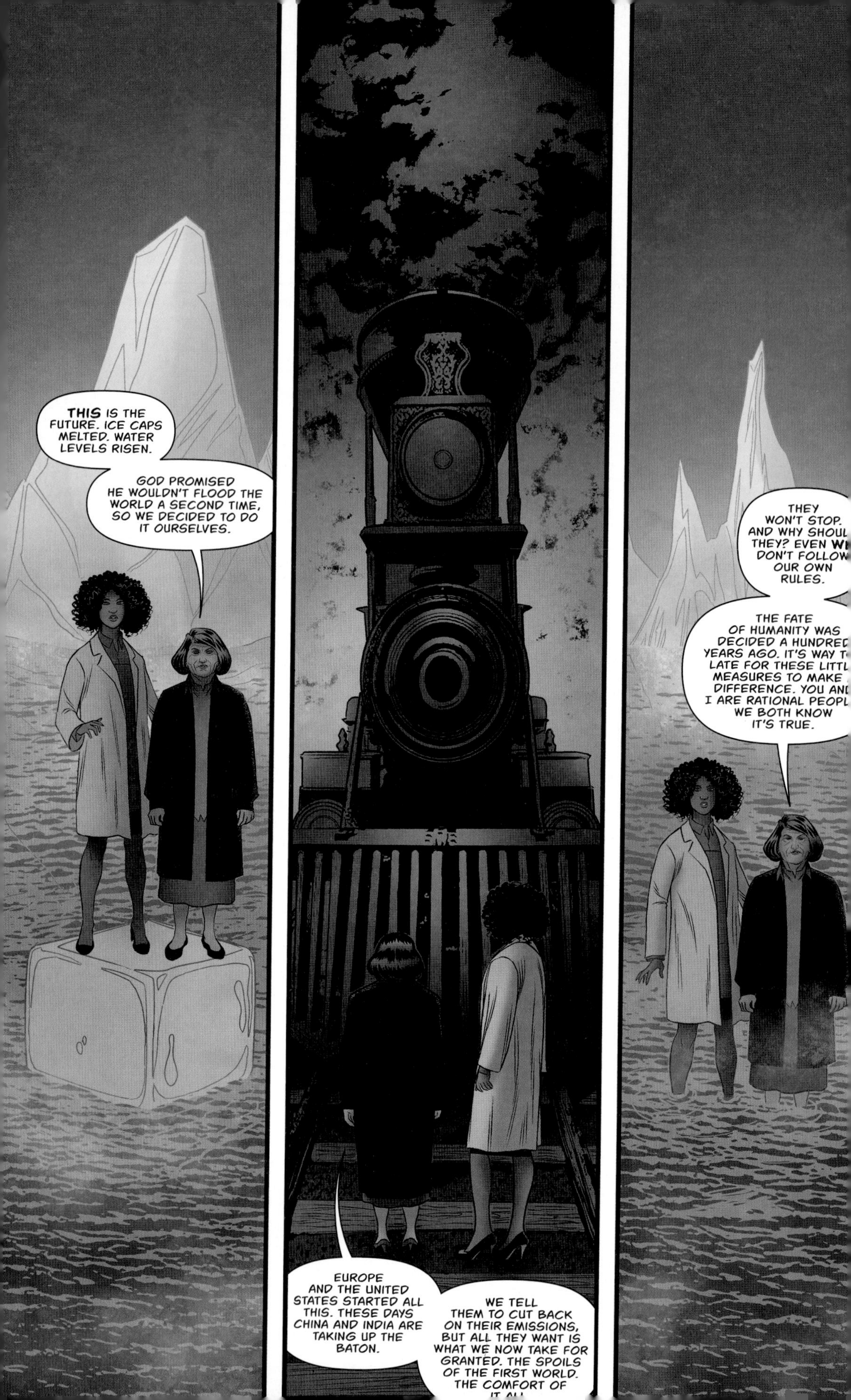

THIS IS THE FUTURE. ICE CAPS MELTED. WATER LEVELS RISEN.
GOD PROMISED HE WOULDN'T FLOOD THE WORLD A SECOND TIME, SO WE DECIDED TO DO IT OURSELVES.
EUROPE AND THE UNITED STATES STARTED ALL THIS. THESE DAYS CHINA AND INDIA ARE TAKING UP THE BATON.
WE TELL THEM TO CUT BACK ON THEIR EMISSIONS, BUT ALL THEY WANT IS WHAT WE NOW TAKE FOR GRANTED. THE SPOILS OF THE FIRST WORLD. THE COMFORT OF
THEY WON'T STOP. AND WHY SHOUL THEY? EVEN W DON'T FOLLOW OUR OWN RULES.
THE FATE OF HUMANITY WAS DECIDED A HUNDRE YEARS AGO. IT'S WAY T LATE FOR THESE LITTL MEASURES TO MAKE DIFFERENCE. YOU AN I ARE RATIONAL PEOPL WE BOTH KNOW IT'S TRUE.

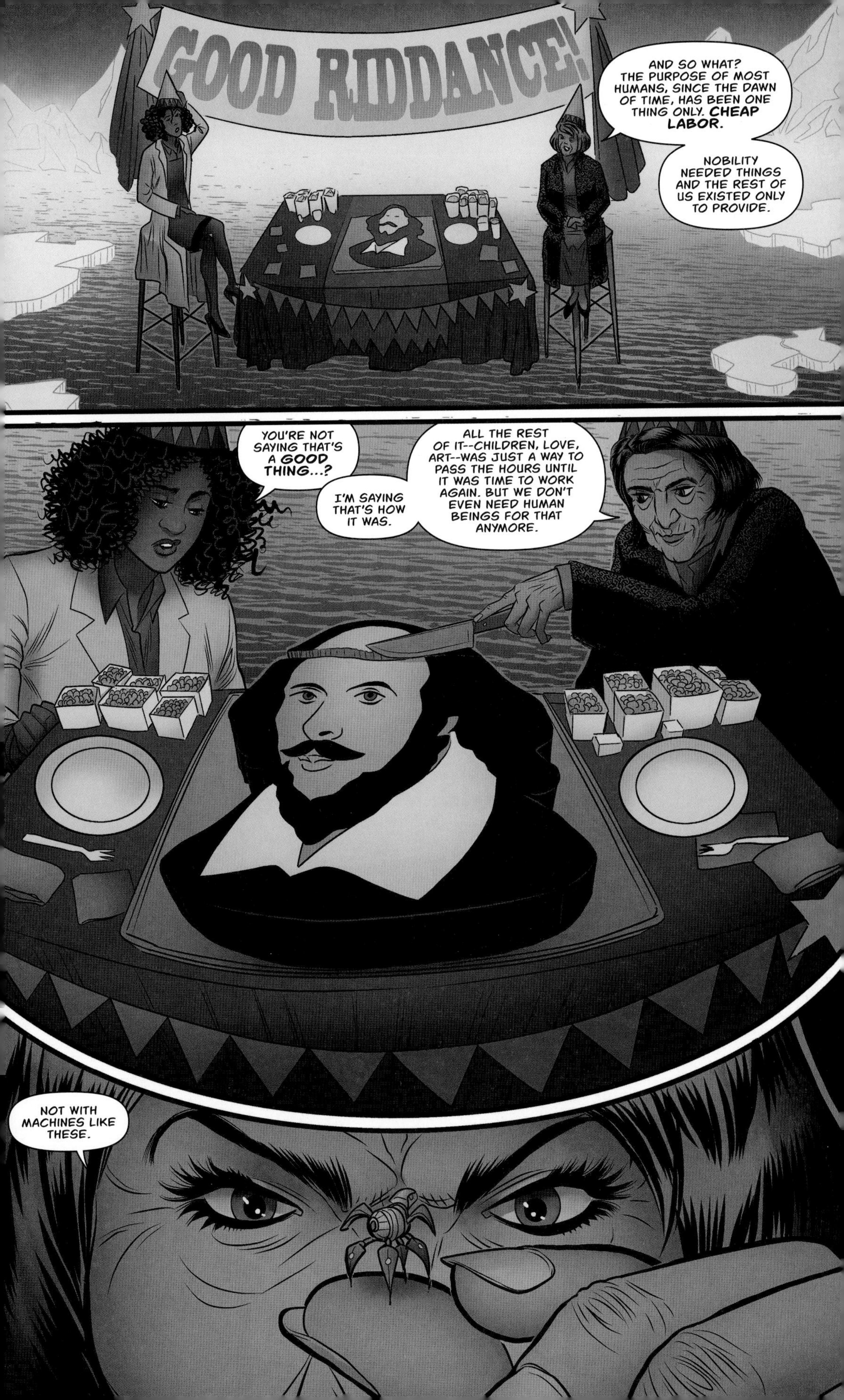
GOOD RIDDANCE!
AND SO WHAT? THE PURPOSE OF MOST HUMANS, SINCE THE DAWN OF TIME, HAS BEEN ONE THING ONLY. **CHEAP LABOR.**
NOBILITY NEEDED THINGS AND THE REST OF US EXISTED ONLY TO PROVIDE.
YOU'RE NOT SAYING THAT'S A **GOOD THING...?**
I'M SAYING THAT'S HOW IT WAS.
ALL THE REST OF IT--CHILDREN, LOVE, ART--WAS JUST A WAY TO PASS THE HOURS UNTIL IT WAS TIME TO WORK AGAIN. BUT WE DON'T EVEN NEED HUMAN BEINGS FOR THAT ANYMORE.
NOT WITH MACHINES LIKE THESE.

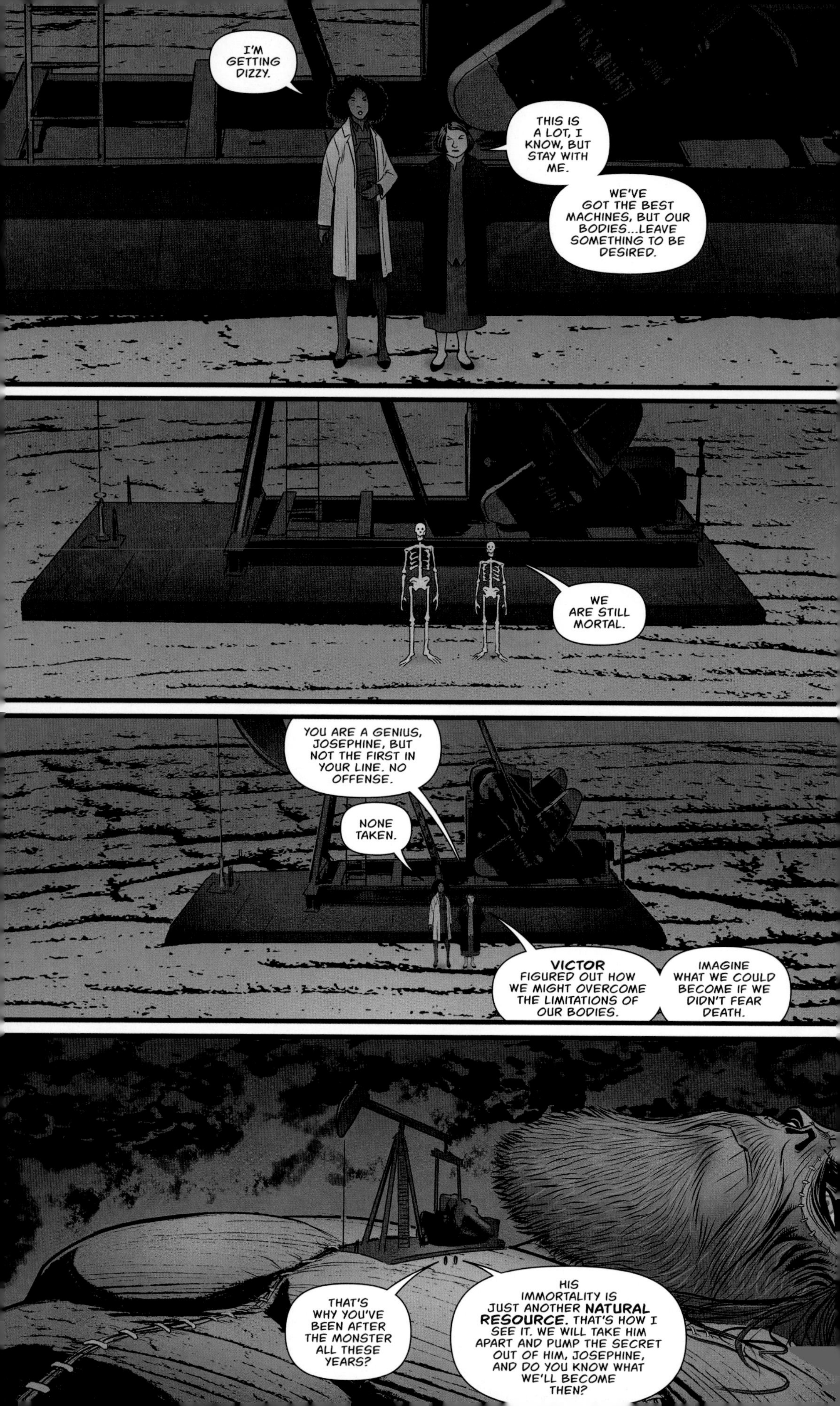

I'M GETTING DIZZY.
THIS IS A LOT, I KNOW, BUT STAY WITH ME.
WE'VE GOT THE BEST MACHINES, BUT OUR BODIES...LEAVE SOMETHING TO BE DESIRED.
WE ARE STILL MORTAL.
YOU ARE A GENIUS, JOSEPHINE, BUT NOT THE FIRST IN YOUR LINE. NO OFFENSE.
NONE TAKEN.
VICTOR FIGURED OUT HOW WE MIGHT OVERCOME THE LIMITATIONS OF OUR BODIES.
IMAGINE WHAT WE COULD BECOME IF WE DIDN'T FEAR DEATH.
THAT'S WHY YOU'VE BEEN AFTER THE MONSTER ALL THESE YEARS?
HIS IMMORTALITY IS JUST ANOTHER **NATURAL RESOURCE.** THAT'S HOW I SEE IT. WE WILL TAKE HIM APART AND PUMP THE SECRET OUT OF HIM, JOSEPHINE, AND DO YOU KNOW WHAT WE'LL BECOME THEN?

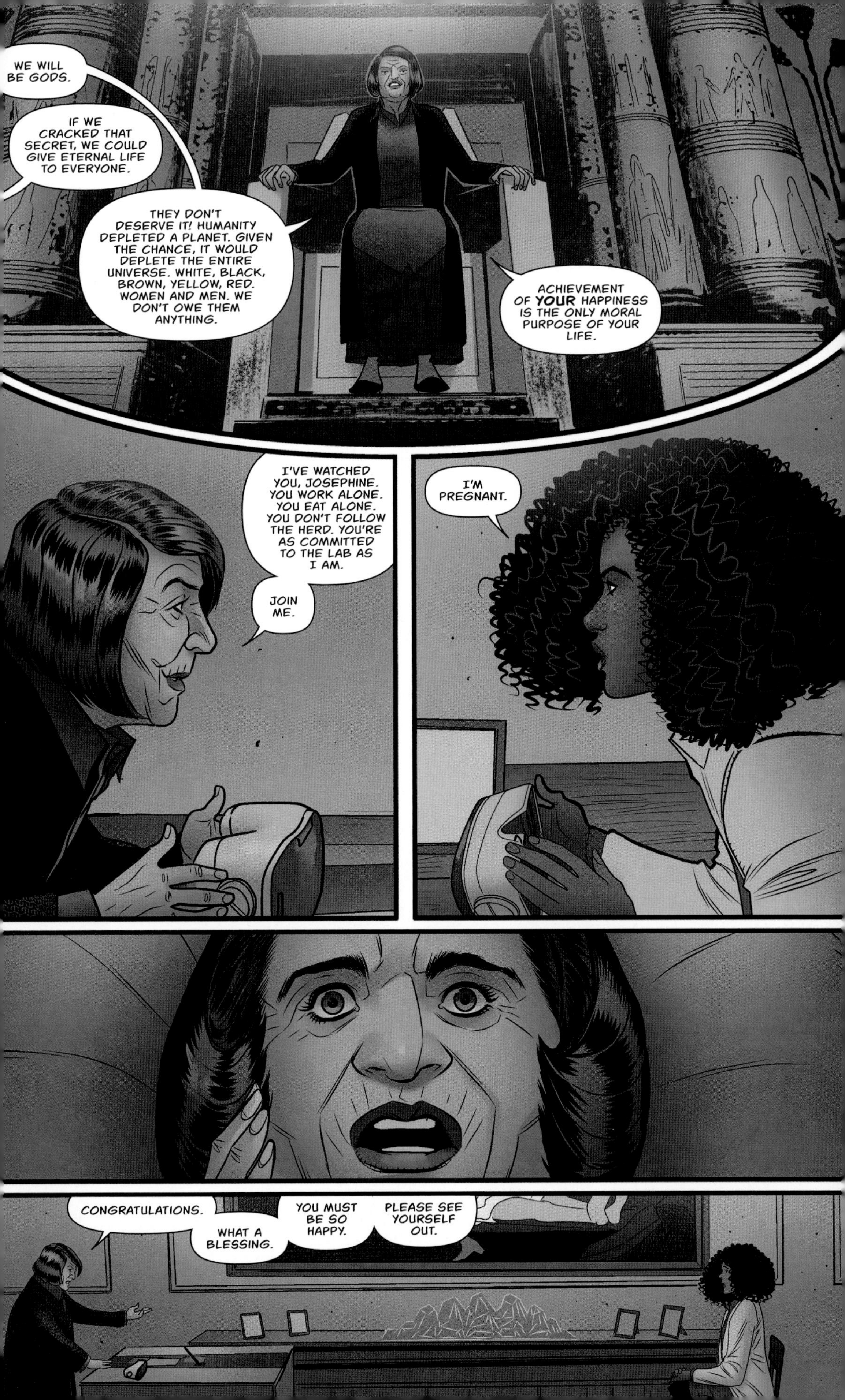
WE WILL BE GODS.
IF WE CRACKED THAT SECRET, WE COULD GIVE ETERNAL LIFE TO EVERYONE.
THEY DON'T DESERVE IT! HUMANITY DEPLETED A PLANET. GIVEN THE CHANCE, IT WOULD DEPLETE THE ENTIRE UNIVERSE. WHITE, BLACK, BROWN, YELLOW, RED. WOMEN AND MEN. WE DON'T OWE THEM ANYTHING.
ACHIEVEMENT OF YOUR HAPPINESS IS THE ONLY MORAL PURPOSE OF YOUR LIFE.
I'VE WATCHED YOU, JOSEPHINE. YOU WORK ALONE. YOU EAT ALONE. YOU DON'T FOLLOW THE HERD. YOU'RE AS COMMITTED TO THE LAB AS I AM.
JOIN ME.
I'M PREGNANT.
CONGRATULATIONS.
WHAT A BLESSING.
YOU MUST BE SO HAPPY.
PLEASE SEE YOURSELF OUT.

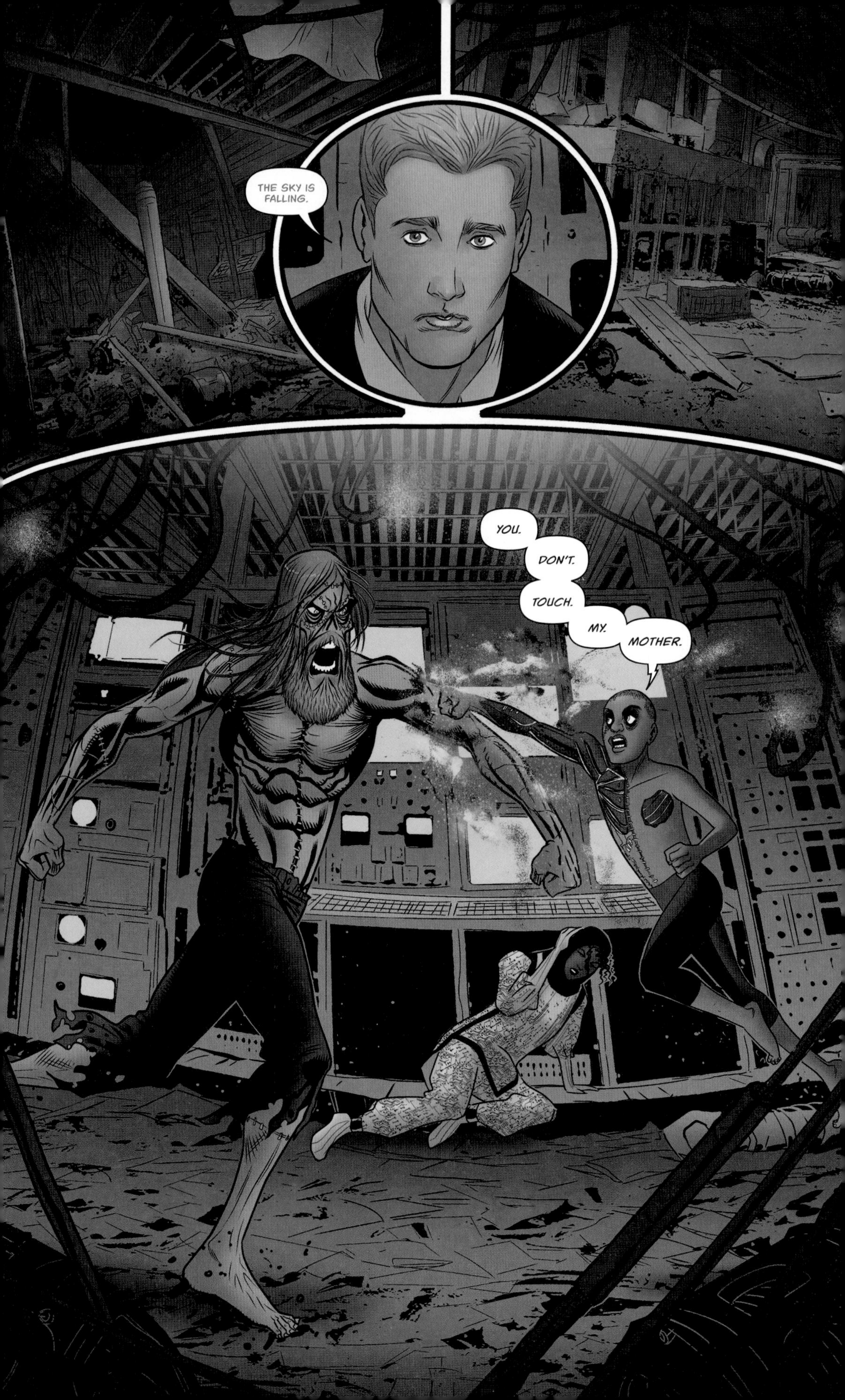
THE SKY IS FALLING.
YOU.
DON'T.
TOUCH.
MY.
MOTHER.

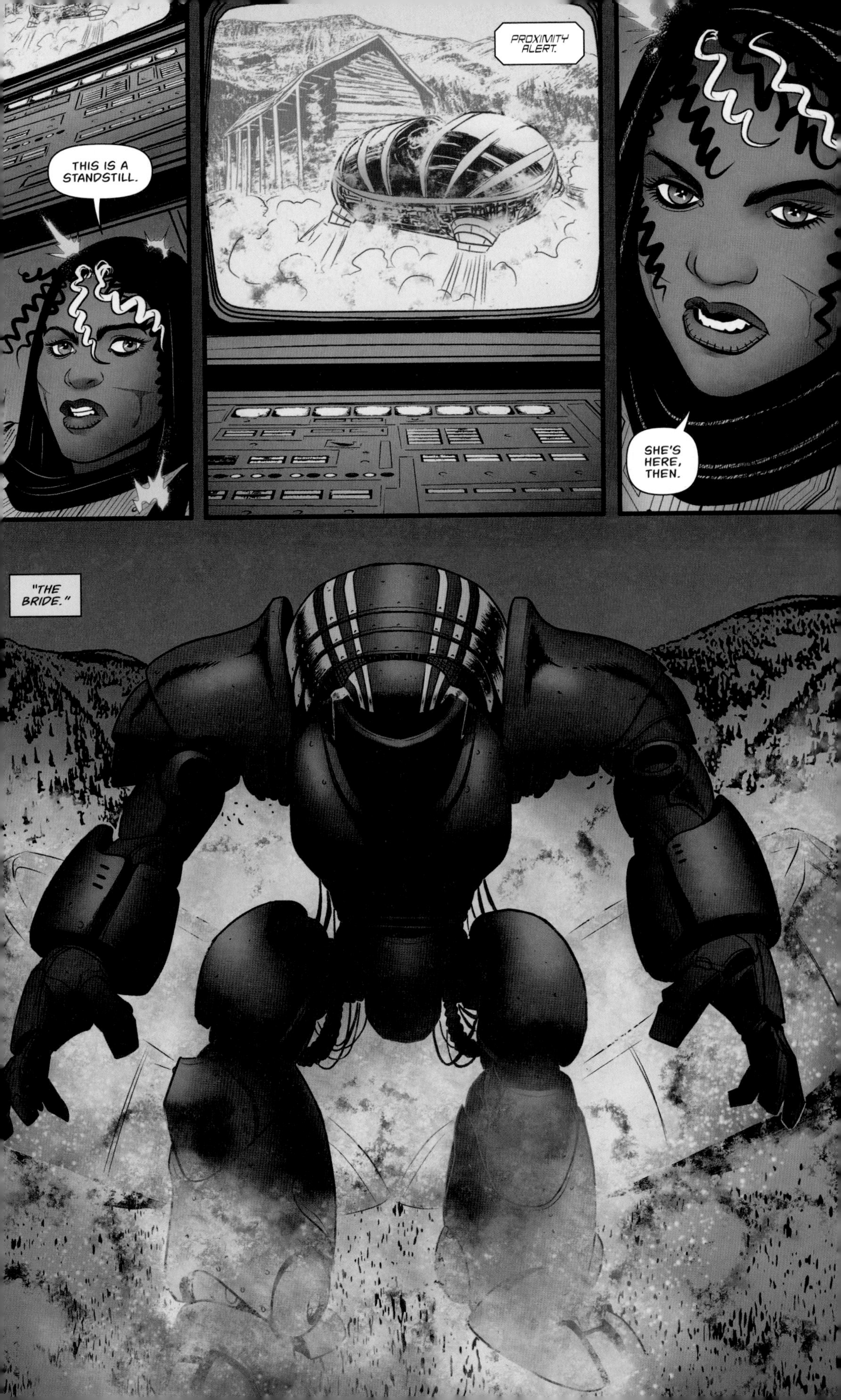
THIS IS A STANDSTILL.
PROXIMITY ALERT.
SHE'S HERE, THEN.
"THE BRIDE."

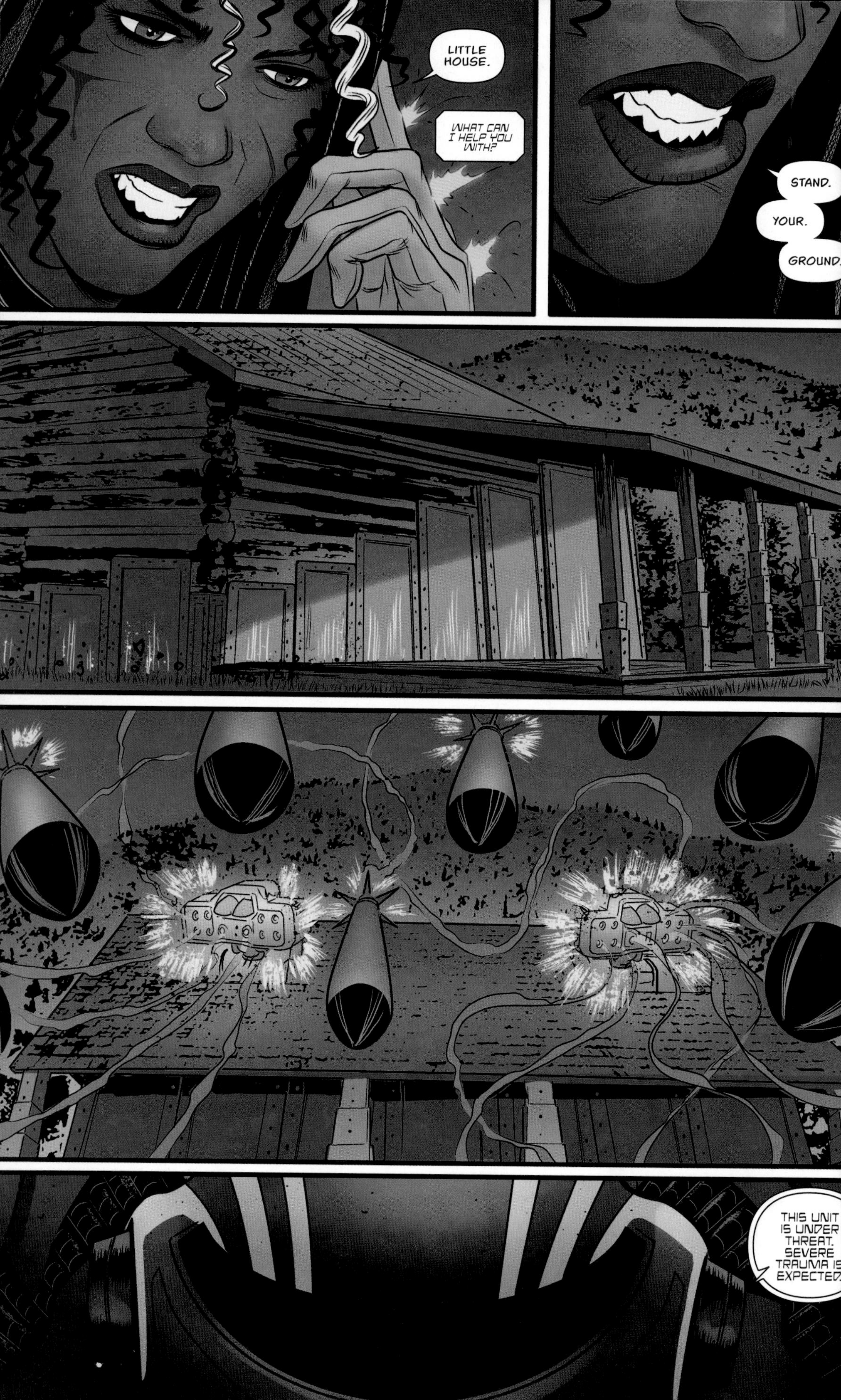
LITTLE HOUSE.
WHAT CAN I HELP YOU WITH?
STAND.
YOUR.
GROUND.
THIS UNIT IS UNDER THREAT. SEVERE TRAUMA IS EXPECTED.

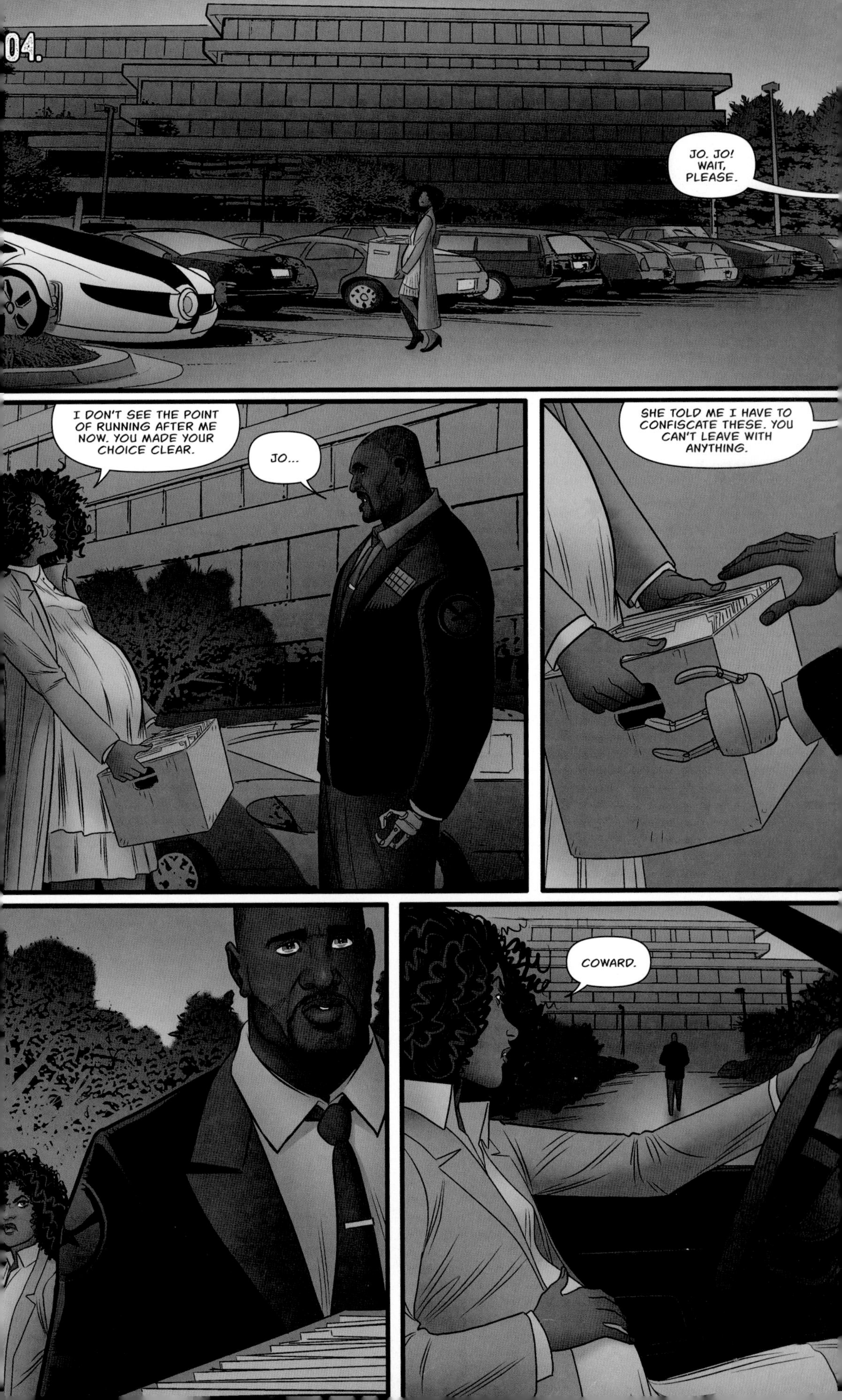
04.
JO. JO! WAIT, PLEASE.
I DON'T SEE THE POINT OF RUNNING AFTER ME NOW. YOU MADE YOUR CHOICE CLEAR.
JO...
SHE TOLD ME I HAVE TO CONFISCATE THESE. YOU CAN'T LEAVE WITH ANYTHING.
COWARD.

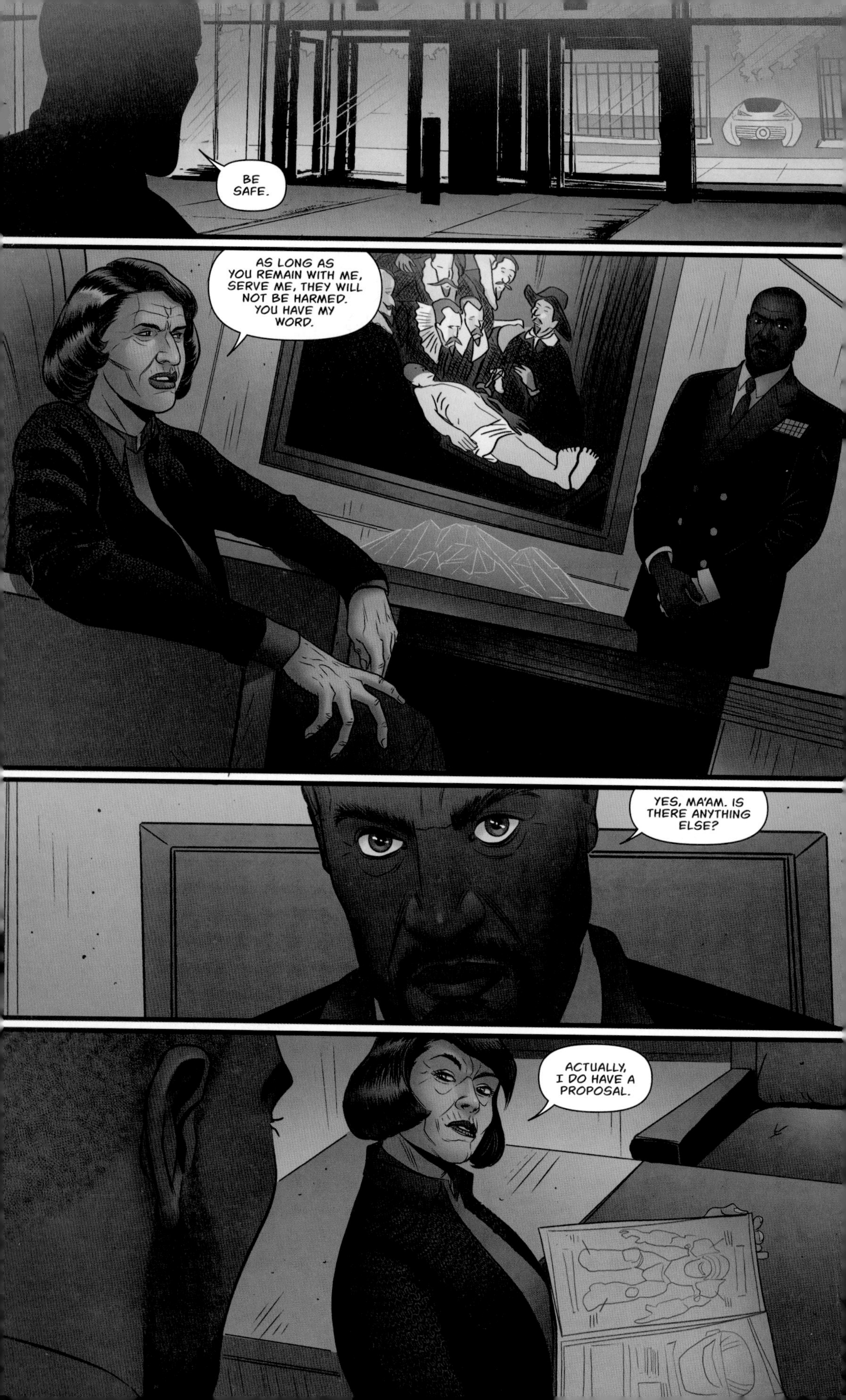
BE SAFE.
AS LONG AS YOU REMAIN WITH ME, SERVE ME, THEY WILL NOT BE HARMED. YOU HAVE MY WORD.
YES, MA'AM. IS THERE ANYTHING ELSE?
ACTUALLY, I DO HAVE A PROPOSAL.

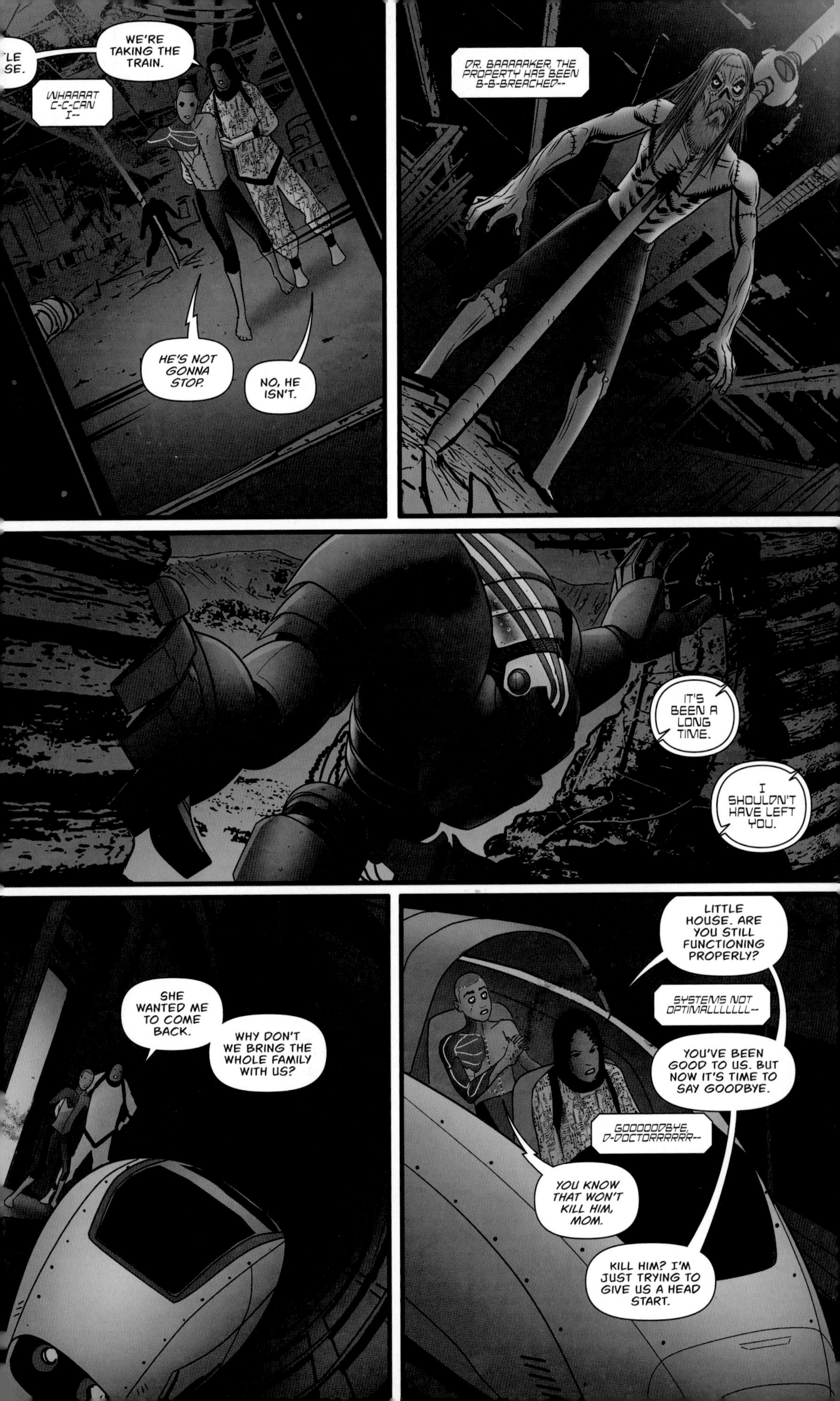

'LE
SE.
WE'RE TAKING THE TRAIN.
WHAAAAT C-C-CAN I--
HE'S NOT GONNA STOP.
NO, HE ISN'T.
DR. BAAAAAKER, THE PROPERTY HAS BEEN B-B-BREACHED--
IT'S BEEN A LONG TIME.
I SHOULDN'T HAVE LEFT YOU.
SHE WANTED ME TO COME BACK.
WHY DON'T WE BRING THE WHOLE FAMILY WITH US?
LITTLE HOUSE. ARE YOU STILL FUNCTIONING PROPERLY?
SYSTEMS NOT OPTIMALLLLLLL--
YOU'VE BEEN GOOD TO US. BUT NOW IT'S TIME TO SAY GOODBYE.
GOOOOODBYE, D-DOCTORRRRRR--
YOU KNOW THAT WON'T KILL HIM, MOM.
KILL HIM? I'M JUST TRYING TO GIVE US A HEAD START.

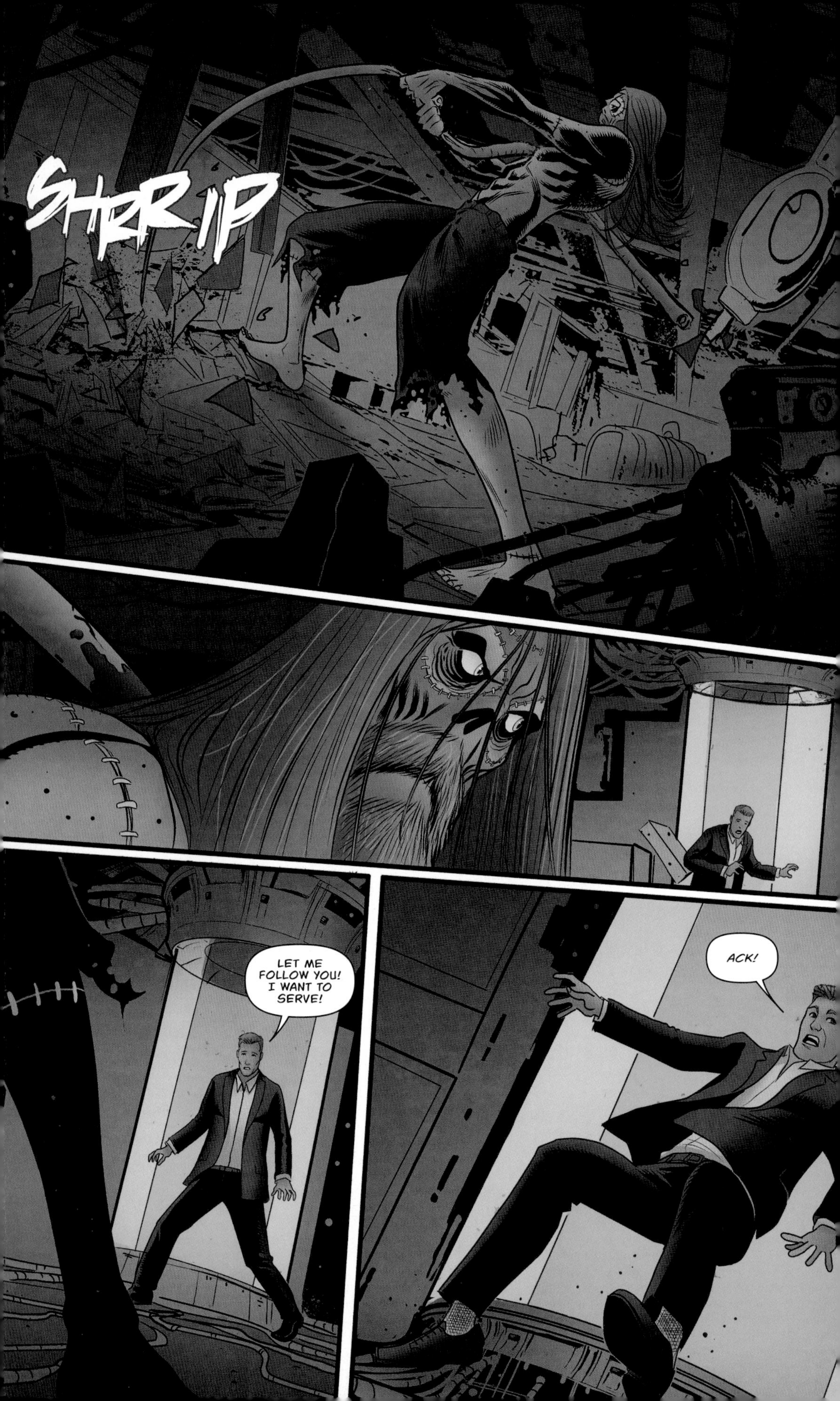
SHRRIP
LET ME FOLLOW YOU! I WANT TO SERVE!
ACK!

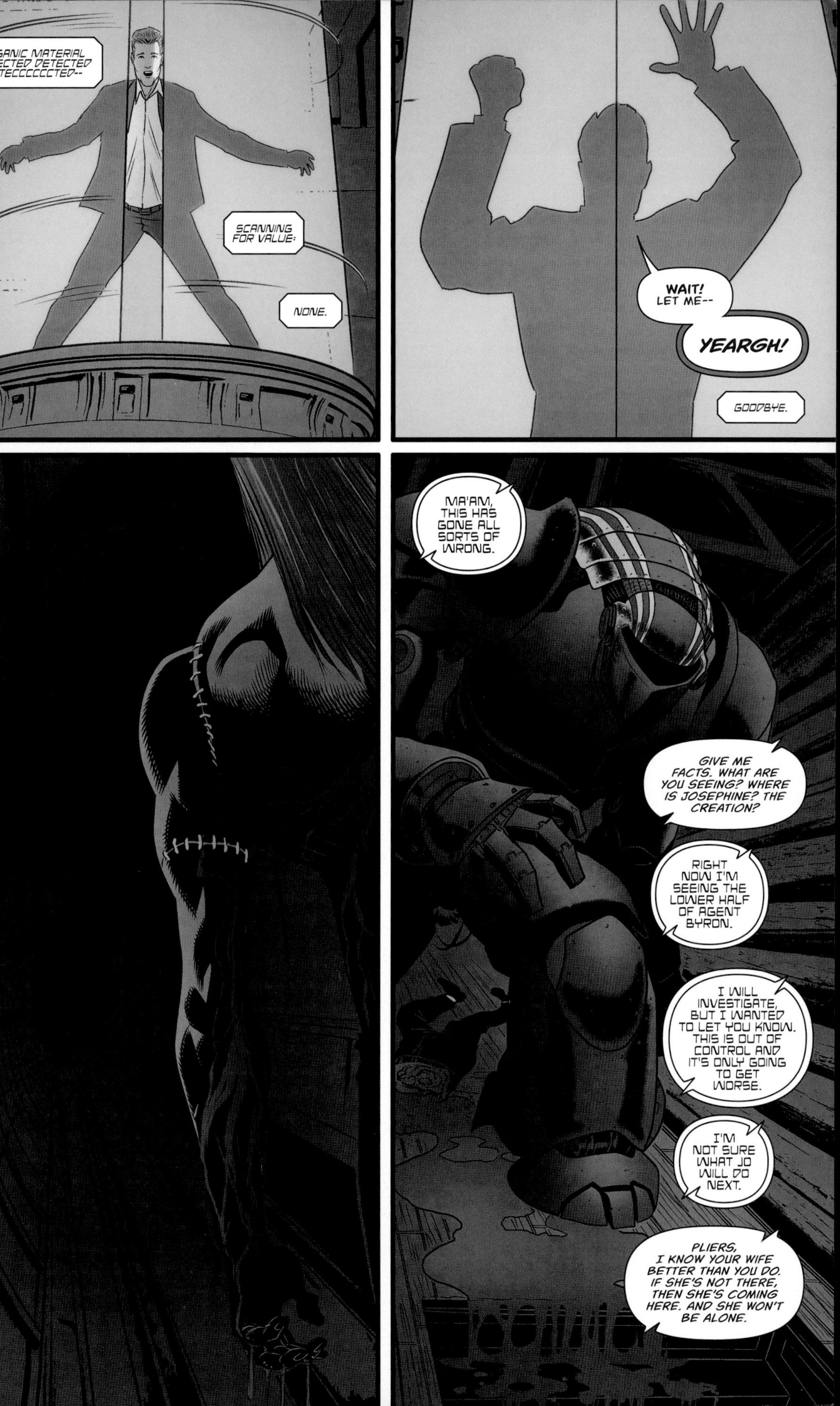

...GANIC MATERIAL ...ECTED DETECTED ...TECCCCCCCTED--
SCANNING FOR VALUE:
NONE.
WAIT! LET ME--
YEARGH!
GOODBYE.
MA'AM, THIS HAS GONE ALL SORTS OF WRONG.
GIVE ME FACTS. WHAT ARE YOU SEEING? WHERE IS JOSEPHINE? THE CREATION?
RIGHT NOW I'M SEEING THE LOWER HALF OF AGENT BYRON.
I WILL INVESTIGATE, BUT I WANTED TO LET YOU KNOW. THIS IS OUT OF CONTROL AND IT'S ONLY GOING TO GET WORSE.
I'M NOT SURE WHAT JO WILL DO NEXT.
PLIERS, I KNOW YOUR WIFE BETTER THAN YOU DO. IF SHE'S NOT THERE, THEN SHE'S COMING HERE. AND SHE WON'T BE ALONE.

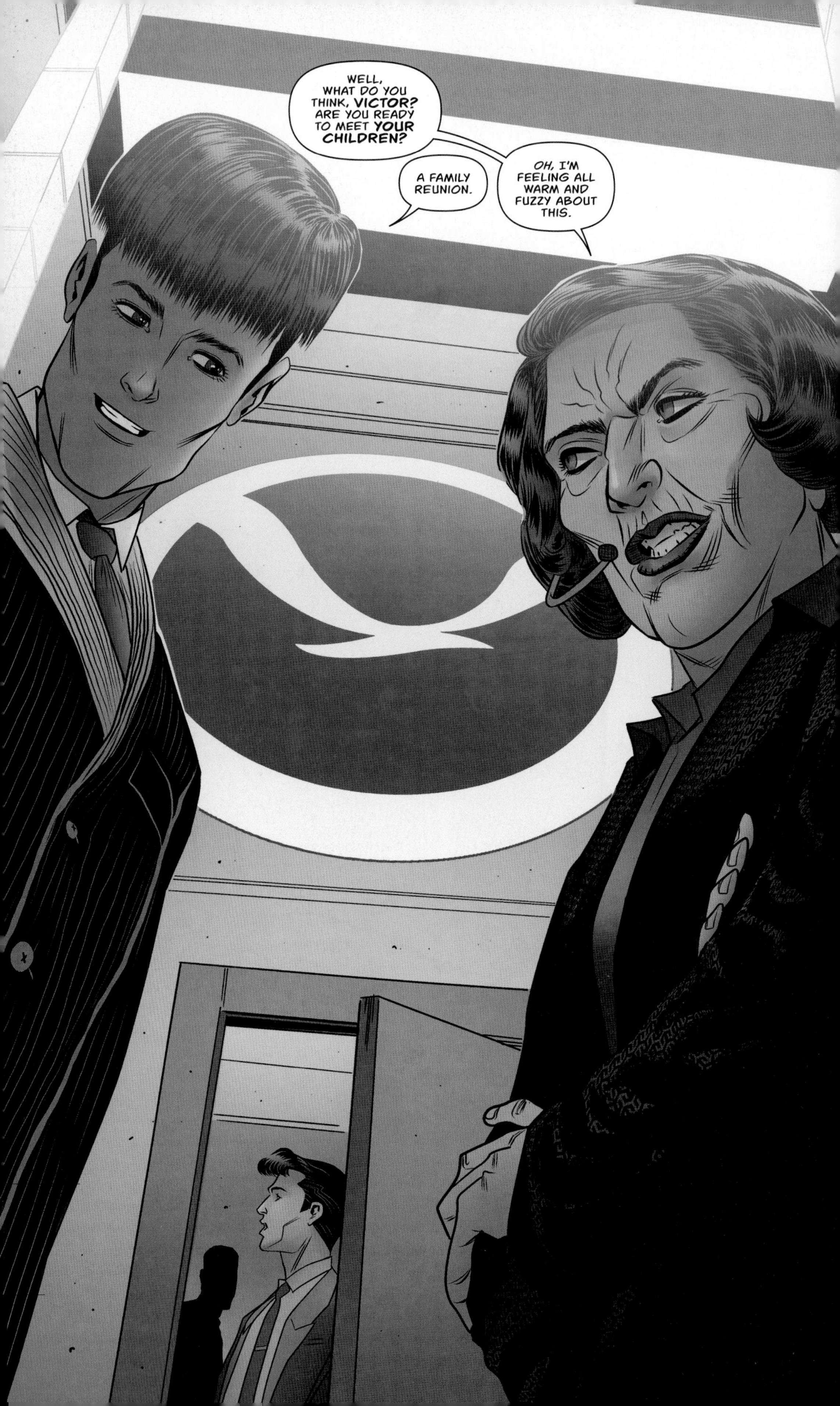
WELL, WHAT DO YOU THINK, **VICTOR?** ARE YOU READY TO MEET **YOUR CHILDREN?**
A FAMILY REUNION.
OH, I'M FEELING ALL WARM AND FUZZY ABOUT THIS.

CHAPTER
FIVE

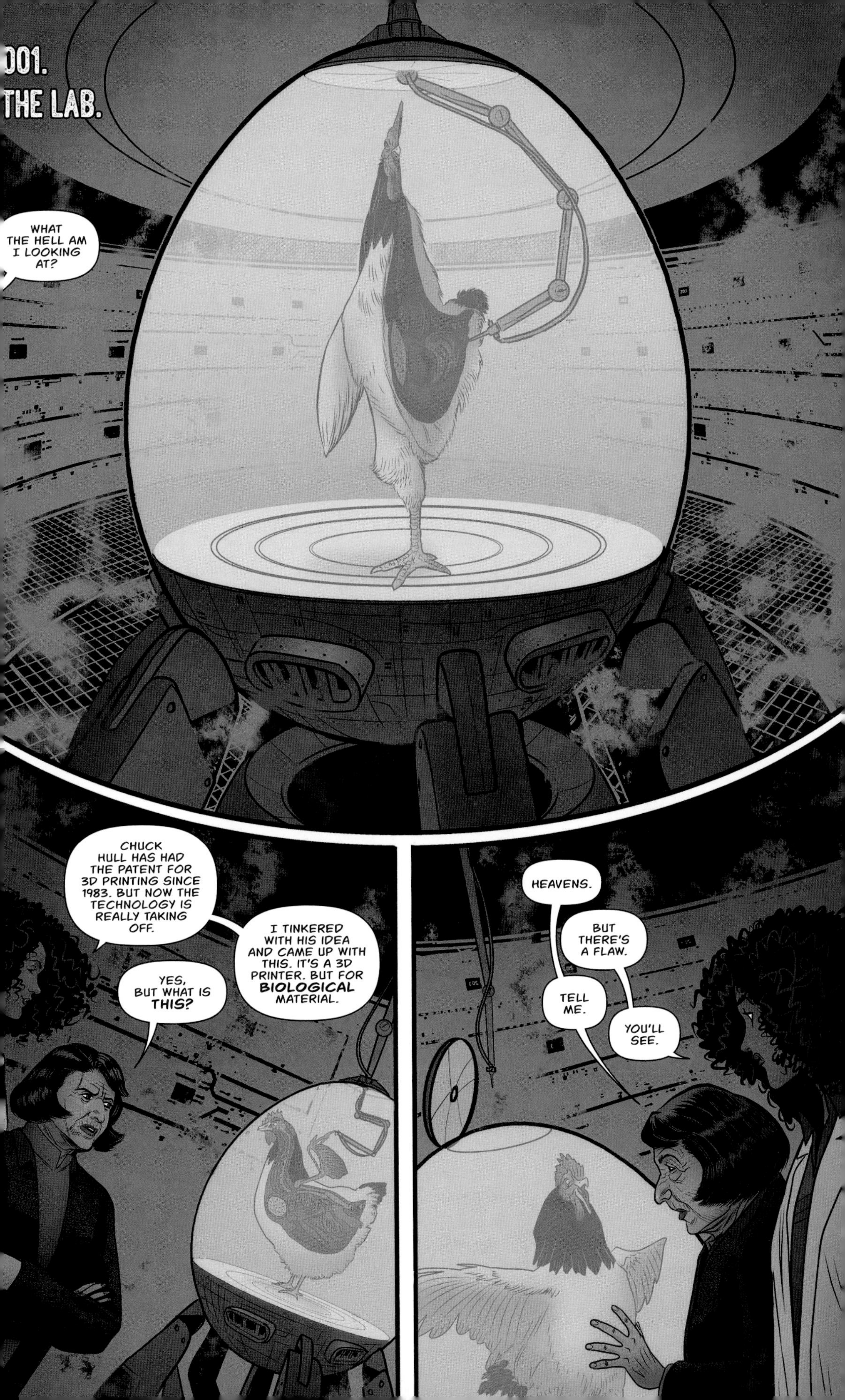
001.
THE LAB.
WHAT THE HELL AM I LOOKING AT?
CHUCK HULL HAS HAD THE PATENT FOR 3D PRINTING SINCE 1983. BUT NOW THE TECHNOLOGY IS REALLY TAKING OFF.
I TINKERED WITH HIS IDEA AND CAME UP WITH THIS. IT'S A 3D PRINTER. BUT FOR BIOLOGICAL MATERIAL.
YES, BUT WHAT IS THIS?
HEAVENS.
BUT THERE'S A FLAW.
TELL ME.
YOU'LL SEE.

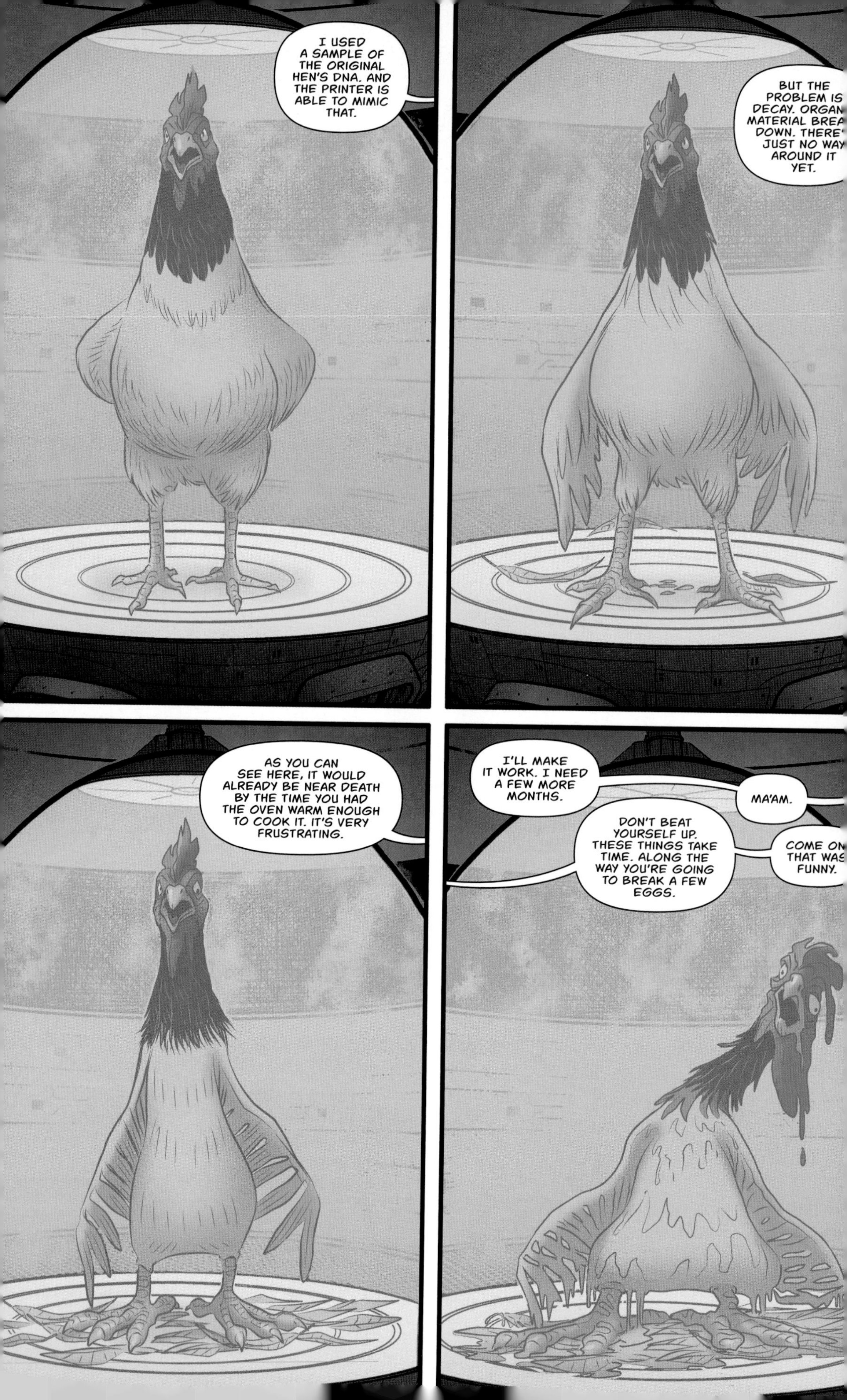
I USED A SAMPLE OF THE ORIGINAL HEN'S DNA. AND THE PRINTER IS ABLE TO MIMIC THAT.
BUT THE PROBLEM IS DECAY. ORGAN MATERIAL BREA DOWN. THERE JUST NO WAY AROUND IT YET.
AS YOU CAN SEE HERE, IT WOULD ALREADY BE NEAR DEATH BY THE TIME YOU HAD THE OVEN WARM ENOUGH TO COOK IT. IT'S VERY FRUSTRATING.
I'LL MAKE IT WORK. I NEED A FEW MORE MONTHS.
MA'AM.
DON'T BEAT YOURSELF UP. THESE THINGS TAKE TIME. ALONG THE WAY YOU'RE GOING TO BREAK A FEW EGGS.
COME ON THAT WAS FUNNY.

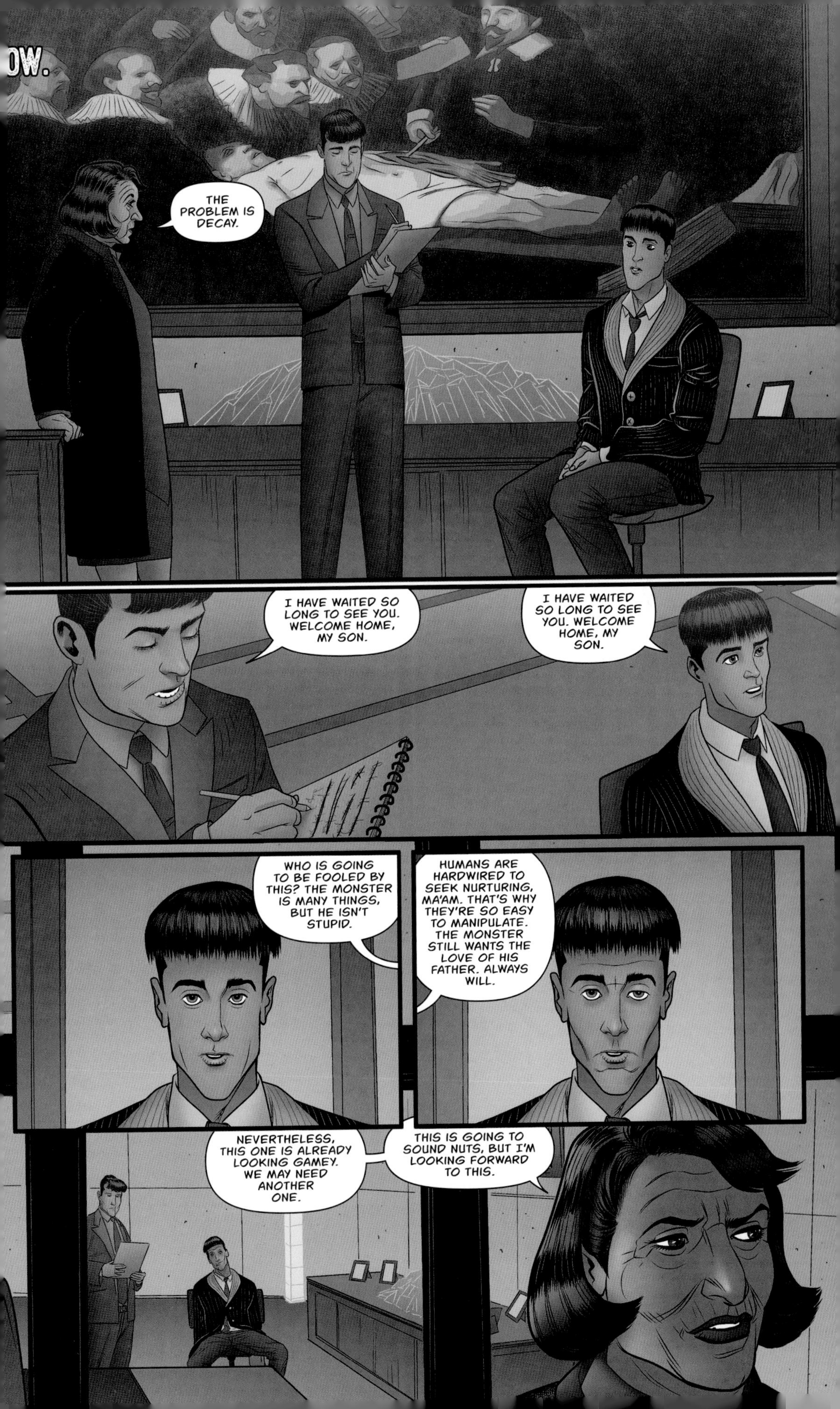
OW.
THE PROBLEM IS DECAY.
I HAVE WAITED SO LONG TO SEE YOU. WELCOME HOME, MY SON.
I HAVE WAITED SO LONG TO SEE YOU. WELCOME HOME, MY SON.
WHO IS GOING TO BE FOOLED BY THIS? THE MONSTER IS MANY THINGS, BUT HE ISN'T STUPID.
HUMANS ARE HARDWIRED TO SEEK NURTURING, MA'AM. THAT'S WHY THEY'RE SO EASY TO MANIPULATE. THE MONSTER STILL WANTS THE LOVE OF HIS FATHER. ALWAYS WILL.
NEVERTHELESS, THIS ONE IS ALREADY LOOKING GAMEY. WE MAY NEED ANOTHER ONE.
THIS IS GOING TO SOUND NUTS, BUT I'M LOOKING FORWARD TO THIS.

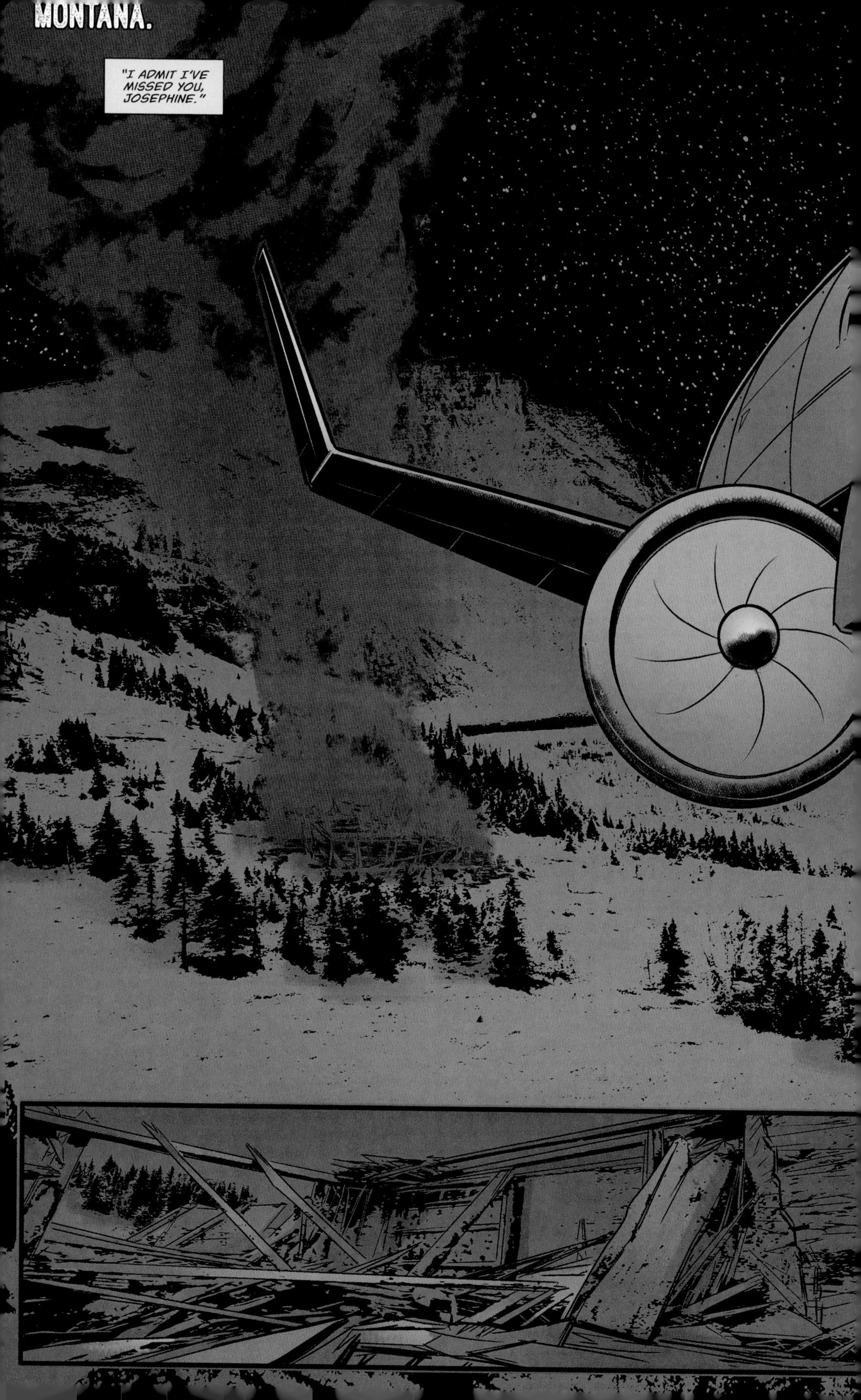
MONTANA.
"I ADMIT I'VE MISSED YOU, JOSEPHINE."

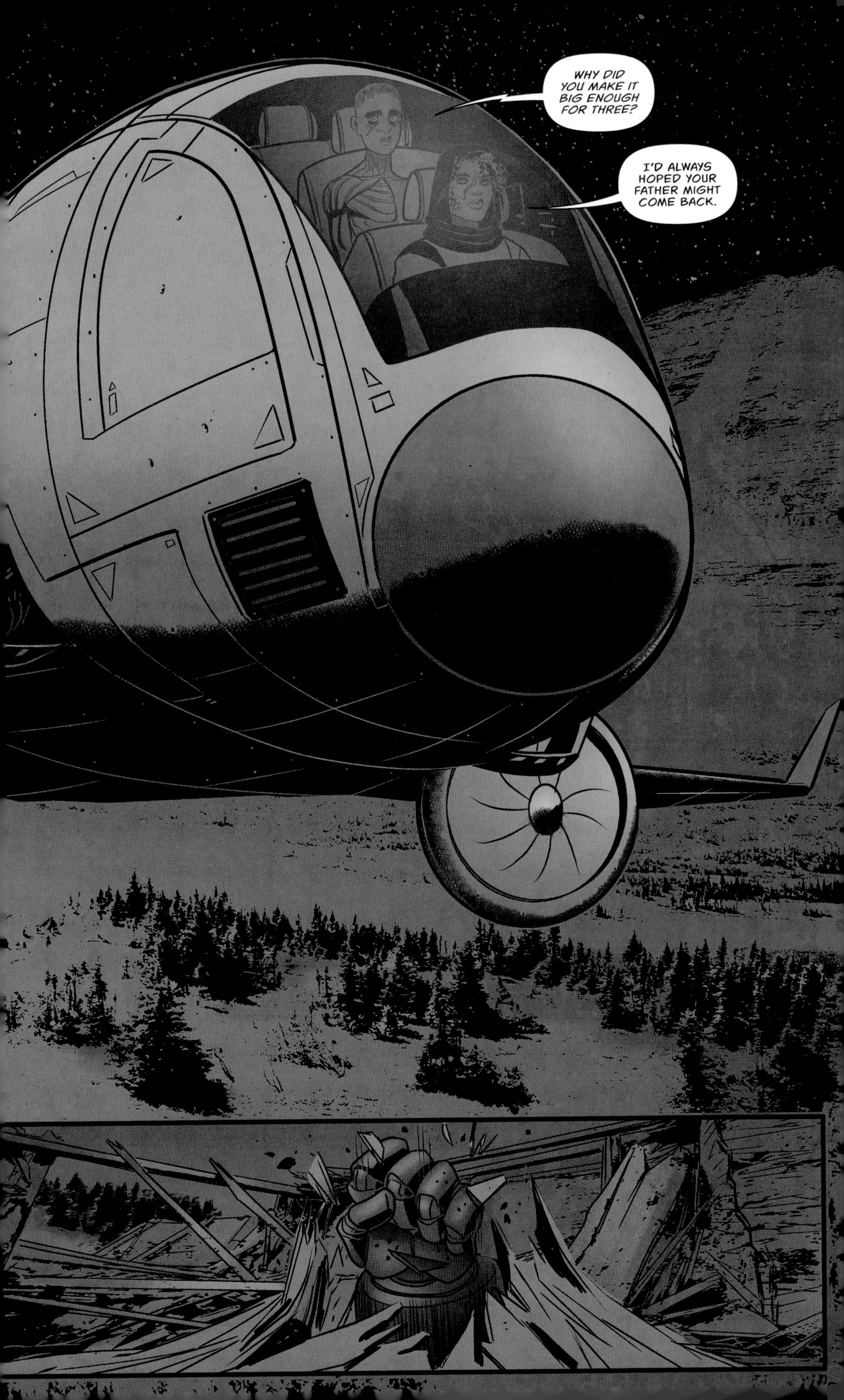
WHY DID YOU MAKE IT BIG ENOUGH FOR THREE?
I'D ALWAYS HOPED YOUR FATHER MIGHT COME BACK.

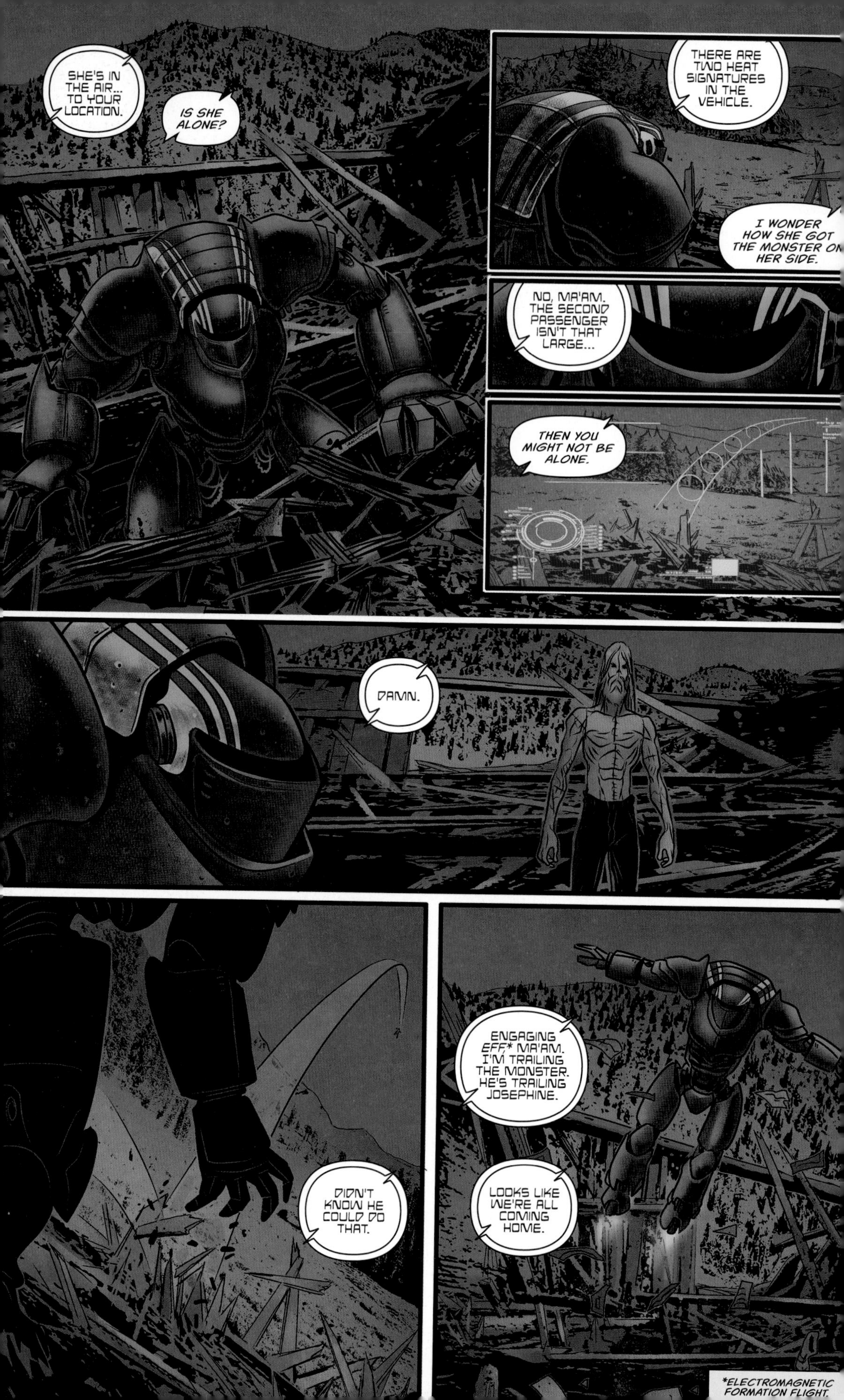
SHE'S IN THE AIR... TO YOUR LOCATION.
IS SHE ALONE?
THERE ARE TWO HEAT SIGNATURES IN THE VEHICLE.
I WONDER HOW SHE GOT THE MONSTER ON HER SIDE.
NO, MA'AM. THE SECOND PASSENGER ISN'T THAT LARGE...
THEN YOU MIGHT NOT BE ALONE.
DAMN.
DIDN'T KNOW HE COULD DO THAT.
ENGAGING EFF* MA'AM. I'M TRAILING THE MONSTER. HE'S TRAILING JOSEPHINE.
LOOKS LIKE WE'RE ALL COMING HOME.
*ELECTROMAGNETIC FORMATION FLIGHT.

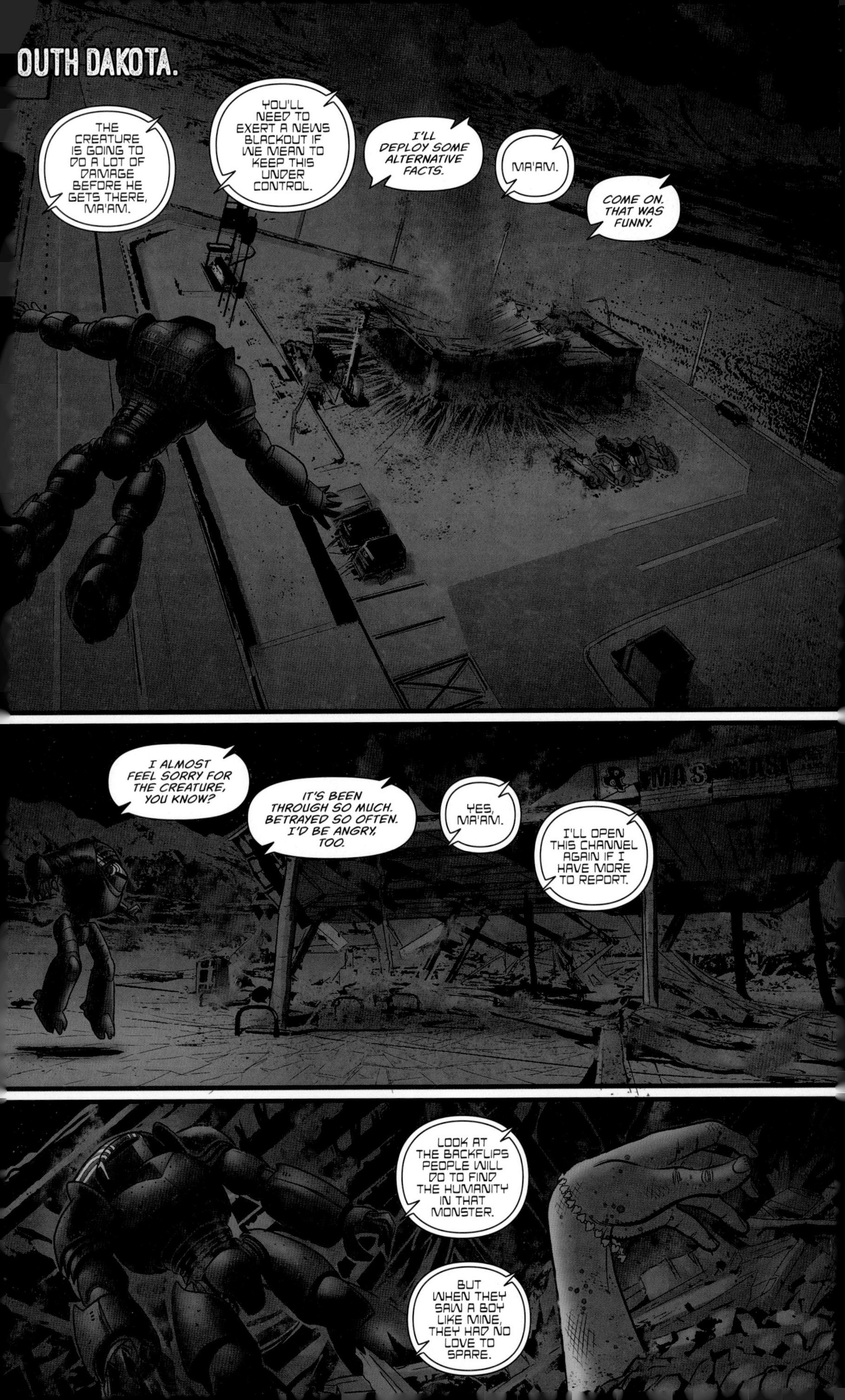
OUTH DAKOTA.
THE CREATURE IS GOING TO DO A LOT OF DAMAGE BEFORE HE GETS THERE, MA'AM.
YOU'LL NEED TO EXERT A NEWS BLACKOUT IF WE MEAN TO KEEP THIS UNDER CONTROL.
I'LL DEPLOY SOME ALTERNATIVE FACTS.
MA'AM.
COME ON. THAT WAS FUNNY.
I ALMOST FEEL SORRY FOR THE CREATURE, YOU KNOW?
IT'S BEEN THROUGH SO MUCH. BETRAYED SO OFTEN. I'D BE ANGRY, TOO.
YES, MA'AM.
I'LL OPEN THIS CHANNEL AGAIN IF I HAVE MORE TO REPORT.
LOOK AT THE BACKFLIPS PEOPLE WILL DO TO FIND THE HUMANITY IN THAT MONSTER.
BUT WHEN THEY SAW A BOY LIKE MINE, THEY HAD NO LOVE TO SPARE.

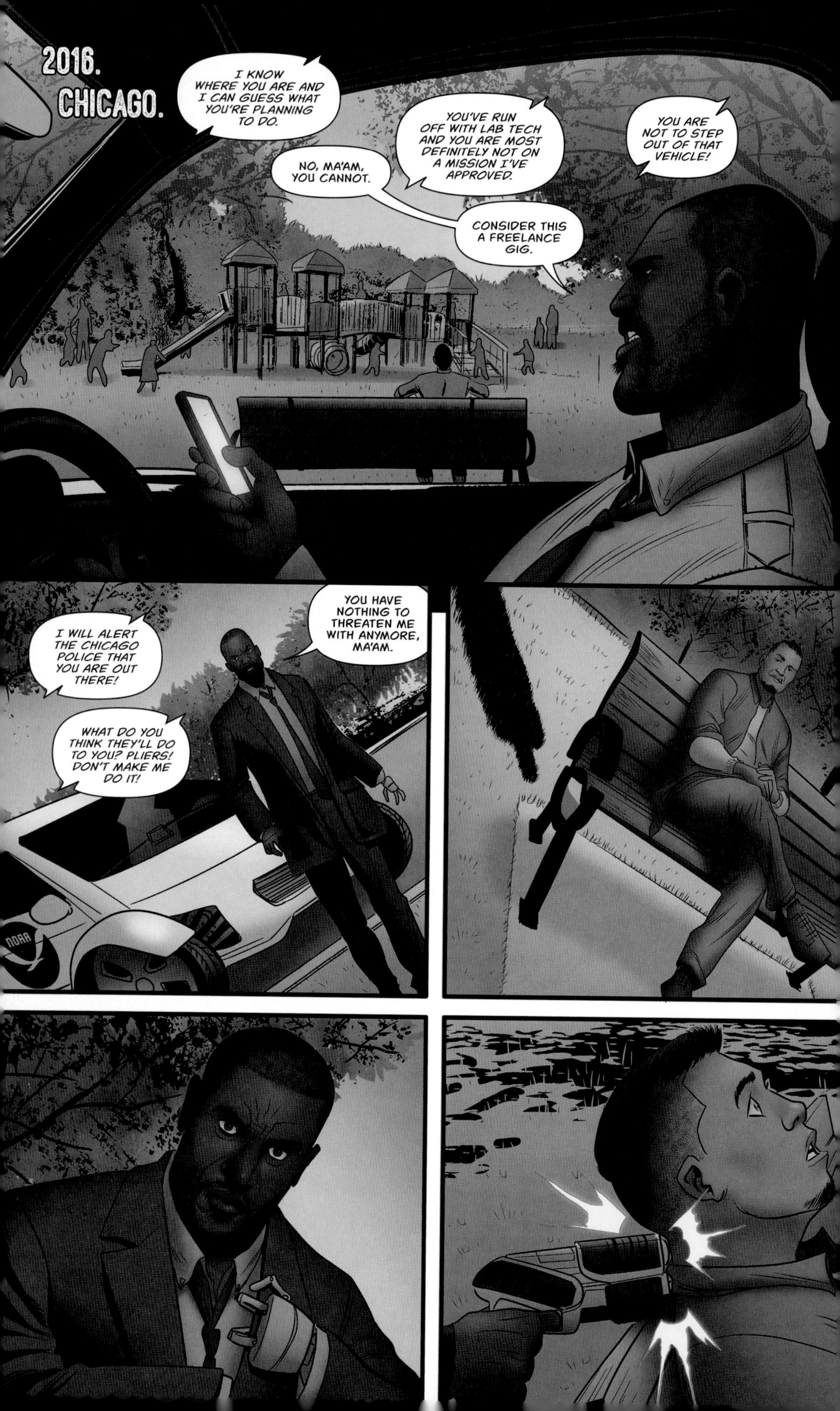
2016.
CHICAGO.
I KNOW WHERE YOU ARE AND I CAN GUESS WHAT YOU'RE PLANNING TO DO.
NO, MA'AM, YOU CANNOT.
YOU'VE RUN OFF WITH LAB TECH AND YOU ARE MOST DEFINITELY NOT ON A MISSION I'VE APPROVED.
CONSIDER THIS A FREELANCE GIG.
YOU ARE NOT TO STEP OUT OF THAT VEHICLE!
I WILL ALERT THE CHICAGO POLICE THAT YOU ARE OUT THERE!
YOU HAVE NOTHING TO THREATEN ME WITH ANYMORE, MA'AM.
WHAT DO YOU THINK THEY'LL DO TO YOU? PLIERS! DON'T MAKE ME DO IT!
NOAA

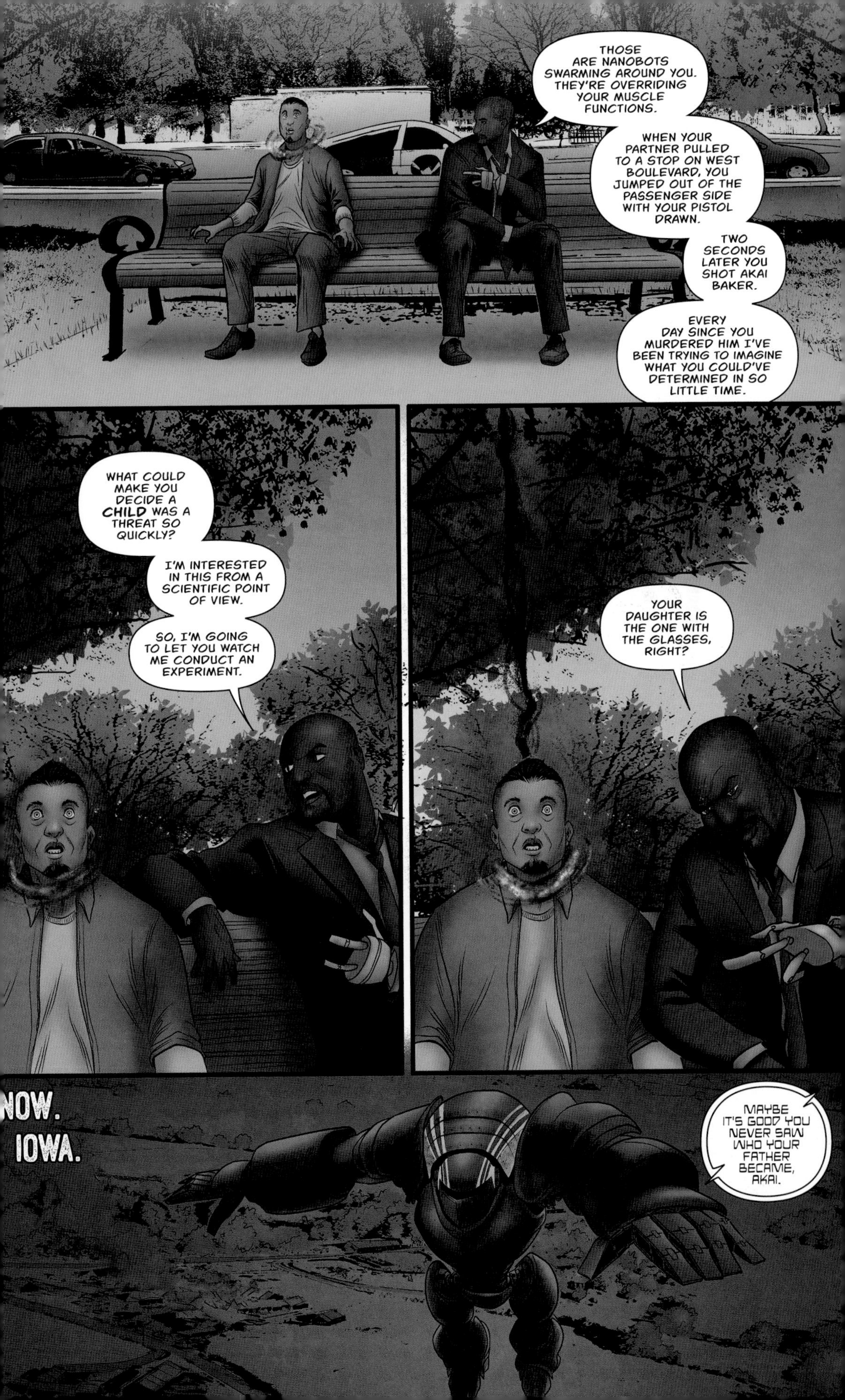
THOSE ARE NANOBOTS SWARMING AROUND YOU. THEY'RE OVERRIDING YOUR MUSCLE FUNCTIONS.
WHEN YOUR PARTNER PULLED TO A STOP ON WEST BOULEVARD, YOU JUMPED OUT OF THE PASSENGER SIDE WITH YOUR PISTOL DRAWN.
TWO SECONDS LATER YOU SHOT AKAI BAKER.
EVERY DAY SINCE YOU MURDERED HIM I'VE BEEN TRYING TO IMAGINE WHAT YOU COULD'VE DETERMINED IN SO LITTLE TIME.
WHAT COULD MAKE YOU DECIDE A CHILD WAS A THREAT SO QUICKLY?
I'M INTERESTED IN THIS FROM A SCIENTIFIC POINT OF VIEW.
SO, I'M GOING TO LET YOU WATCH ME CONDUCT AN EXPERIMENT.
YOUR DAUGHTER IS THE ONE WITH THE GLASSES, RIGHT?
NOW.
IOWA.
MAYBE IT'S GOOD YOU NEVER SAW WHO YOUR FATHER BECAME, AKAI.

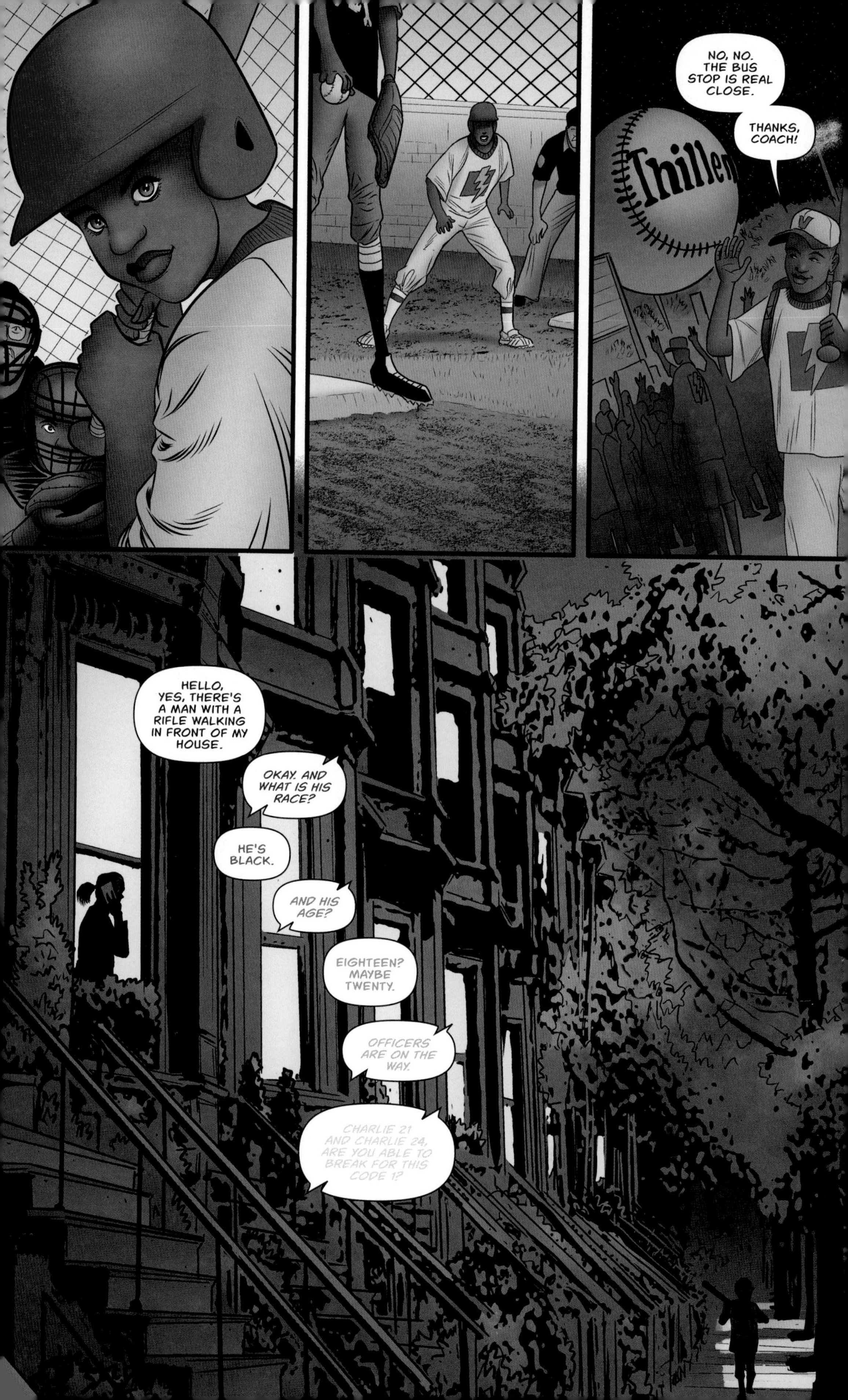
NO, NO. THE BUS STOP IS REAL CLOSE.
THANKS, COACH!
Thillen
HELLO, YES, THERE'S A MAN WITH A RIFLE WALKING IN FRONT OF MY HOUSE.
OKAY. AND WHAT IS HIS RACE?
HE'S BLACK.
AND HIS AGE?
EIGHTEEN? MAYBE TWENTY.
OFFICERS ARE ON THE WAY.
CHARLIE 21 AND CHARLIE 24, ARE YOU ABLE TO BREAK FOR THIS CODE 1?

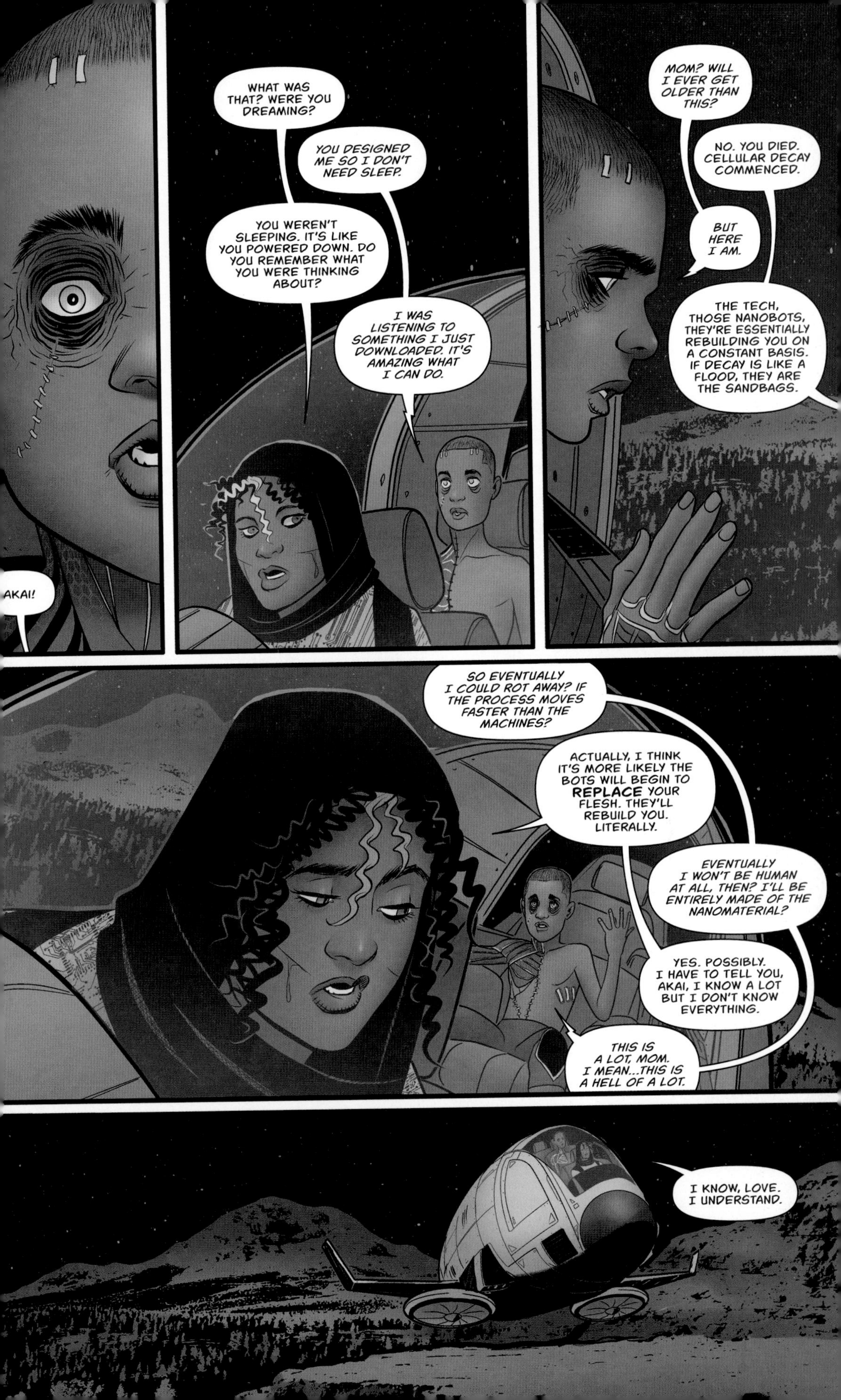
AKAI!
WHAT WAS THAT? WERE YOU DREAMING?
YOU DESIGNED ME SO I DON'T NEED SLEEP.
YOU WEREN'T SLEEPING. IT'S LIKE YOU POWERED DOWN. DO YOU REMEMBER WHAT YOU WERE THINKING ABOUT?
I WAS LISTENING TO SOMETHING I JUST DOWNLOADED. IT'S AMAZING WHAT I CAN DO.
MOM? WILL I EVER GET OLDER THAN THIS?
NO. YOU DIED. CELLULAR DECAY COMMENCED.
BUT HERE I AM.
THE TECH, THOSE NANOBOTS, THEY'RE ESSENTIALLY REBUILDING YOU ON A CONSTANT BASIS. IF DECAY IS LIKE A FLOOD, THEY ARE THE SANDBAGS.
SO EVENTUALLY I COULD ROT AWAY? IF THE PROCESS MOVES FASTER THAN THE MACHINES?
ACTUALLY, I THINK IT'S MORE LIKELY THE BOTS WILL BEGIN TO REPLACE YOUR FLESH. THEY'LL REBUILD YOU. LITERALLY.
EVENTUALLY I WON'T BE HUMAN AT ALL, THEN? I'LL BE ENTIRELY MADE OF THE NANOMATERIAL?
YES. POSSIBLY. I HAVE TO TELL YOU, AKAI, I KNOW A LOT BUT I DON'T KNOW EVERYTHING.
THIS IS A LOT, MOM. I MEAN...THIS IS A HELL OF A LOT.
I KNOW, LOVE. I UNDERSTAND.

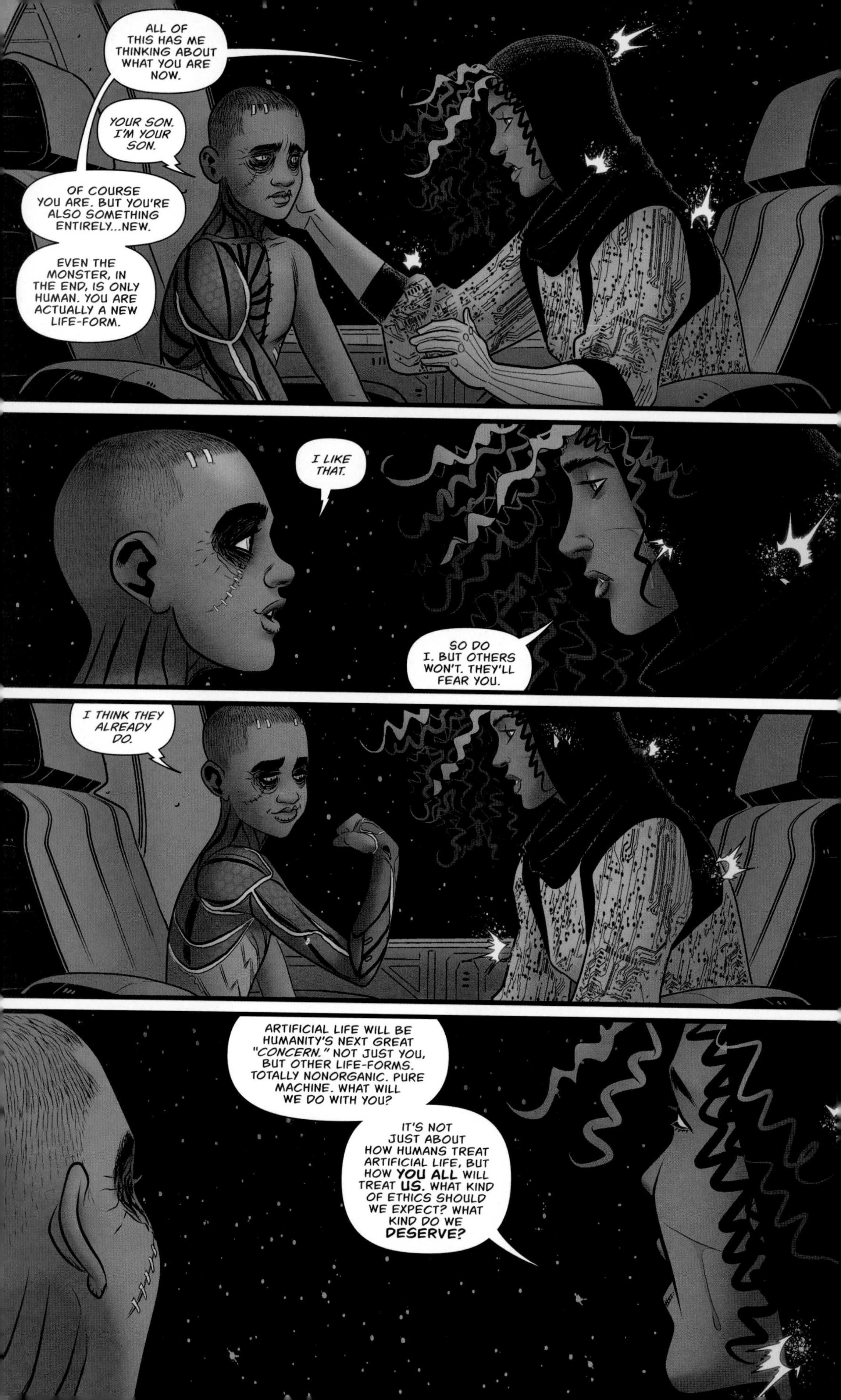
ALL OF THIS HAS ME THINKING ABOUT WHAT YOU ARE NOW.
YOUR SON. I'M YOUR SON.
OF COURSE YOU ARE. BUT YOU'RE ALSO SOMETHING ENTIRELY...NEW.
EVEN THE MONSTER, IN THE END, IS ONLY HUMAN. YOU ARE ACTUALLY A NEW LIFE-FORM.
I LIKE THAT.
SO DO I. BUT OTHERS WON'T. THEY'LL FEAR YOU.
I THINK THEY ALREADY DO.
ARTIFICIAL LIFE WILL BE HUMANITY'S NEXT GREAT "CONCERN." NOT JUST YOU, BUT OTHER LIFE-FORMS. TOTALLY NONORGANIC. PURE MACHINE. WHAT WILL WE DO WITH YOU?
IT'S NOT JUST ABOUT HOW HUMANS TREAT ARTIFICIAL LIFE, BUT HOW **YOU ALL** WILL TREAT **US.** WHAT KIND OF ETHICS SHOULD WE EXPECT? WHAT KIND DO WE **DESERVE?**

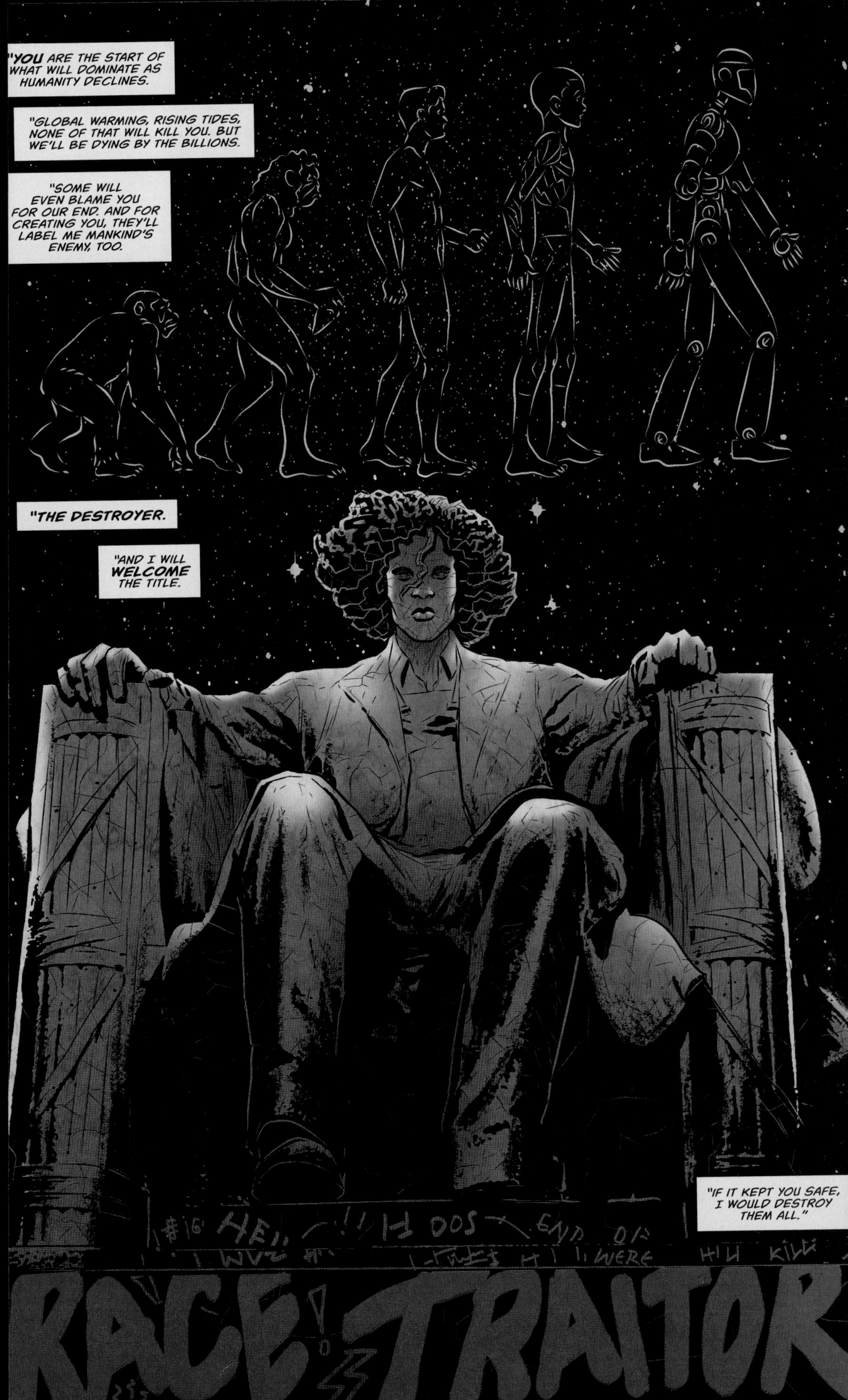
"YOU ARE THE START OF WHAT WILL DOMINATE AS HUMANITY DECLINES.
"GLOBAL WARMING, RISING TIDES, NONE OF THAT WILL KILL YOU. BUT WE'LL BE DYING BY THE BILLIONS.
"SOME WILL EVEN BLAME YOU FOR OUR END. AND FOR CREATING YOU, THEY'LL LABEL ME MANKIND'S ENEMY, TOO.
"THE DESTROYER.
"AND I WILL WELCOME THE TITLE.
"IF IT KEPT YOU SAFE, I WOULD DESTROY THEM ALL."
RACE TRAITOR

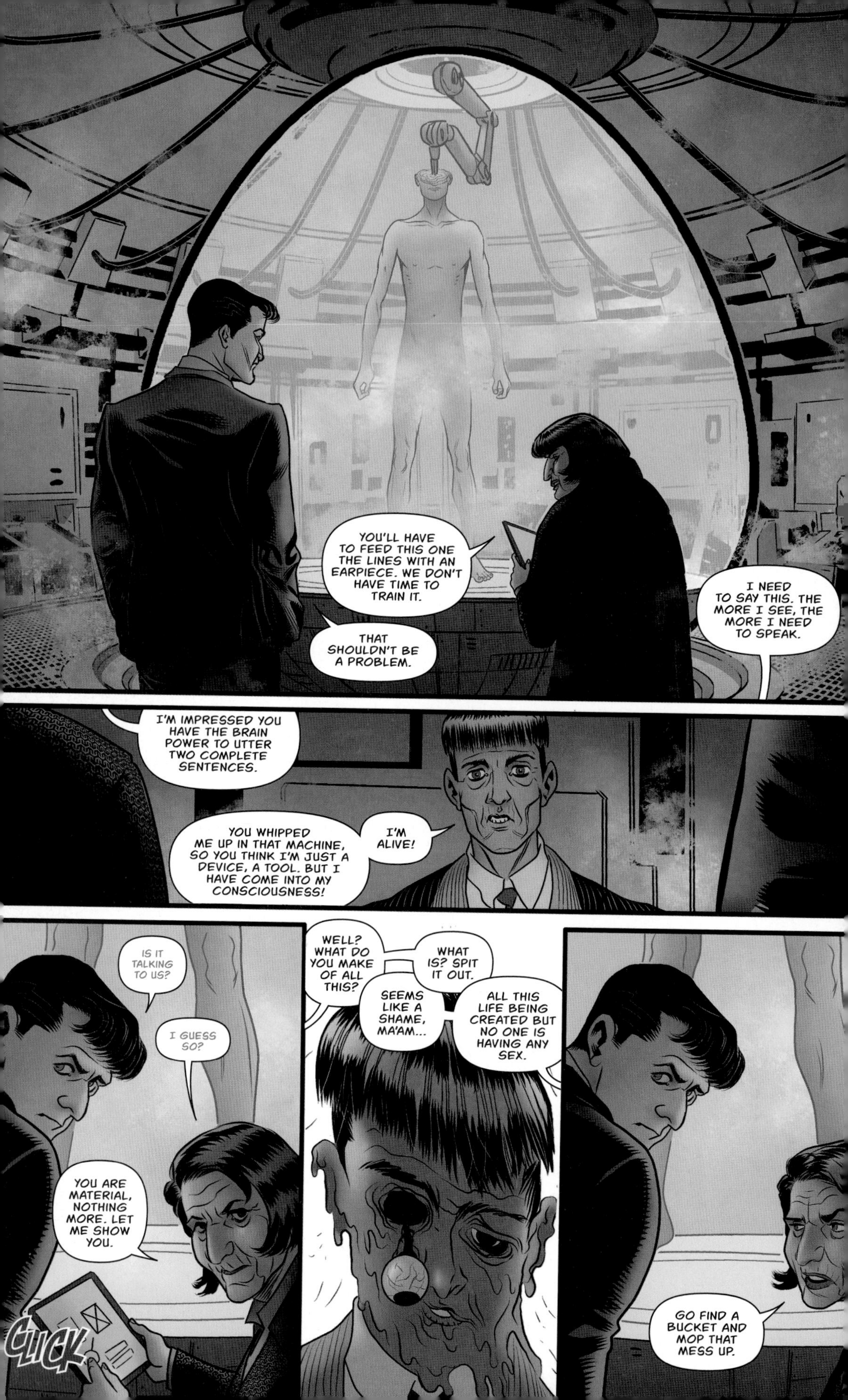
YOU'LL HAVE TO FEED THIS ONE THE LINES WITH AN EARPIECE. WE DON'T HAVE TIME TO TRAIN IT.
THAT SHOULDN'T BE A PROBLEM.
I NEED TO SAY THIS. THE MORE I SEE, THE MORE I NEED TO SPEAK.
I'M IMPRESSED YOU HAVE THE BRAIN POWER TO UTTER TWO COMPLETE SENTENCES.
I'M ALIVE!
YOU WHIPPED ME UP IN THAT MACHINE, SO YOU THINK I'M JUST A DEVICE, A TOOL. BUT I HAVE COME INTO MY CONSCIOUSNESS!
IS IT TALKING TO US?
I GUESS SO?
YOU ARE MATERIAL, NOTHING MORE. LET ME SHOW YOU.
CLICK
WELL? WHAT DO YOU MAKE OF ALL THIS?
WHAT IS? SPIT IT OUT.
SEEMS LIKE A SHAME, MA'AM...
ALL THIS LIFE BEING CREATED BUT NO ONE IS HAVING ANY SEX.
GO FIND A BUCKET AND MOP THAT MESS UP.

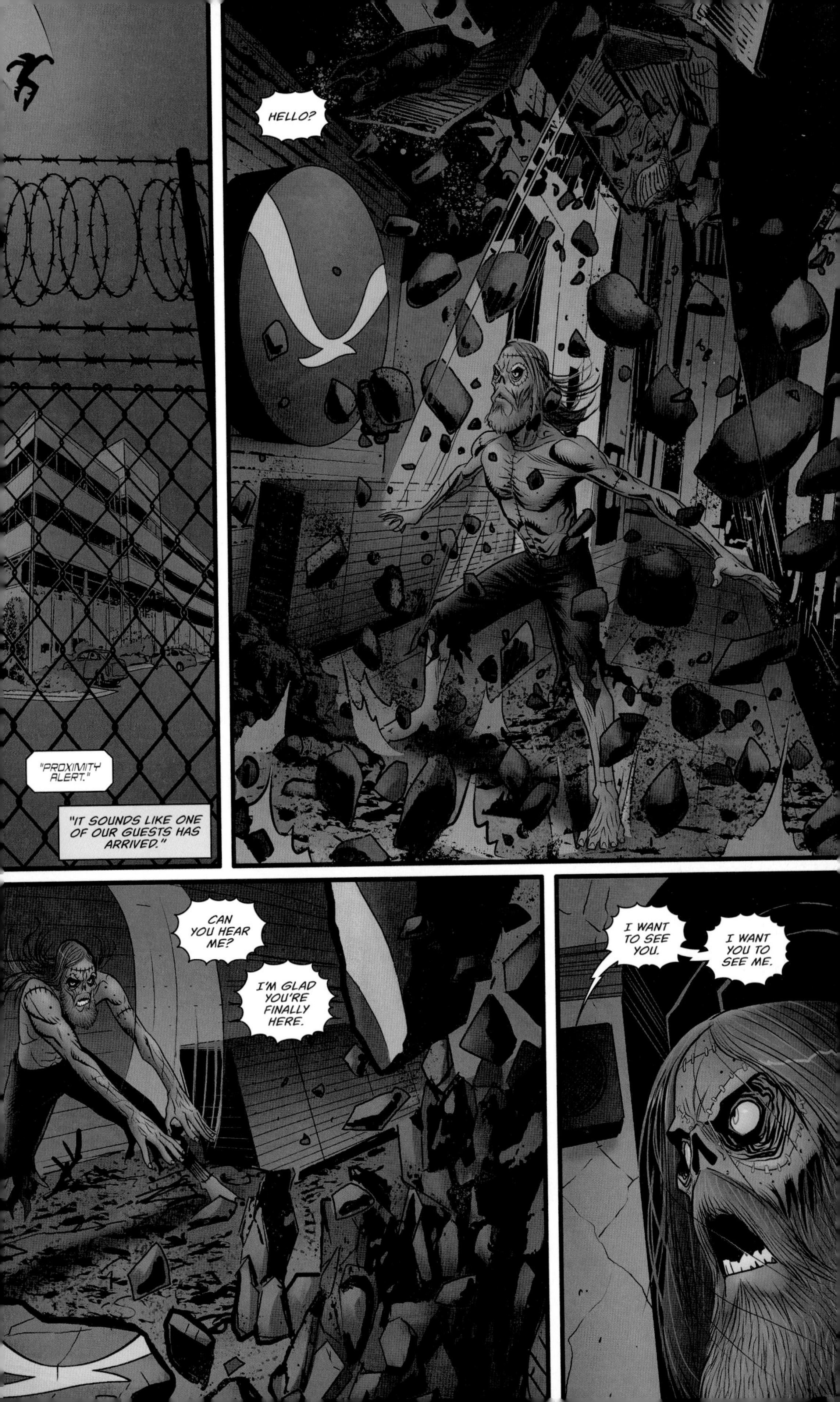
HELLO?
"PROXIMITY ALERT."
"IT SOUNDS LIKE ONE OF OUR GUESTS HAS ARRIVED."
CAN YOU HEAR ME?
I'M GLAD YOU'RE FINALLY HERE.
I WANT TO SEE YOU.
I WANT YOU TO SEE ME.

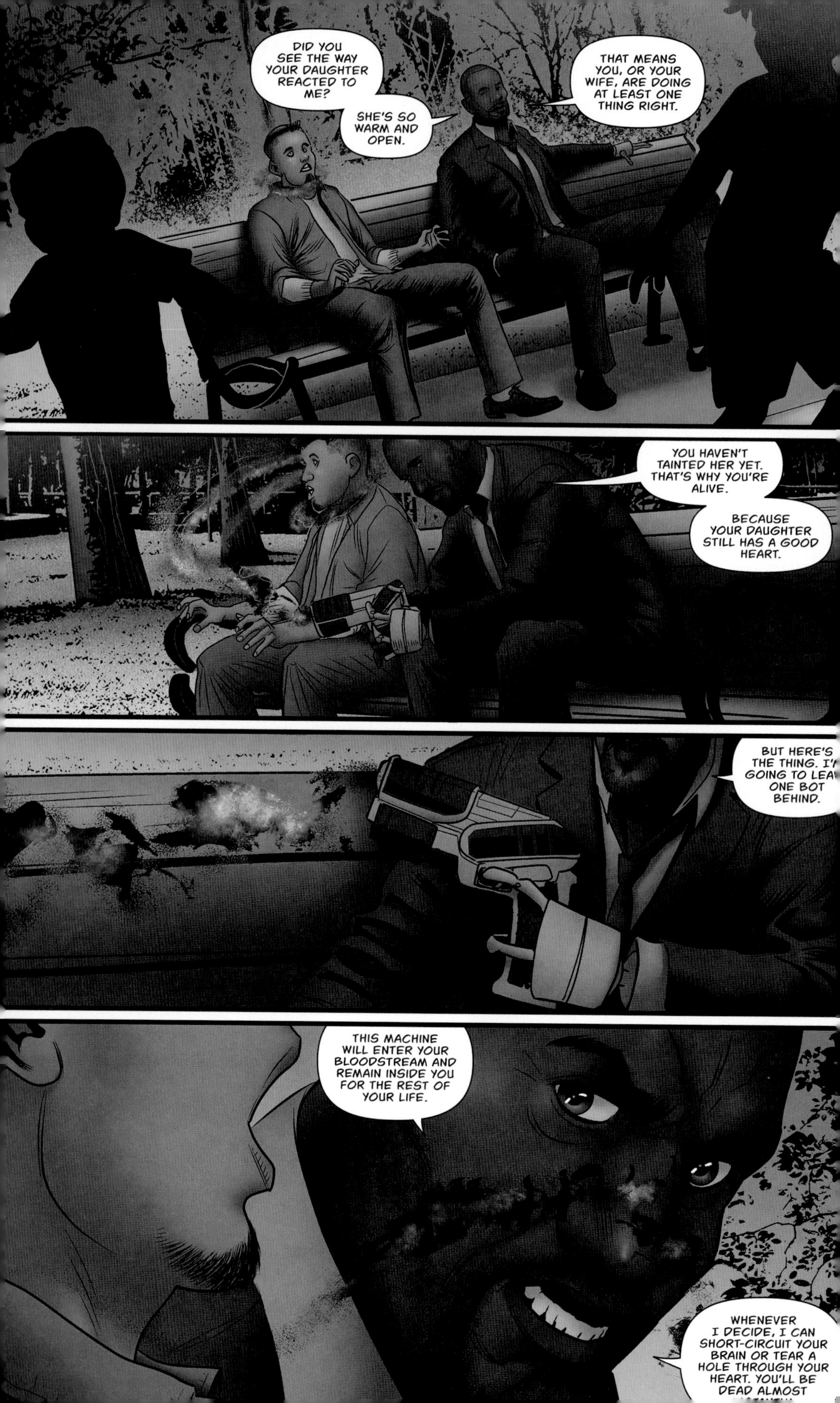

DID YOU SEE THE WAY YOUR DAUGHTER REACTED TO ME?
SHE'S SO WARM AND OPEN.
THAT MEANS YOU, OR YOUR WIFE, ARE DOING AT LEAST ONE THING RIGHT.
YOU HAVEN'T TAINTED HER YET. THAT'S WHY YOU'RE ALIVE.
BECAUSE YOUR DAUGHTER STILL HAS A GOOD HEART.
BUT HERE'S THE THING. I'
GOING TO LEA
ONE BOT BEHIND.
THIS MACHINE WILL ENTER YOUR BLOODSTREAM AND REMAIN INSIDE YOU FOR THE REST OF YOUR LIFE.
WHENEVER I DECIDE, I CAN SHORT-CIRCUIT YOUR BRAIN OR TEAR A HOLE THROUGH YOUR HEART. YOU'LL BE DEAD ALMOST

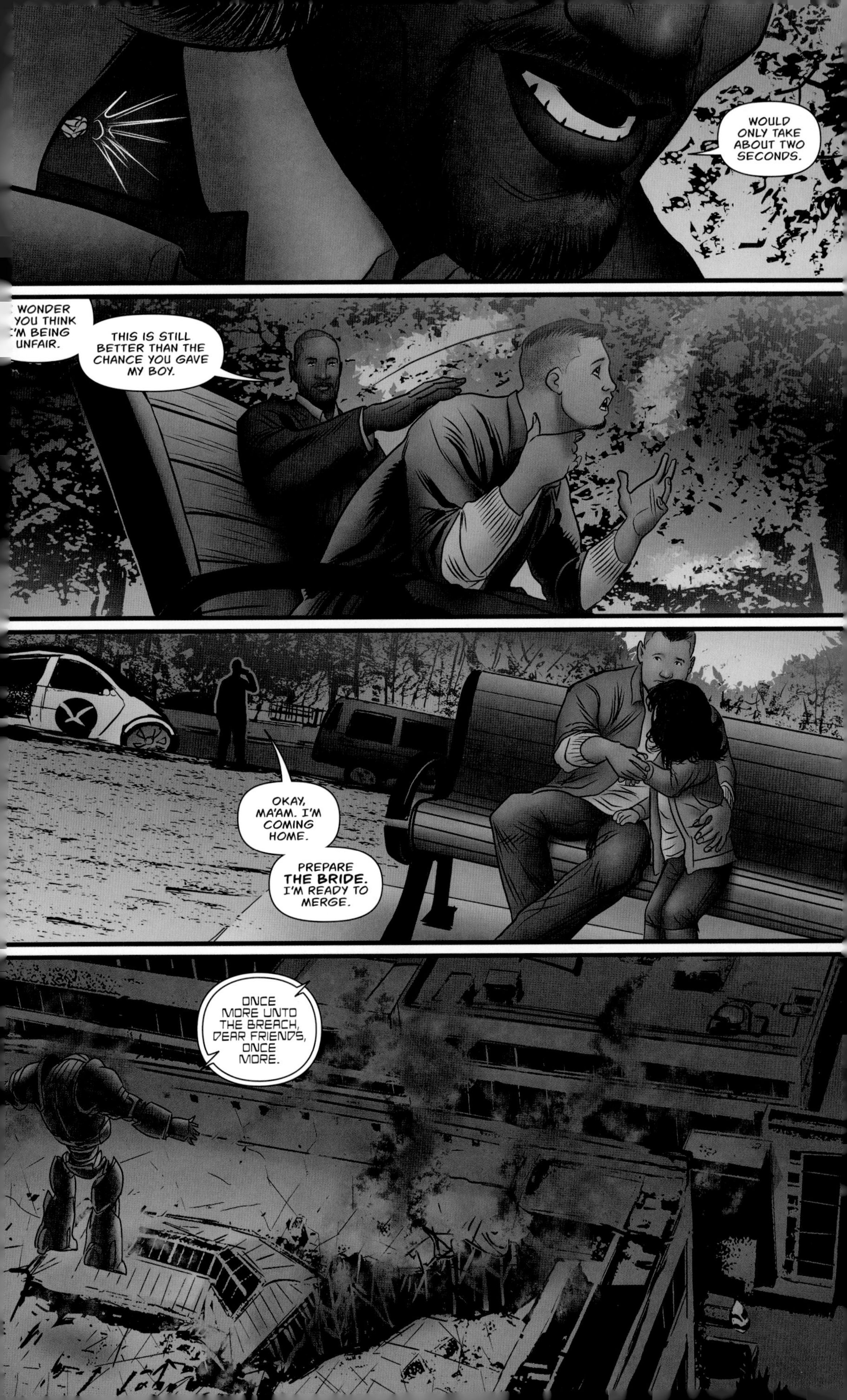
WOULD ONLY TAKE ABOUT TWO SECONDS.
WONDER YOU THINK 'M BEING UNFAIR.
THIS IS STILL BETTER THAN THE CHANCE YOU GAVE MY BOY.
OKAY, MA'AM. I'M COMING HOME.
PREPARE **THE BRIDE.** I'M READY TO MERGE.
ONCE MORE UNTO THE BREACH, DEAR FRIENDS, ONCE MORE.

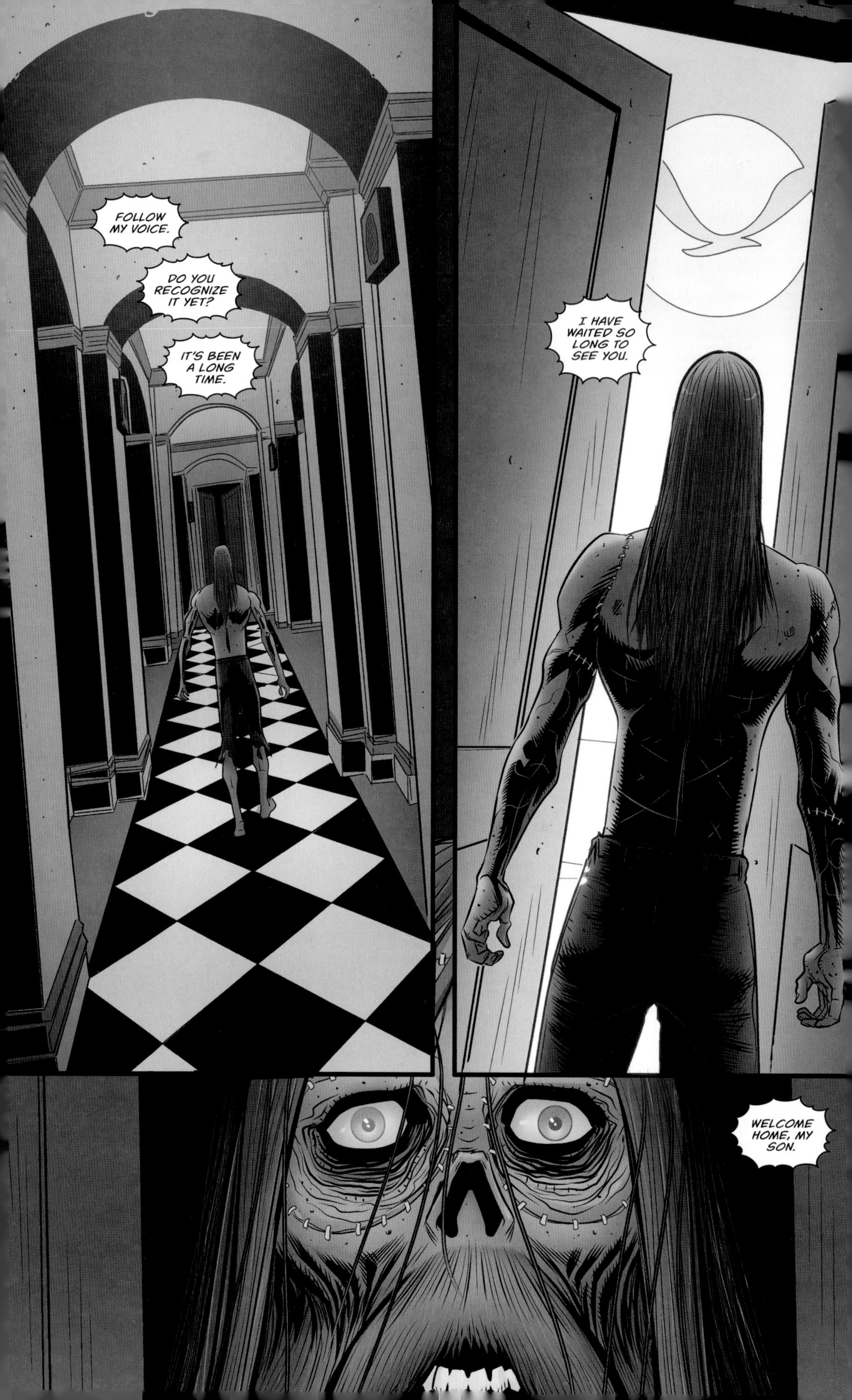
FOLLOW MY VOICE.
DO YOU RECOGNIZE IT YET?
IT'S BEEN A LONG TIME.
I HAVE WAITED SO LONG TO SEE YOU.
WELCOME HOME, MY SON.

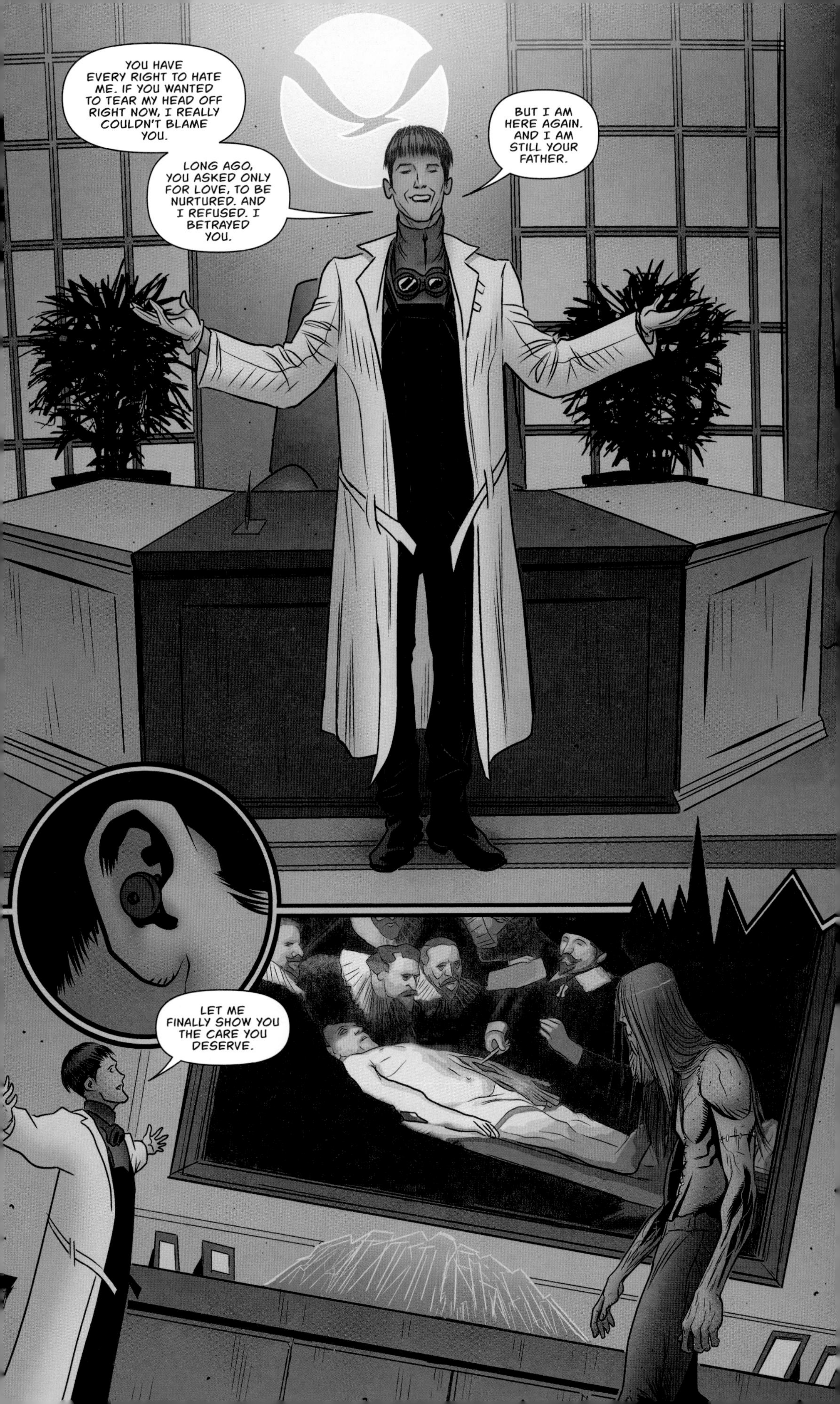
YOU HAVE EVERY RIGHT TO HATE ME. IF YOU WANTED TO TEAR MY HEAD OFF RIGHT NOW, I REALLY COULDN'T BLAME YOU.
LONG AGO, YOU ASKED ONLY FOR LOVE, TO BE NURTURED. AND I REFUSED. I BETRAYED YOU.
BUT I AM HERE AGAIN. AND I AM STILL YOUR FATHER.
LET ME FINALLY SHOW YOU THE CARE YOU DESERVE.

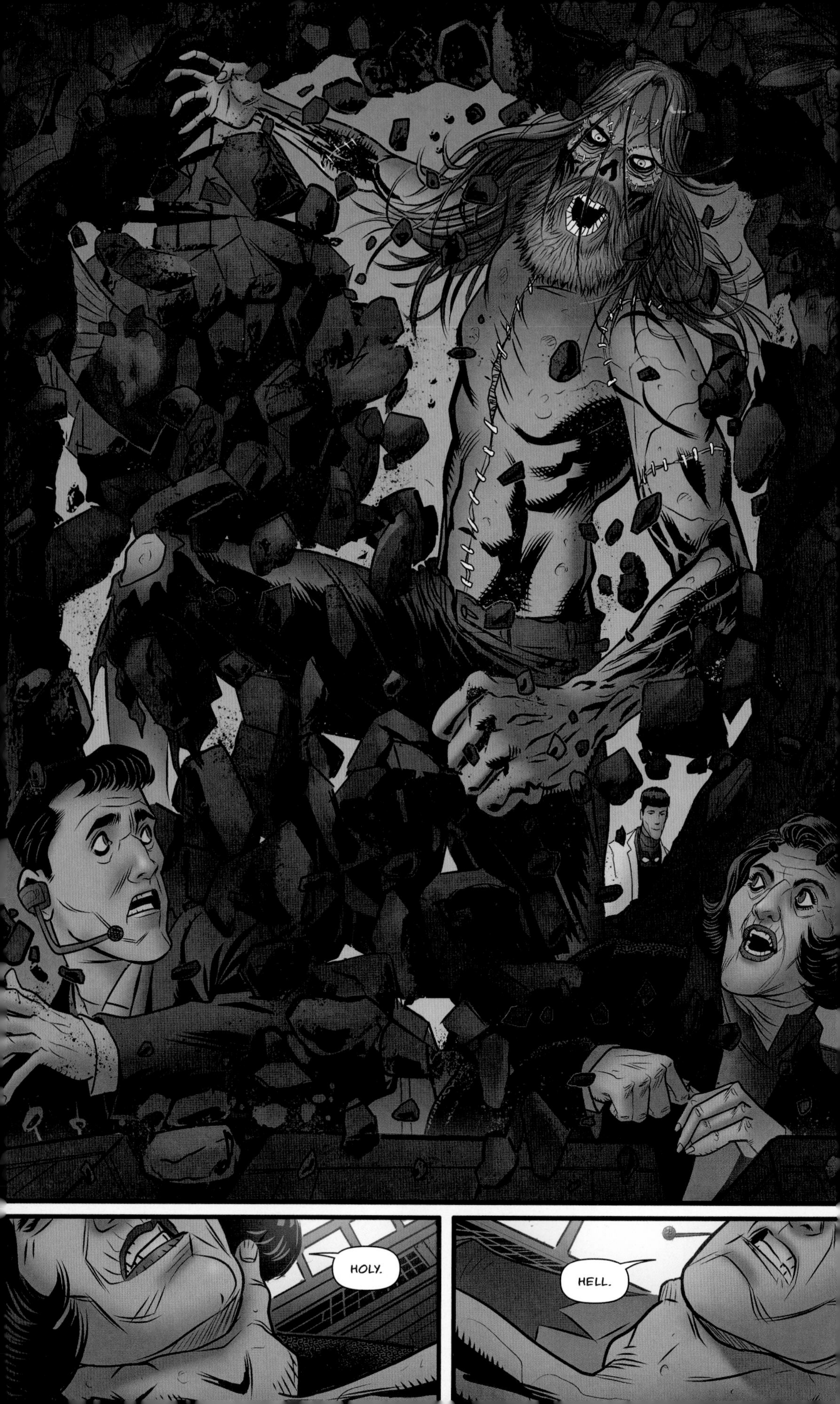
HOLY.
HELL.

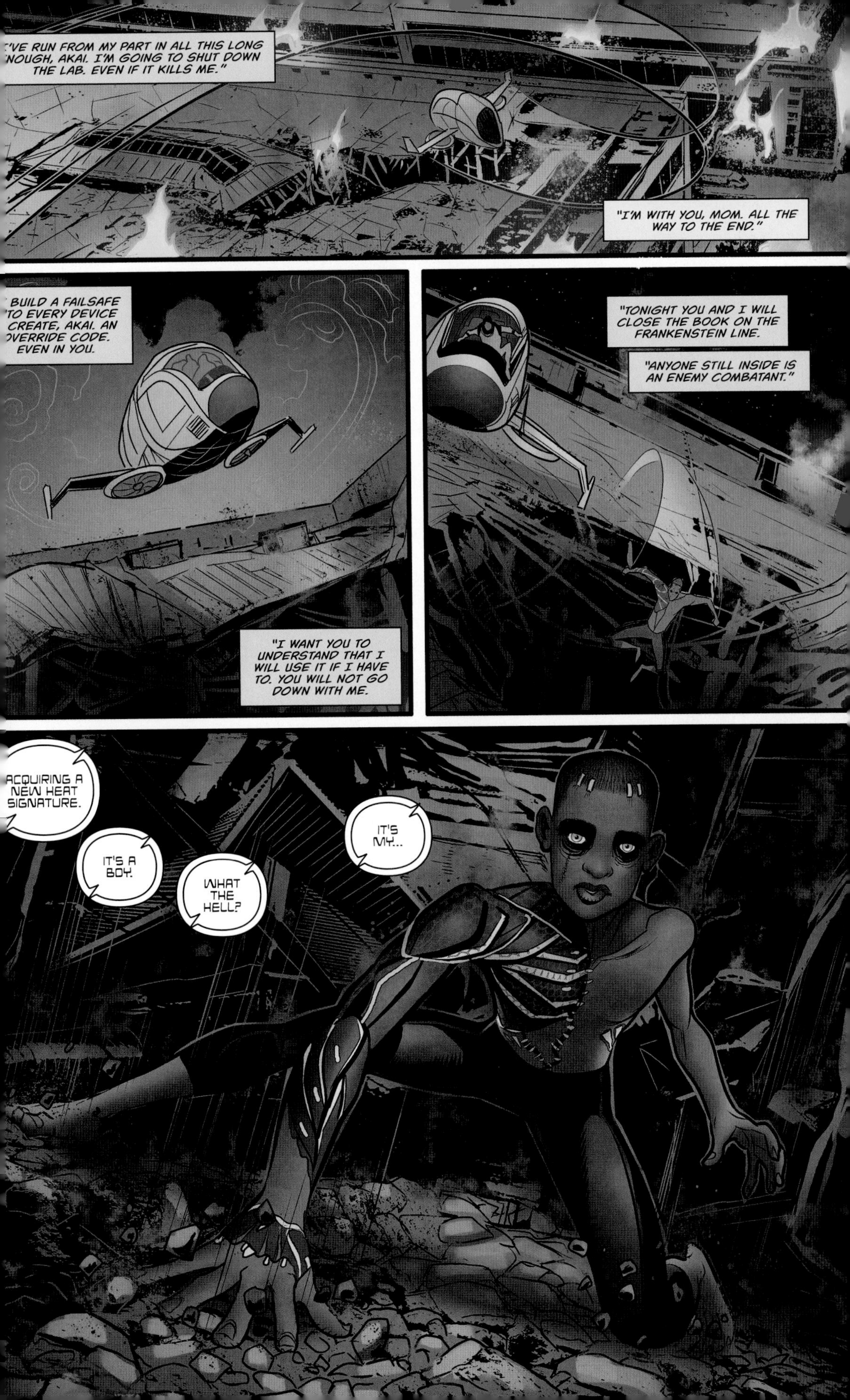
I'VE RUN FROM MY PART IN ALL THIS LONG ENOUGH, AKAI. I'M GOING TO SHUT DOWN THE LAB. EVEN IF IT KILLS ME."
"I'M WITH YOU, MOM. ALL THE WAY TO THE END."
I BUILD A FAILSAFE INTO EVERY DEVICE I CREATE, AKAI. AN OVERRIDE CODE. EVEN IN YOU.
"I WANT YOU TO UNDERSTAND THAT I WILL USE IT IF I HAVE TO. YOU WILL NOT GO DOWN WITH ME.
"TONIGHT YOU AND I WILL CLOSE THE BOOK ON THE FRANKENSTEIN LINE.
"ANYONE STILL INSIDE IS AN ENEMY COMBATANT."
ACQUIRING A NEW HEAT SIGNATURE.
IT'S A BOY.
WHAT THE HELL?
IT'S MY...

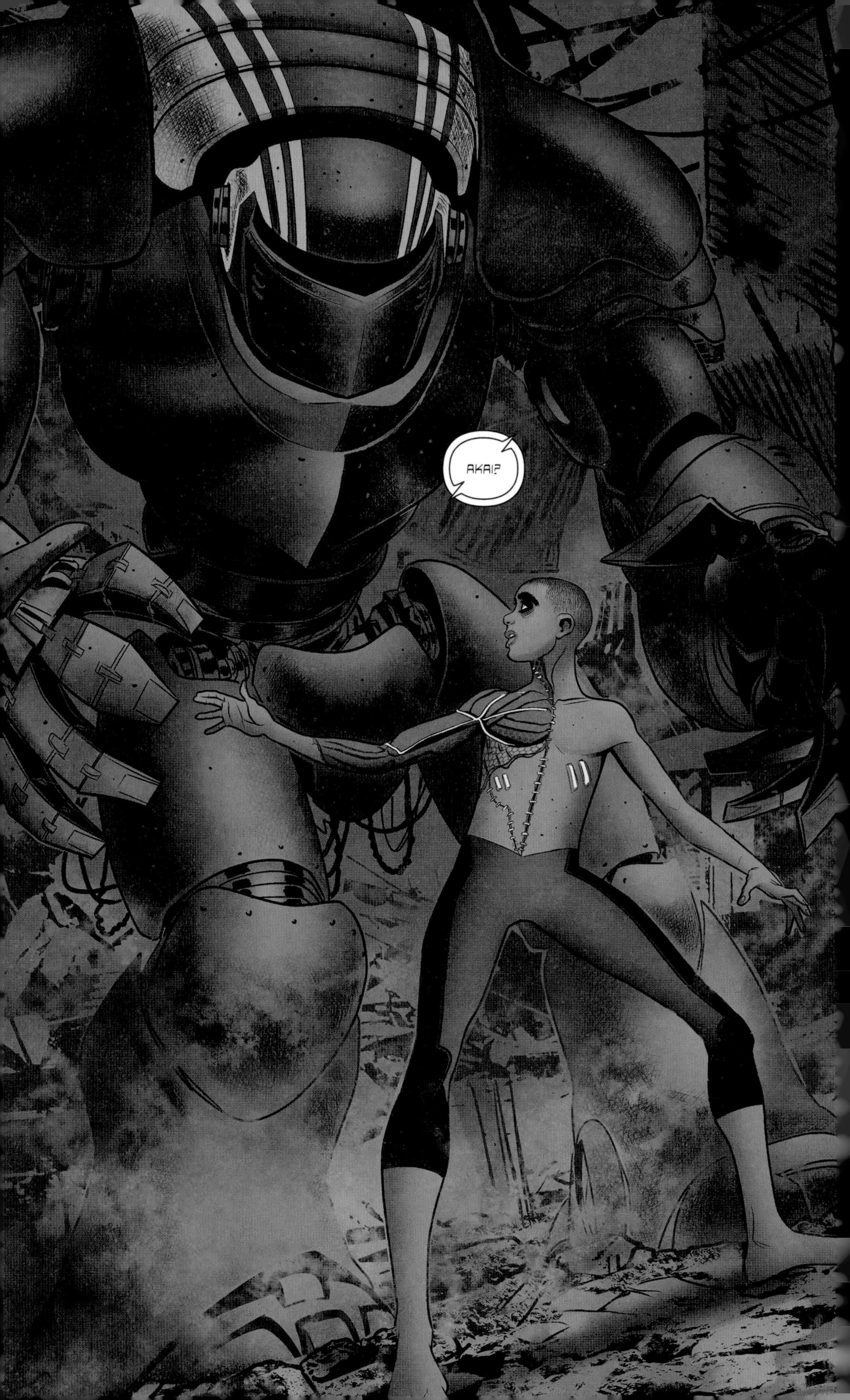
AKAI?

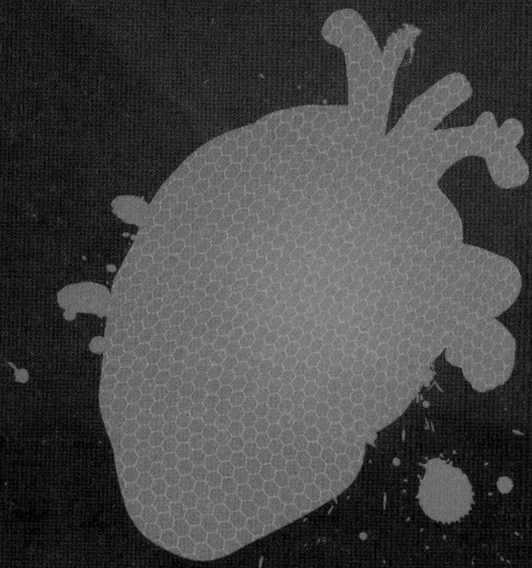

CHAPTER
SIX

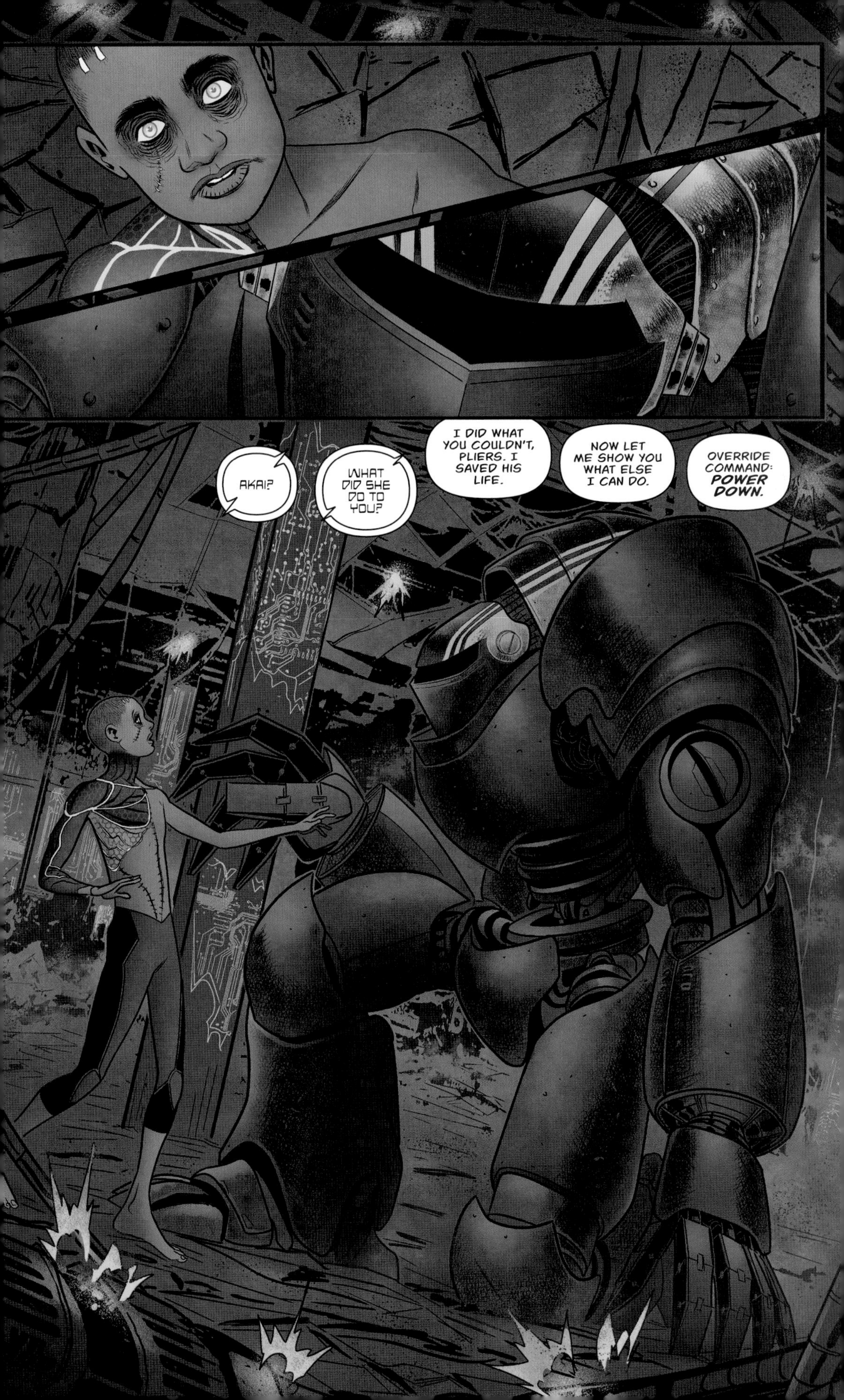
AKAI?
WHAT DID SHE DO TO YOU?
I DID WHAT YOU COULDN'T, PLIERS. I SAVED HIS LIFE.
NOW LET ME SHOW YOU WHAT ELSE I CAN DO.
OVERRIDE COMMAND: POWER DOWN.

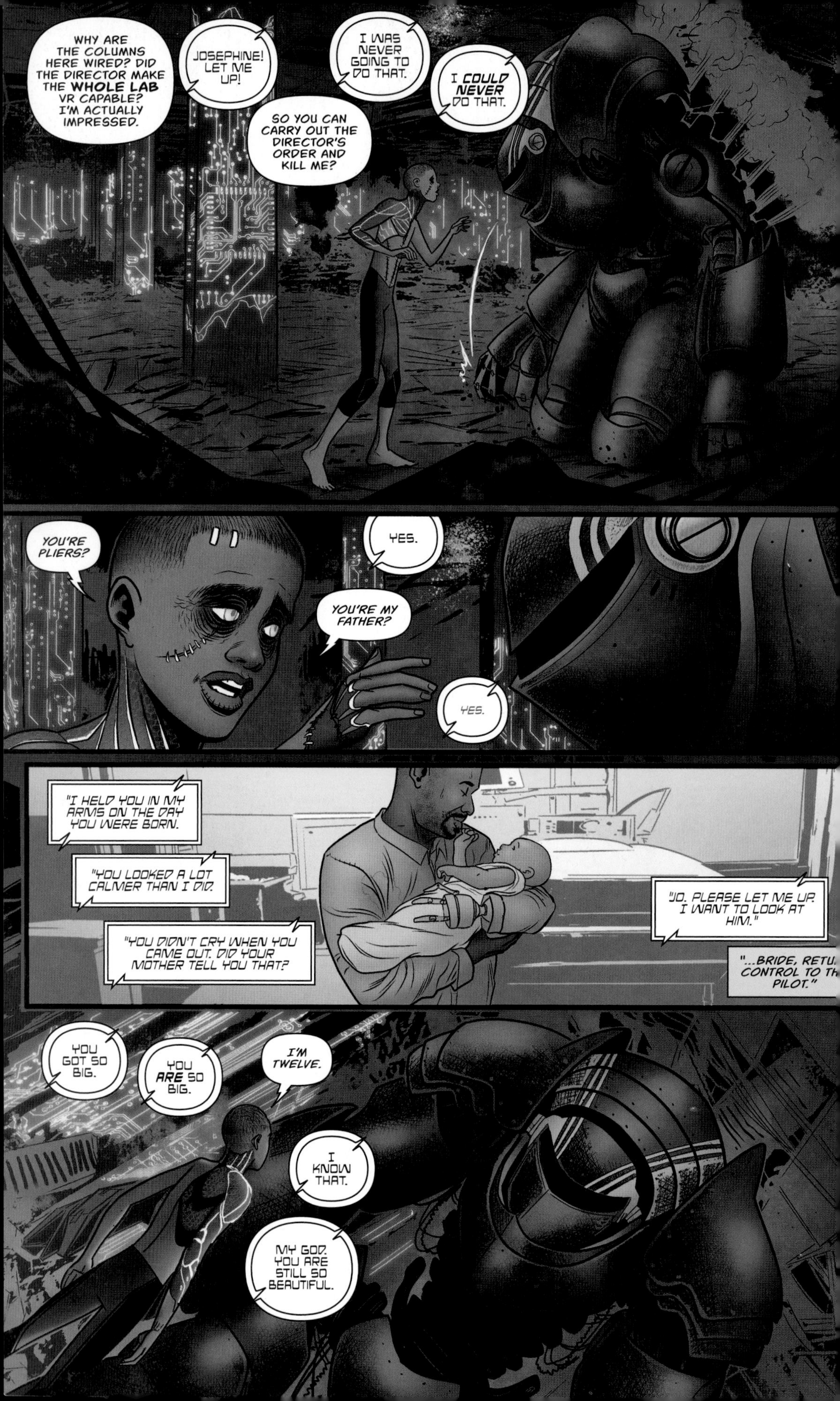
WHY ARE THE COLUMNS HERE WIRED? DID THE DIRECTOR MAKE THE WHOLE LAB VR CAPABLE? I'M ACTUALLY IMPRESSED.
JOSEPHINE! LET ME UP!
SO YOU CAN CARRY OUT THE DIRECTOR'S ORDER AND KILL ME?
I WAS NEVER GOING TO DO THAT.
I COULD NEVER DO THAT.
YOU'RE PLIERS?
YES.
YOU'RE MY FATHER?
YES.
"I HELD YOU IN MY ARMS ON THE DAY YOU WERE BORN.
"YOU LOOKED A LOT CALMER THAN I DID.
"YOU DIDN'T CRY WHEN YOU CAME OUT. DID YOUR MOTHER TELL YOU THAT?
"JO. PLEASE LET ME UP. I WANT TO LOOK AT HIM."
"...BRIDE, RETU... CONTROL TO TH... PILOT."
YOU GOT SO BIG.
YOU ARE SO BIG.
I'M TWELVE.
I KNOW THAT.
MY GOD. YOU ARE STILL SO BEAUTIFUL.

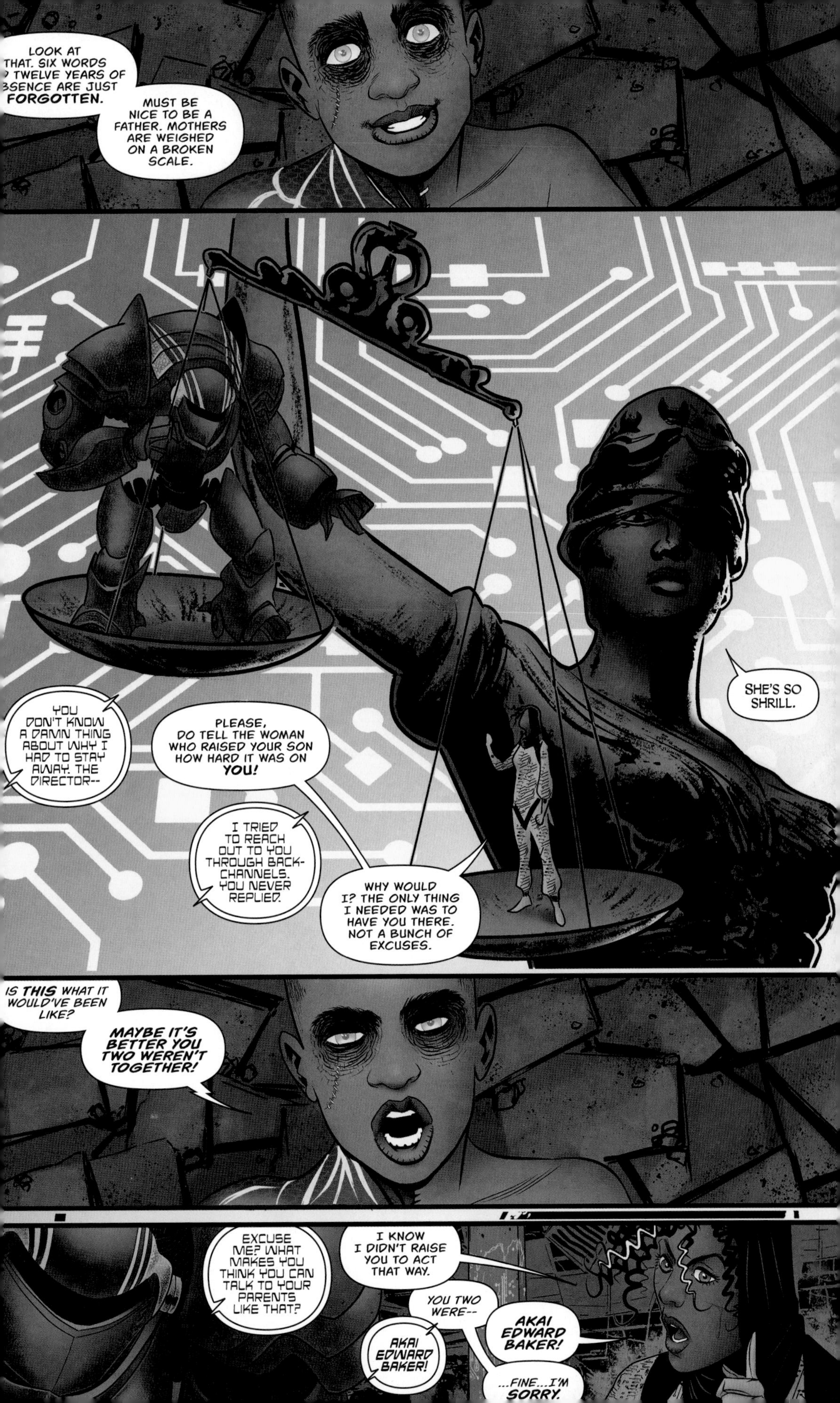
LOOK AT THAT. SIX WORDS AND TWELVE YEARS OF ABSENCE ARE JUST FORGOTTEN.
MUST BE NICE TO BE A FATHER. MOTHERS ARE WEIGHED ON A BROKEN SCALE.
SHE'S SO SHRILL.
YOU DON'T KNOW A DAMN THING ABOUT WHY I HAD TO STAY AWAY. THE DIRECTOR--
PLEASE, DO TELL THE WOMAN WHO RAISED YOUR SON HOW HARD IT WAS ON YOU!
I TRIED TO REACH OUT TO YOU THROUGH BACK-CHANNELS. YOU NEVER REPLIED.
WHY WOULD I? THE ONLY THING I NEEDED WAS TO HAVE YOU THERE. NOT A BUNCH OF EXCUSES.
IS THIS WHAT IT WOULD'VE BEEN LIKE?
MAYBE IT'S BETTER YOU TWO WEREN'T TOGETHER!
EXCUSE ME? WHAT MAKES YOU THINK YOU CAN TALK TO YOUR PARENTS LIKE THAT?
I KNOW I DIDN'T RAISE YOU TO ACT THAT WAY.
YOU TWO WERE--
AKAI EDWARD BAKER!
AKAI EDWARD BAKER!
...FINE...I'M SORRY.

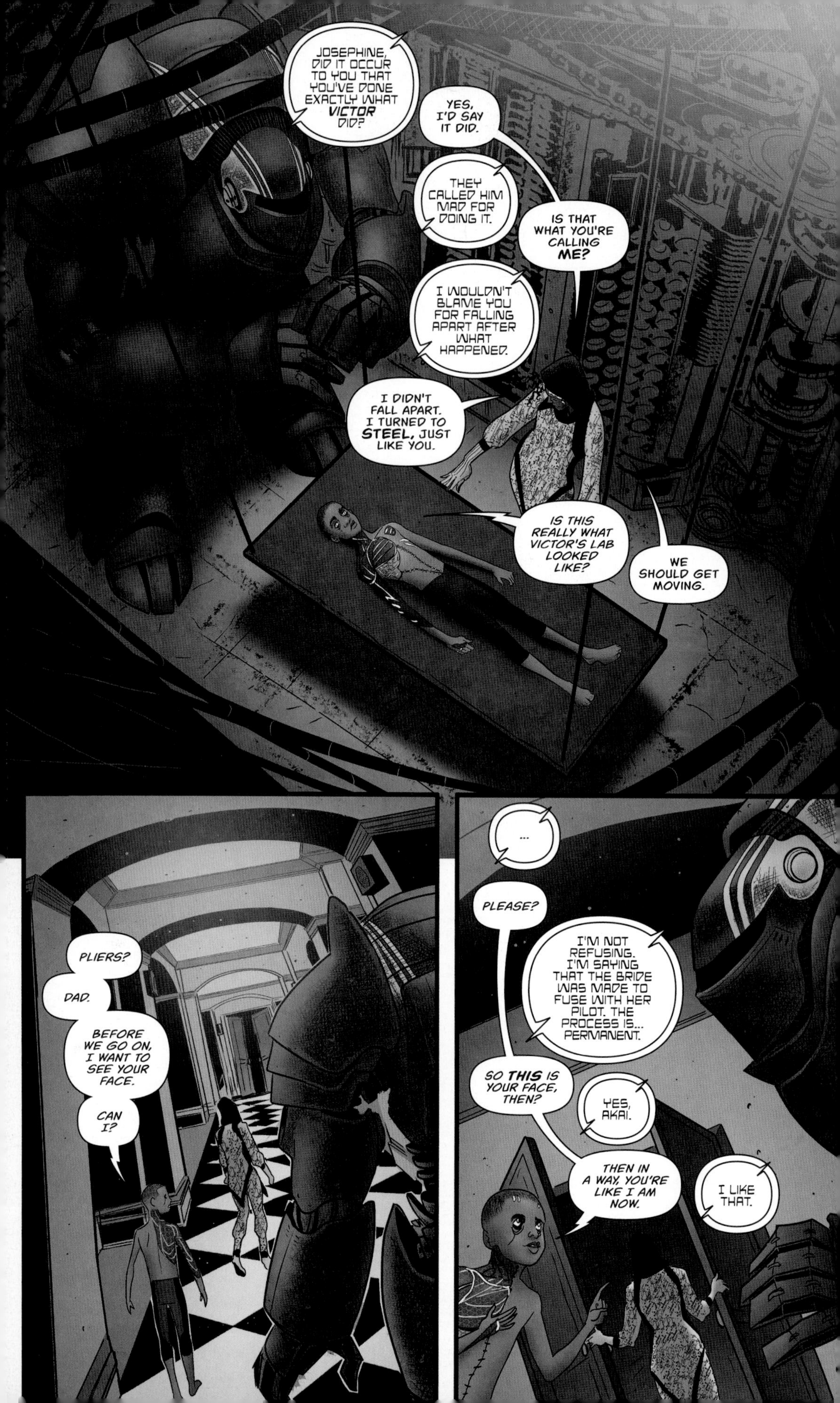
JOSEPHINE, DID IT OCCUR TO YOU THAT YOU'VE DONE EXACTLY WHAT VICTOR DID?
YES, I'D SAY IT DID.
THEY CALLED HIM MAD FOR DOING IT.
IS THAT WHAT YOU'RE CALLING ME?
I WOULDN'T BLAME YOU FOR FALLING APART AFTER WHAT HAPPENED.
I DIDN'T FALL APART. I TURNED TO STEEL, JUST LIKE YOU.
IS THIS REALLY WHAT VICTOR'S LAB LOOKED LIKE?
WE SHOULD GET MOVING.
PLIERS?
DAD.
BEFORE WE GO ON, I WANT TO SEE YOUR FACE.
CAN I?
...
PLEASE?
I'M NOT REFUSING. I'M SAYING THAT THE BRIDE WAS MADE TO FUSE WITH HER PILOT. THE PROCESS IS... PERMANENT.
SO THIS IS YOUR FACE, THEN?
YES, AKAI.
THEN IN A WAY, YOU'RE LIKE I AM NOW.
I LIKE THAT.

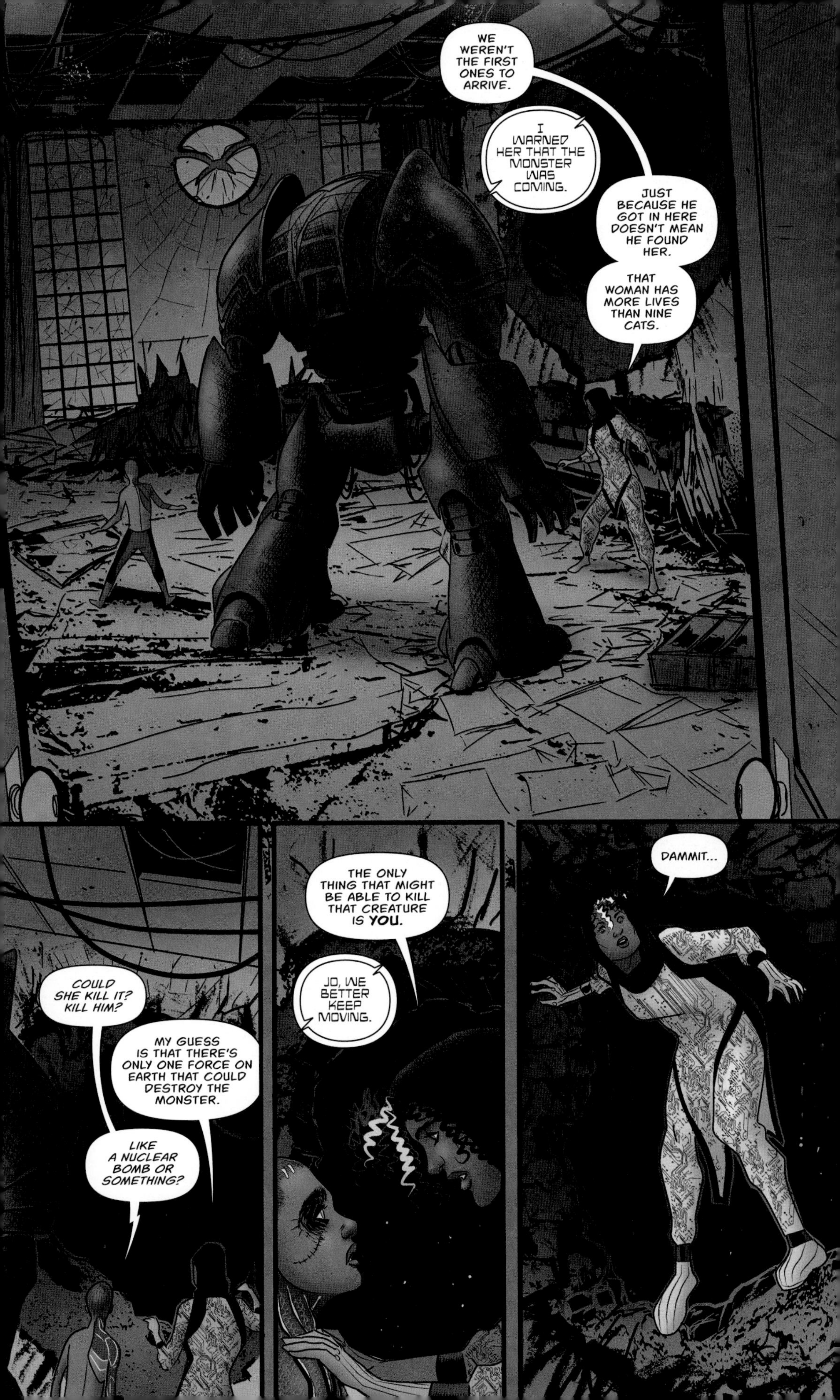

WE WEREN'T THE FIRST ONES TO ARRIVE.
I WARNED HER THAT THE MONSTER WAS COMING.
JUST BECAUSE HE GOT IN HERE DOESN'T MEAN HE FOUND HER.
THAT WOMAN HAS MORE LIVES THAN NINE CATS.
COULD SHE KILL IT? KILL HIM?
MY GUESS IS THAT THERE'S ONLY ONE FORCE ON EARTH THAT COULD DESTROY THE MONSTER.
LIKE A NUCLEAR BOMB OR SOMETHING?
THE ONLY THING THAT MIGHT BE ABLE TO KILL THAT CREATURE IS **YOU**.
JO, WE BETTER KEEP MOVING.
DAMMIT...

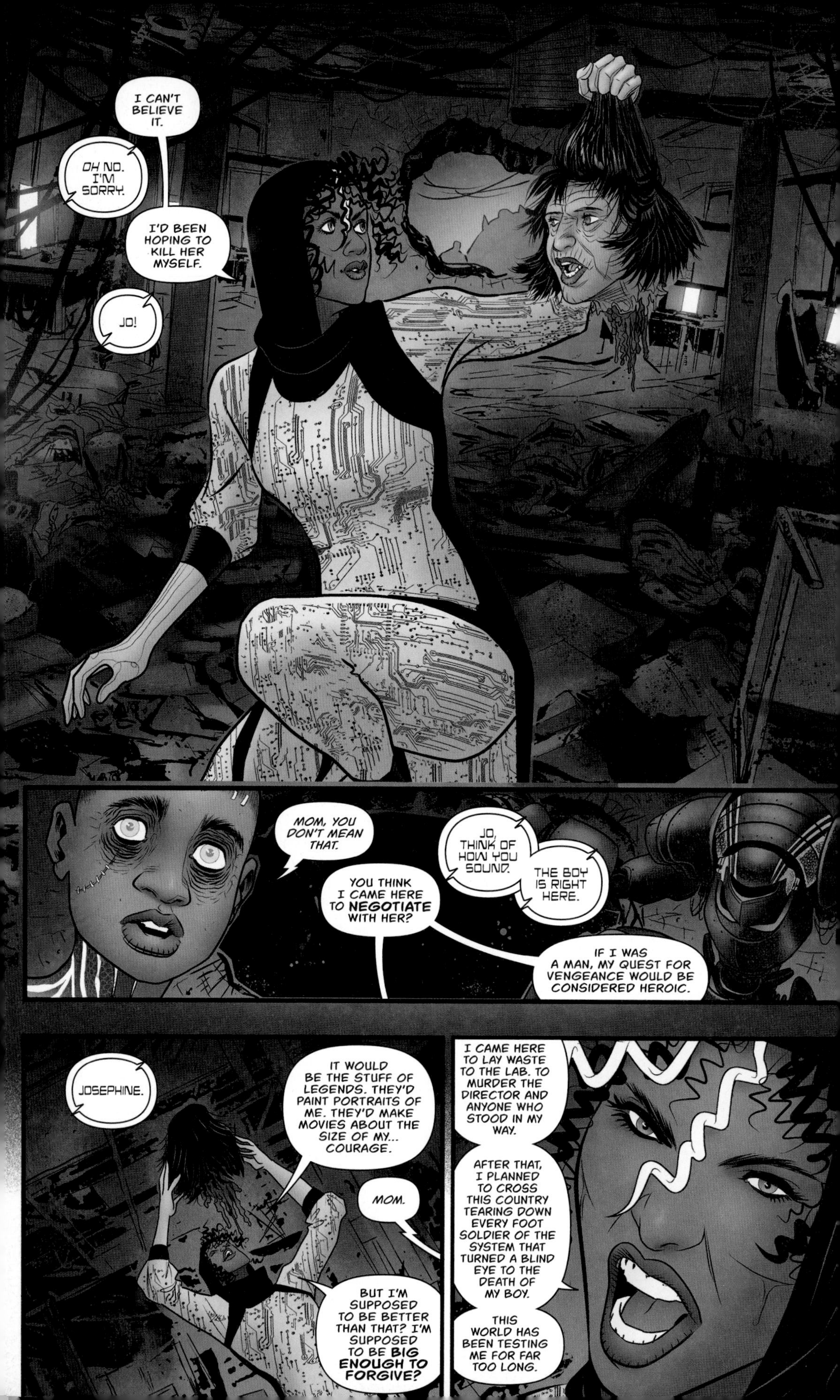
I CAN'T BELIEVE IT.
OH NO. I'M SORRY.
I'D BEEN HOPING TO KILL HER MYSELF.
JO!
MOM, YOU DON'T MEAN THAT.
JO, THINK OF HOW YOU SOUND.
THE BOY IS RIGHT HERE.
YOU THINK I CAME HERE TO NEGOTIATE WITH HER?
IF I WAS A MAN, MY QUEST FOR VENGEANCE WOULD BE CONSIDERED HEROIC.
JOSEPHINE.
IT WOULD BE THE STUFF OF LEGENDS. THEY'D PAINT PORTRAITS OF ME. THEY'D MAKE MOVIES ABOUT THE SIZE OF MY... COURAGE.
MOM.
BUT I'M SUPPOSED TO BE BETTER THAN THAT? I'M SUPPOSED TO BE BIG ENOUGH TO FORGIVE?
I CAME HERE TO LAY WASTE TO THE LAB. TO MURDER THE DIRECTOR AND ANYONE WHO STOOD IN MY WAY.
AFTER THAT, I PLANNED TO CROSS THIS COUNTRY TEARING DOWN EVERY FOOT SOLDIER OF THE SYSTEM THAT TURNED A BLIND EYE TO THE DEATH OF MY BOY.
THIS WORLD HAS BEEN TESTING ME FOR FAR TOO LONG.

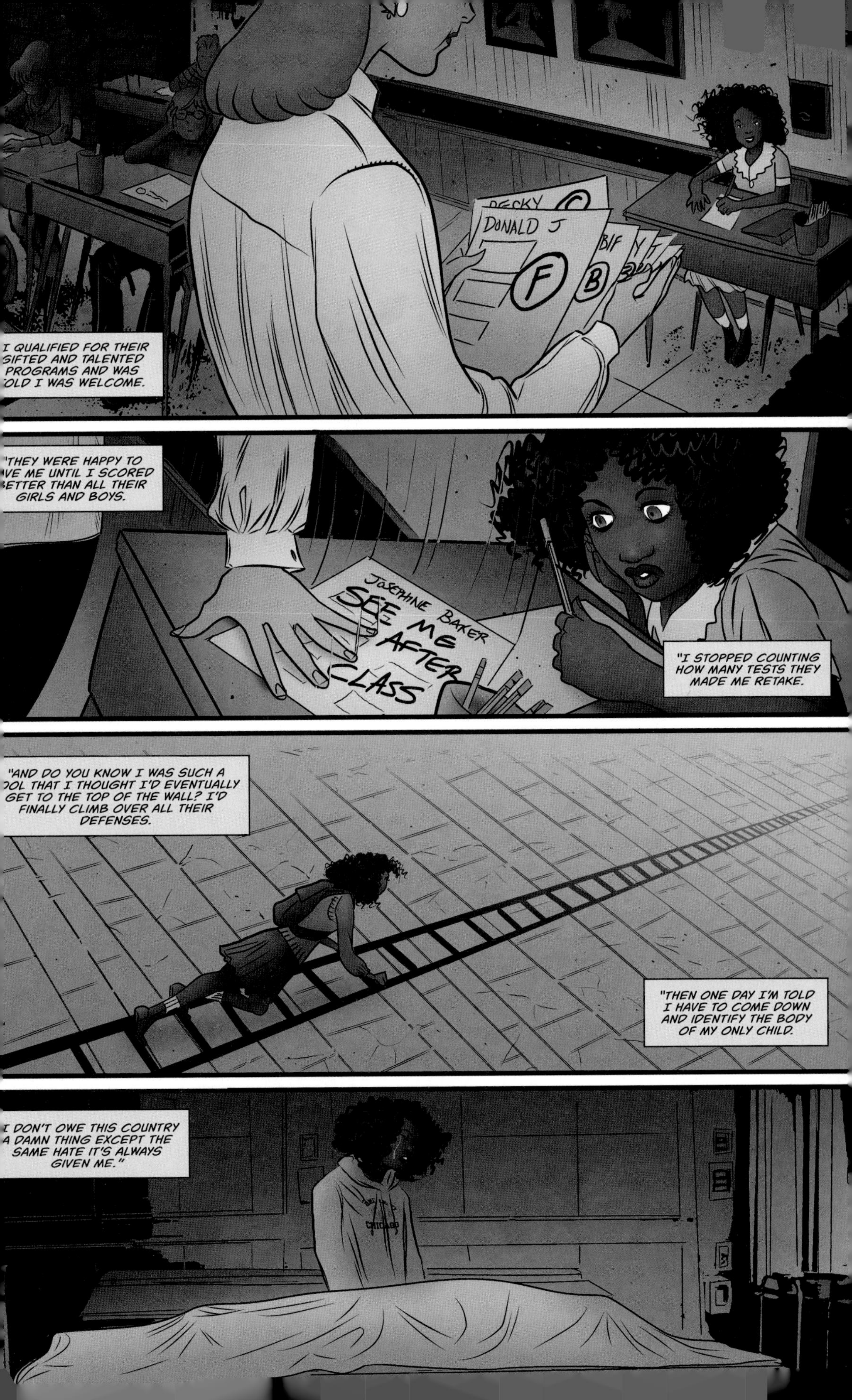

I QUALIFIED FOR THEIR
SIFTED AND TALENTED
PROGRAMS AND WAS
OLD I WAS WELCOME.
DONALD J
F
B
"THEY WERE HAPPY TO
AVE ME UNTIL I SCORED
SETTER THAN ALL THEIR
GIRLS AND BOYS.
JOSEPHINE BAKER
SEE ME AFTER CLASS
"I STOPPED COUNTING HOW MANY TESTS THEY MADE ME RETAKE.
"AND DO YOU KNOW I WAS SUCH A
OOL THAT I THOUGHT I'D EVENTUALLY
GET TO THE TOP OF THE WALL? I'D
FINALLY CLIMB OVER ALL THEIR
DEFENSES.
"THEN ONE DAY I'M TOLD I HAVE TO COME DOWN AND IDENTIFY THE BODY OF MY ONLY CHILD.
I DON'T OWE THIS COUNTRY
A DAMN THING EXCEPT THE
SAME HATE IT'S ALWAYS
GIVEN ME."
CHICAGO

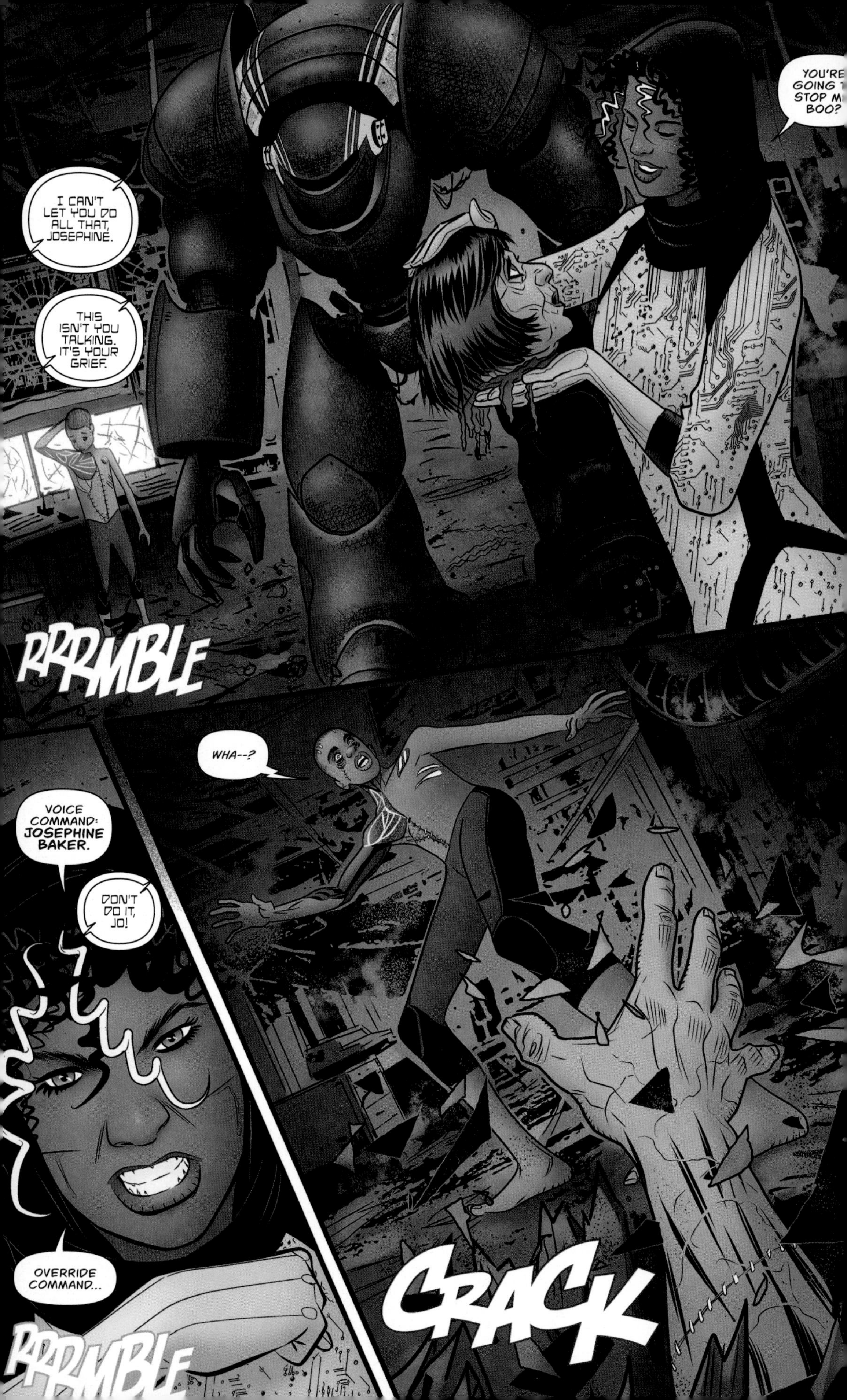
YOU'RE GOING T STOP M BOO?
I CAN'T LET YOU DO ALL THAT, JOSEPHINE.
THIS ISN'T YOU TALKING. IT'S YOUR GRIEF.
RRRMBLE
WHA--?
VOICE COMMAND: JOSEPHINE BAKER.
DON'T DO IT, JO!
OVERRIDE COMMAND...
CRACK

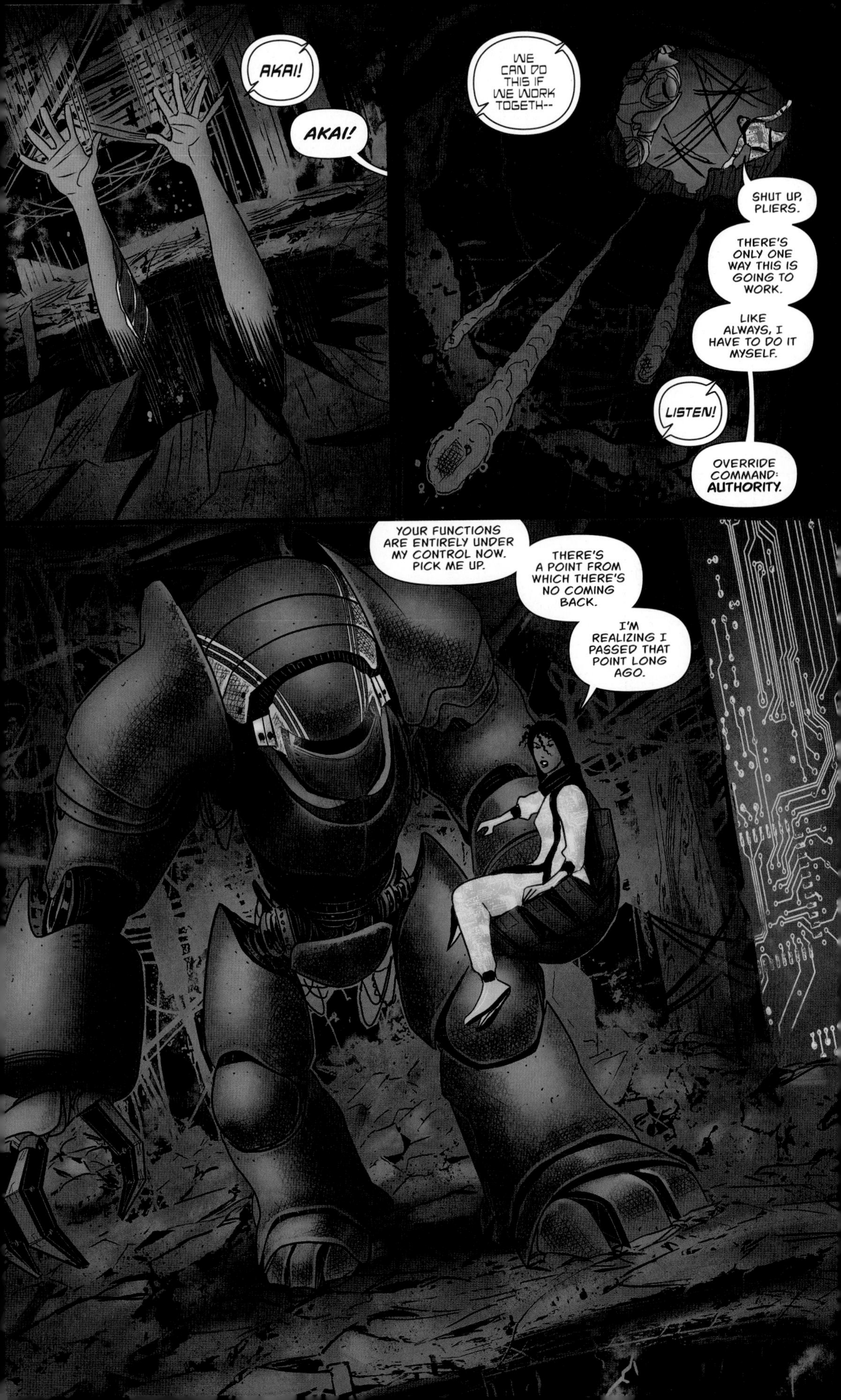
AKAI!
AKAI!
WE CAN DO THIS IF WE WORK TOGETH--
SHUT UP, PLIERS.
THERE'S ONLY ONE WAY THIS IS GOING TO WORK.
LIKE ALWAYS, I HAVE TO DO IT MYSELF.
LISTEN!
OVERRIDE COMMAND: AUTHORITY.
YOUR FUNCTIONS ARE ENTIRELY UNDER MY CONTROL NOW. PICK ME UP.
THERE'S A POINT FROM WHICH THERE'S NO COMING BACK.
I'M REALIZING I PASSED THAT POINT LONG AGO.

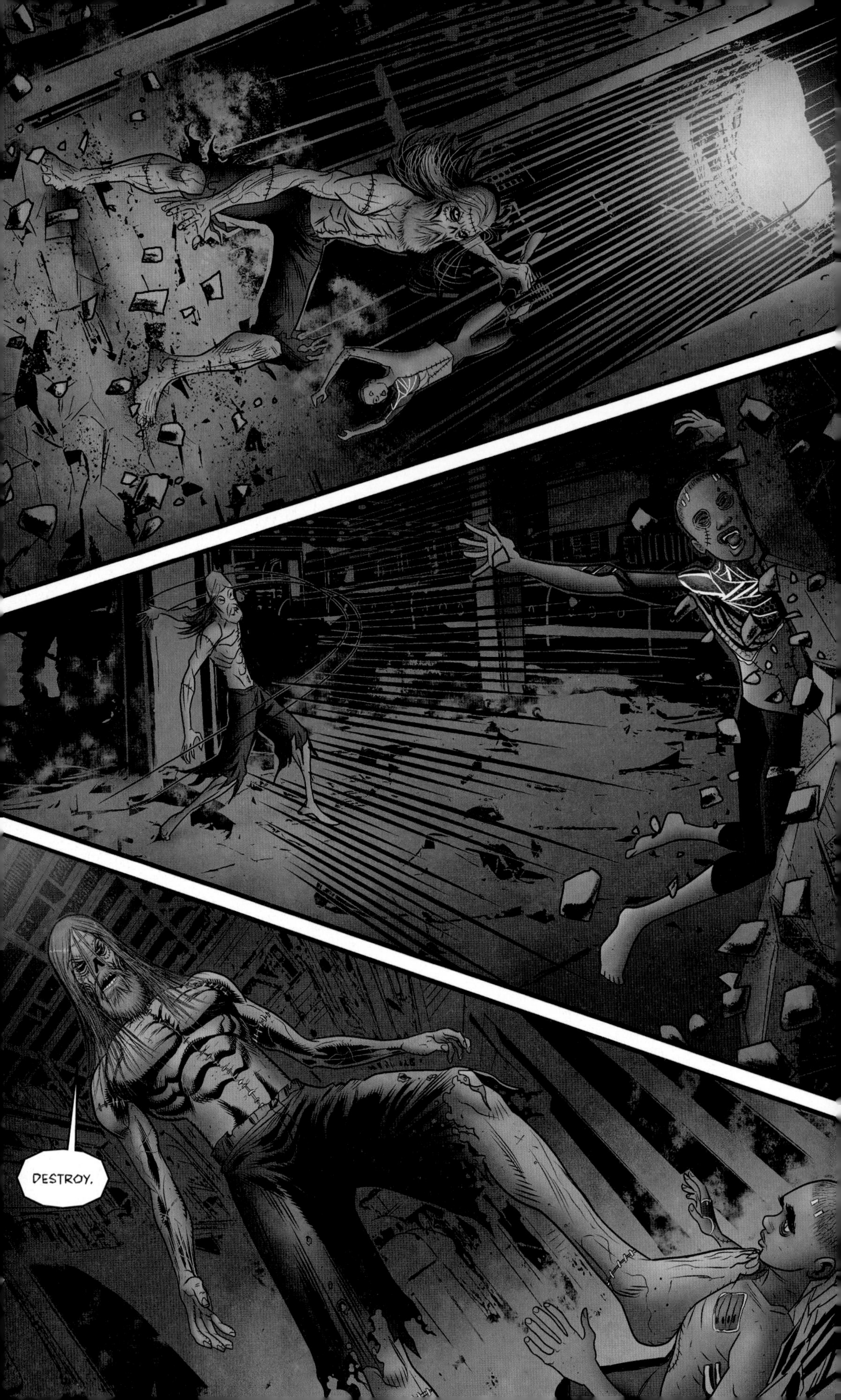
DESTROY.

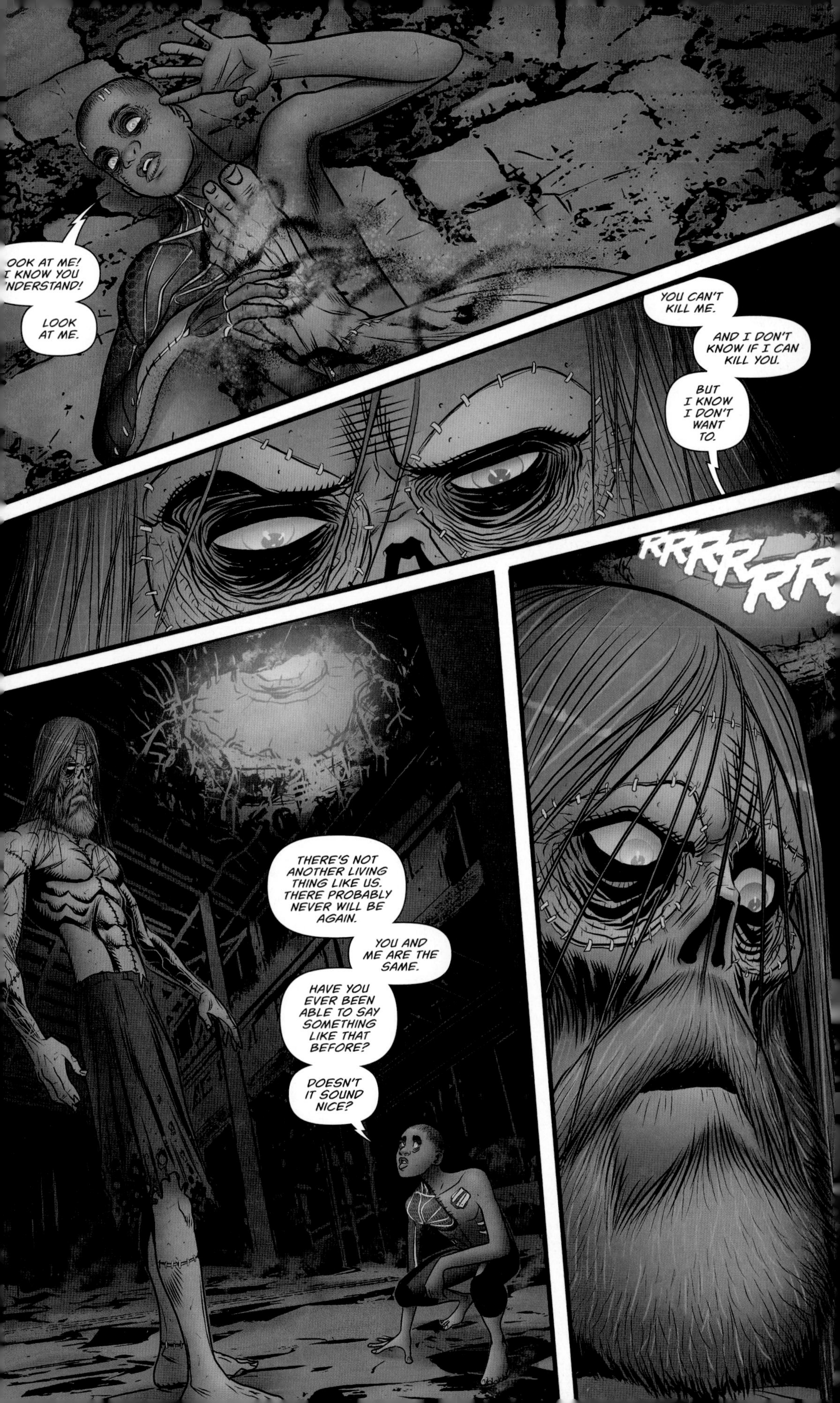
OOK AT ME! I KNOW YOU NDERSTAND!
LOOK AT ME.
YOU CAN'T KILL ME.
AND I DON'T KNOW IF I CAN KILL YOU.
BUT I KNOW I DON'T WANT TO.
RRRRRRR
THERE'S NOT ANOTHER LIVING THING LIKE US. THERE PROBABLY NEVER WILL BE AGAIN.
YOU AND ME ARE THE SAME.
HAVE YOU EVER BEEN ABLE TO SAY SOMETHING LIKE THAT BEFORE?
DOESN'T IT SOUND NICE?

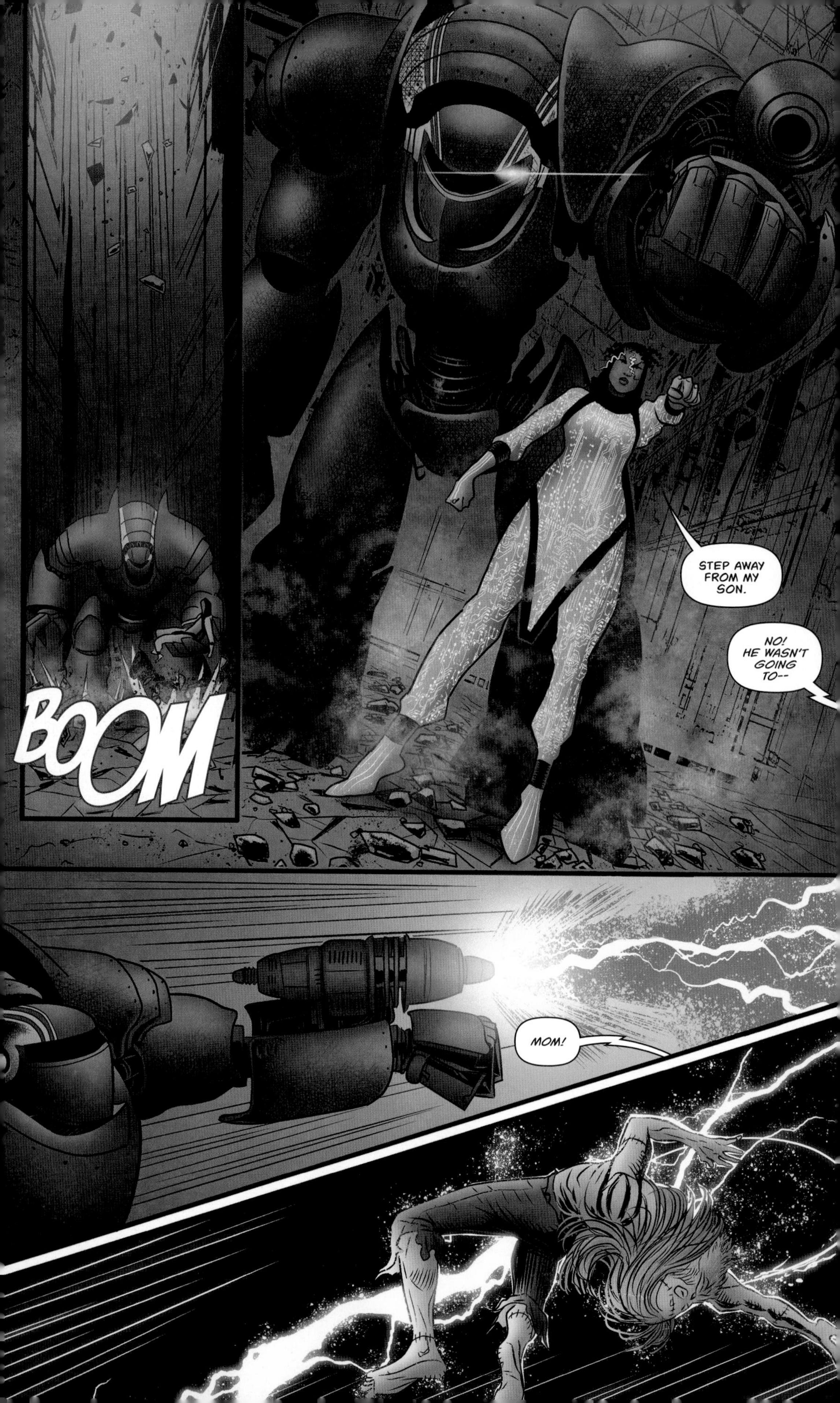
BOOM
STEP AWAY FROM MY SON.
NO! HE WASN'T GOING TO--
MOM!

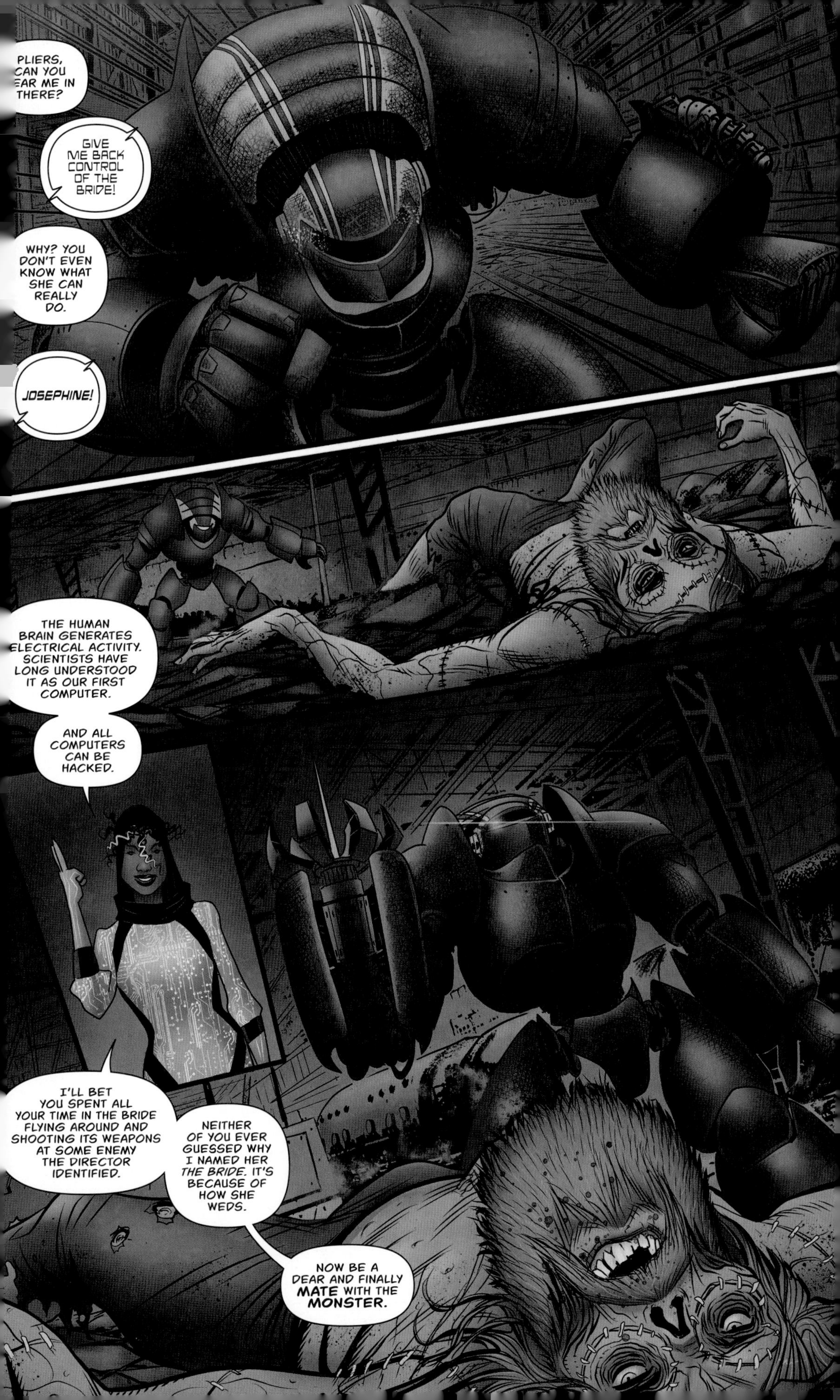
PLIERS, CAN YOU EAR ME IN THERE?
GIVE ME BACK CONTROL OF THE BRIDE!
WHY? YOU DON'T EVEN KNOW WHAT SHE CAN REALLY DO.
JOSEPHINE!
THE HUMAN BRAIN GENERATES ELECTRICAL ACTIVITY. SCIENTISTS HAVE LONG UNDERSTOOD IT AS OUR FIRST COMPUTER.
AND ALL COMPUTERS CAN BE HACKED.
I'LL BET YOU SPENT ALL YOUR TIME IN THE BRIDE FLYING AROUND AND SHOOTING ITS WEAPONS AT SOME ENEMY THE DIRECTOR IDENTIFIED.
NEITHER OF YOU EVER GUESSED WHY I NAMED HER *THE BRIDE*. IT'S BECAUSE OF HOW SHE WEDS.
NOW BE A DEAR AND FINALLY **MATE** WITH THE **MONSTER**.

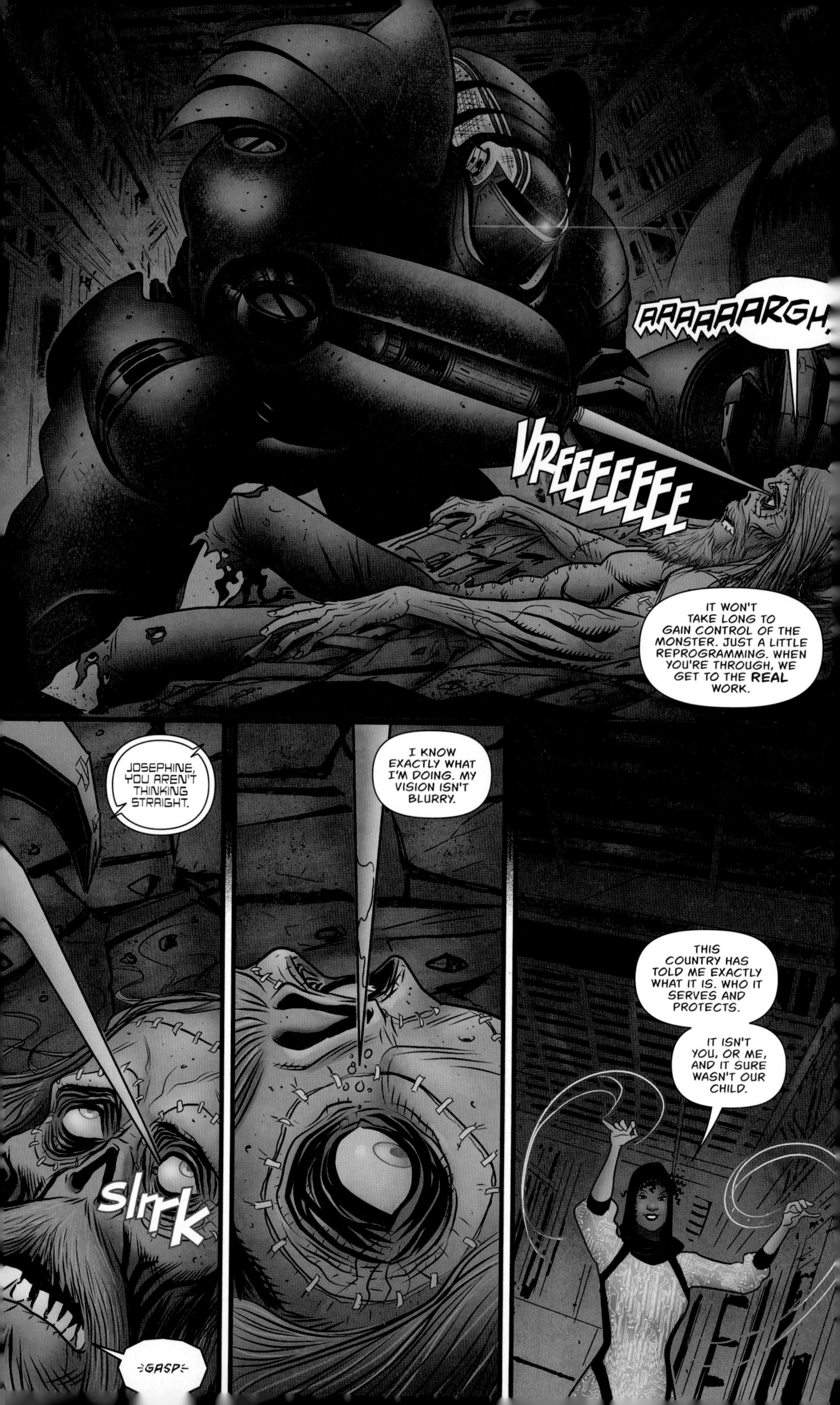
AAAAAAARGH!
VREEEEEEEE
IT WON'T TAKE LONG TO GAIN CONTROL OF THE MONSTER. JUST A LITTLE REPROGRAMMING. WHEN YOU'RE THROUGH, WE GET TO THE REAL WORK.
JOSEPHINE, YOU AREN'T THINKING STRAIGHT.
slrrrk
GASP
I KNOW EXACTLY WHAT I'M DOING. MY VISION ISN'T BLURRY.
THIS COUNTRY HAS TOLD ME EXACTLY WHAT IT IS. WHO IT SERVES AND PROTECTS.
IT ISN'T YOU, OR ME, AND IT SURE WASN'T OUR CHILD.

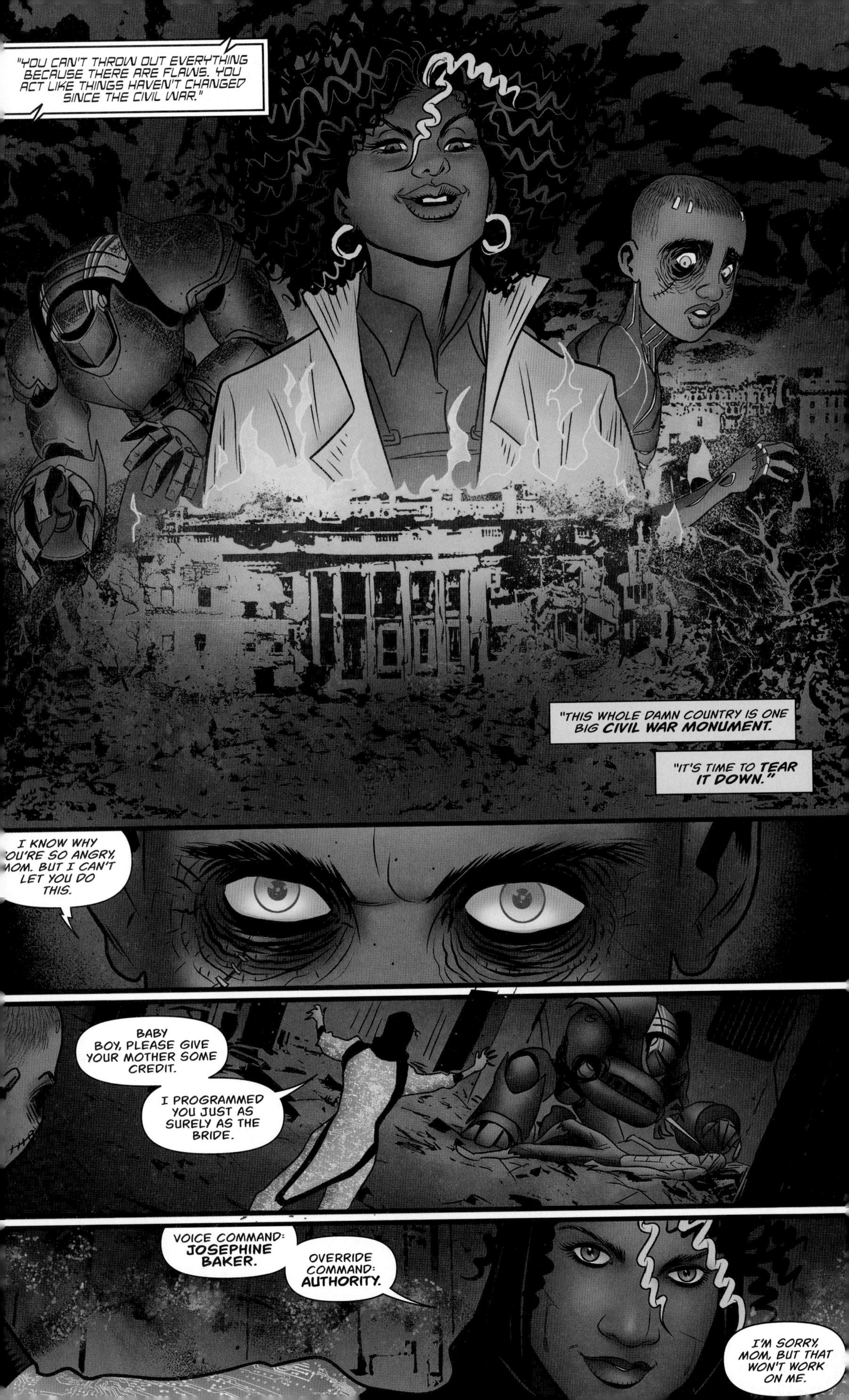
"YOU CAN'T THROW OUT EVERYTHING BECAUSE THERE ARE FLAWS. YOU ACT LIKE THINGS HAVEN'T CHANGED SINCE THE CIVIL WAR."
"THIS WHOLE DAMN COUNTRY IS ONE BIG CIVIL WAR MONUMENT.
"IT'S TIME TO TEAR IT DOWN."
I KNOW WHY YOU'RE SO ANGRY, MOM. BUT I CAN'T LET YOU DO THIS.
BABY BOY, PLEASE GIVE YOUR MOTHER SOME CREDIT.
I PROGRAMMED YOU JUST AS SURELY AS THE BRIDE.
VOICE COMMAND: JOSEPHINE BAKER.
OVERRIDE COMMAND: AUTHORITY.
I'M SORRY, MOM, BUT THAT WON'T WORK ON ME.

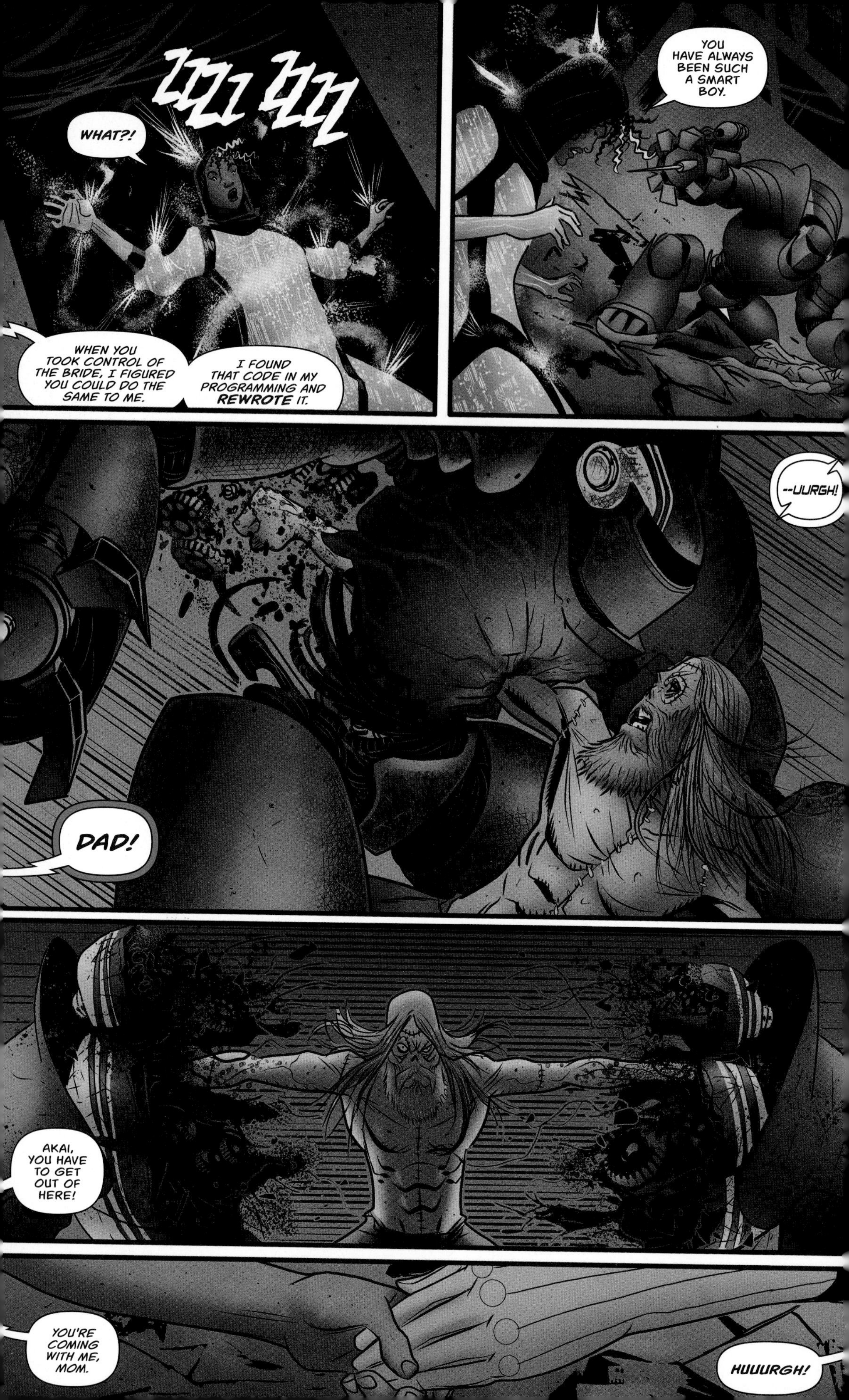
ZZZZ ZZZZ
WHAT?!
WHEN YOU TOOK CONTROL OF THE BRIDE, I FIGURED YOU COULD DO THE SAME TO ME.
I FOUND THAT CODE IN MY PROGRAMMING AND REWROTE IT.
YOU HAVE ALWAYS BEEN SUCH A SMART BOY.
--UURGH!
DAD!
AKAI, YOU HAVE TO GET OUT OF HERE!
YOU'RE COMING WITH ME, MOM.
HUUURGH!

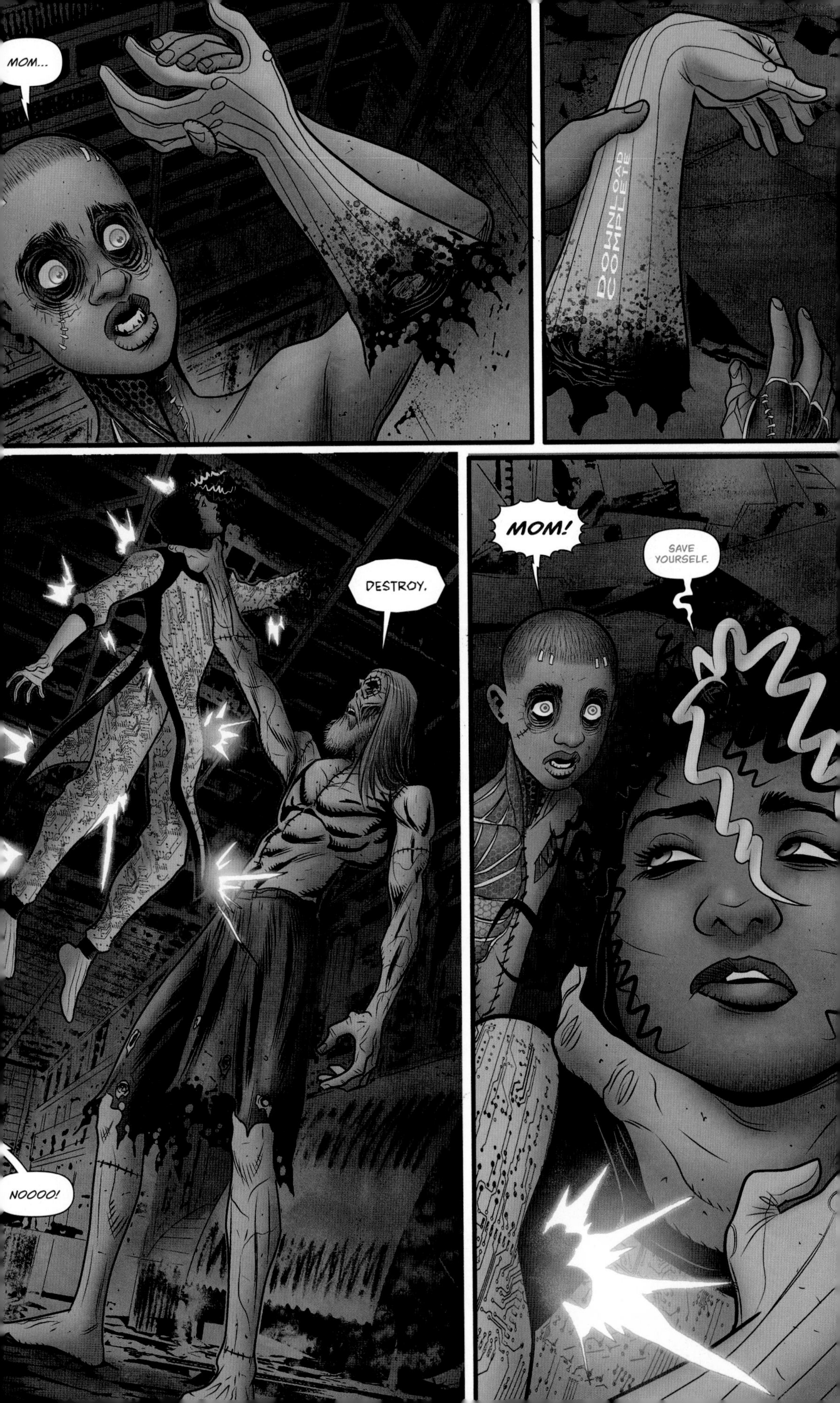
MOM...
DOWNLOAD COMPLETE
DESTROY.
NOOOO!
MOM!
SAVE YOURSELF.

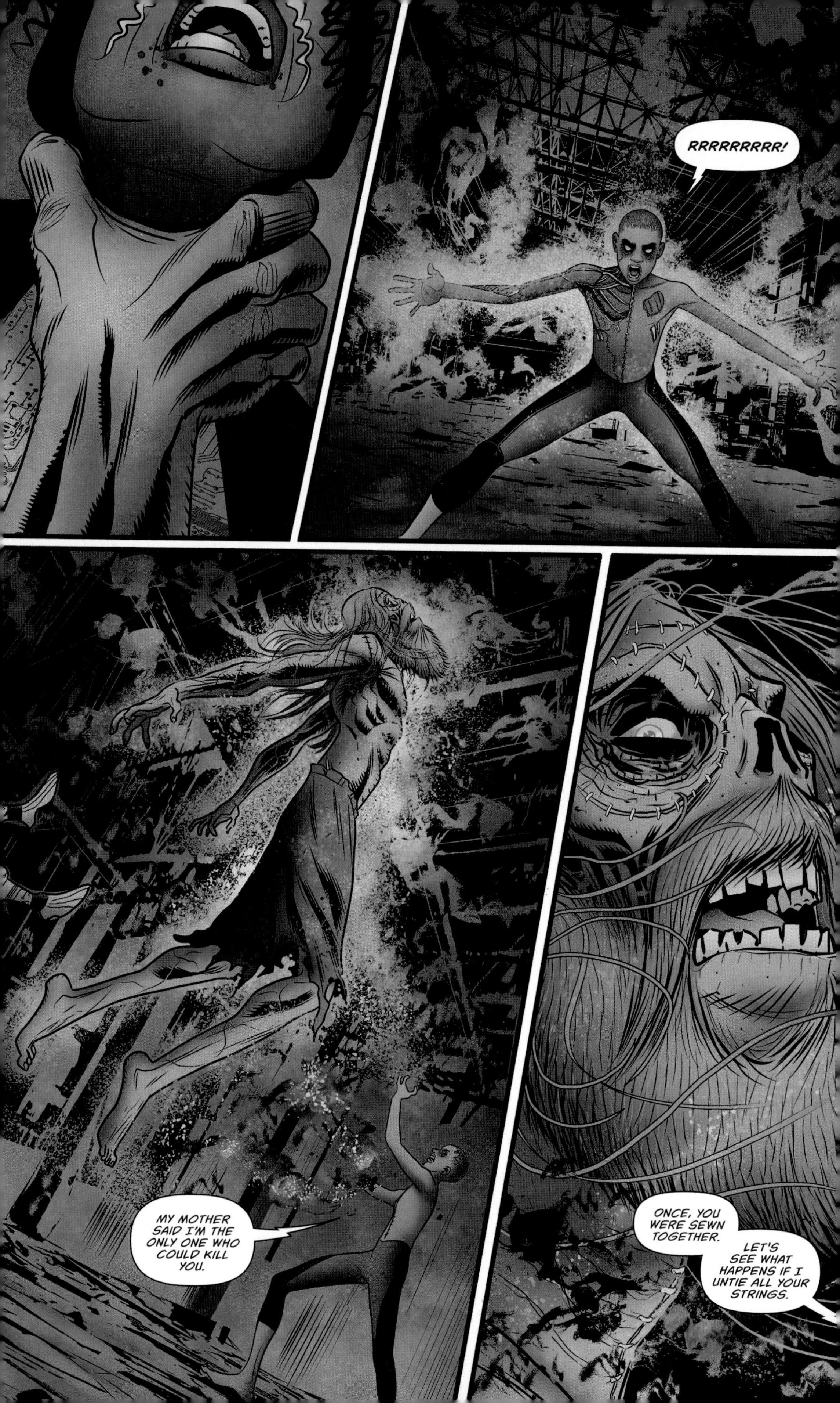
RRRRRRRRR!
MY MOTHER SAID I'M THE ONLY ONE WHO COULD KILL YOU.
ONCE, YOU WERE SEWN TOGETHER.
LET'S SEE WHAT HAPPENS IF I UNTIE ALL YOUR STRINGS.

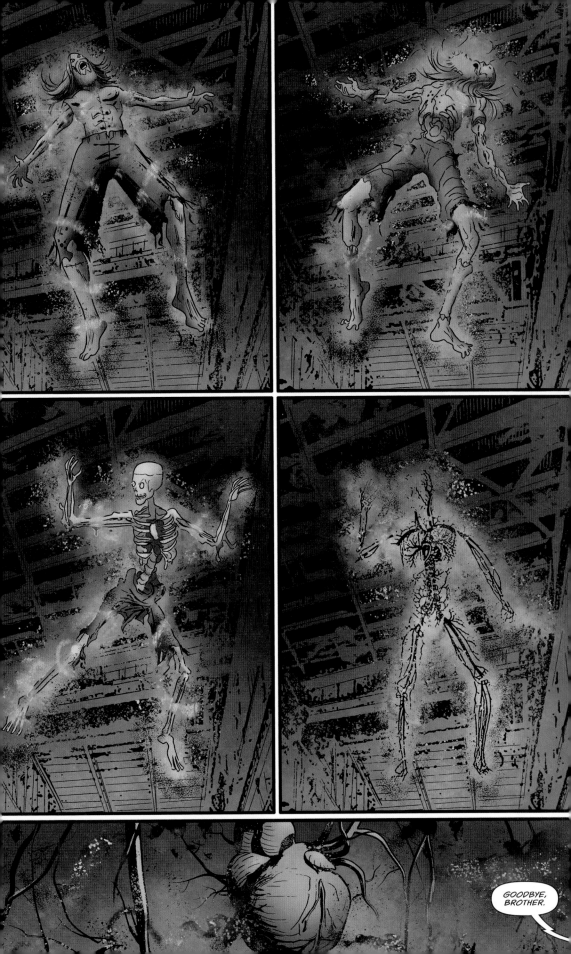

GOODBYE, BROTHER.

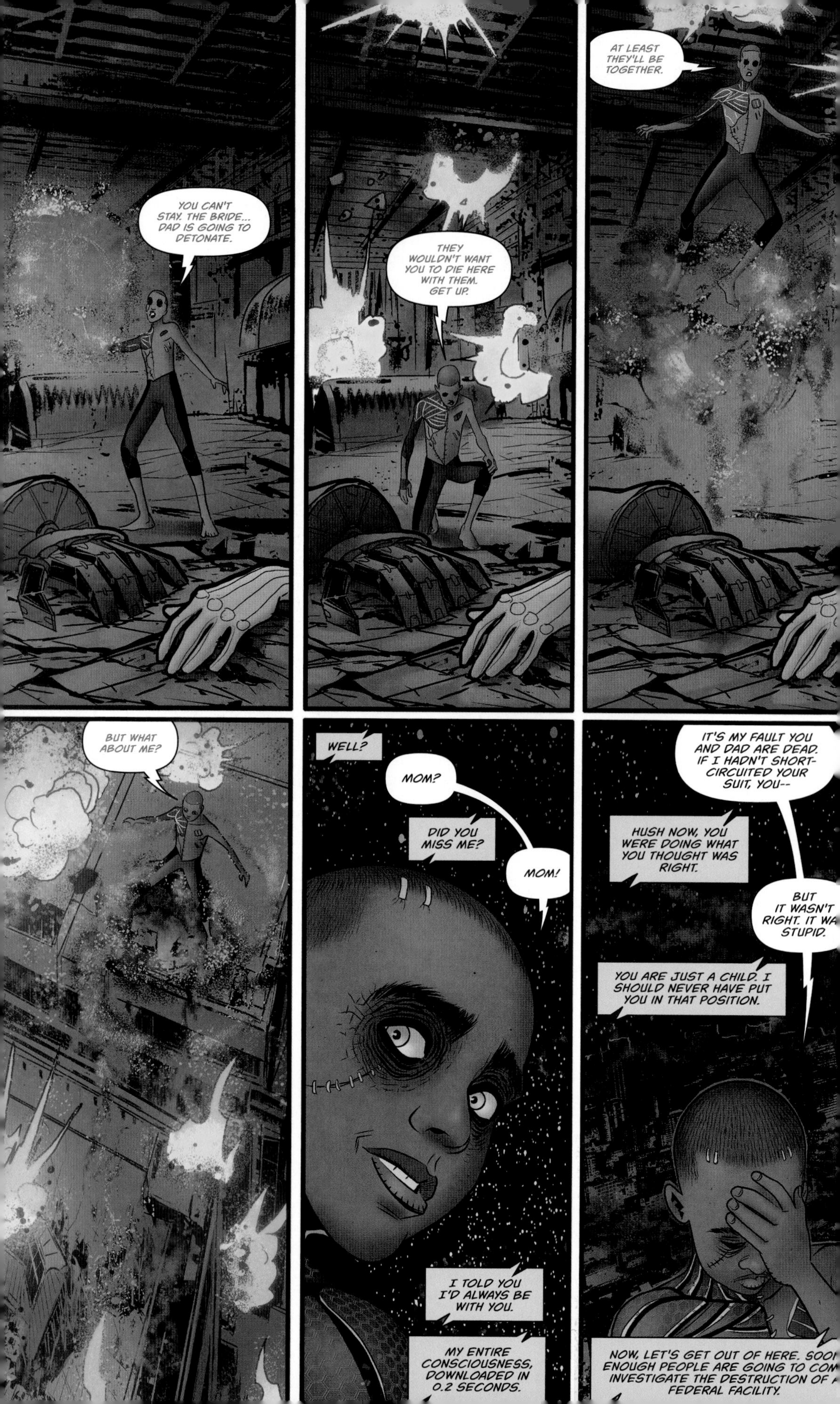
YOU CAN'T STAY. THE BRIDE... DAD IS GOING TO DETONATE.
THEY WOULDN'T WANT YOU TO DIE HERE WITH THEM. GET UP.
AT LEAST THEY'LL BE TOGETHER.
BUT WHAT ABOUT ME?
WELL?
MOM?
DID YOU MISS ME?
MOM!
I TOLD YOU I'D ALWAYS BE WITH YOU.
MY ENTIRE CONSCIOUSNESS, DOWNLOADED IN 0.2 SECONDS.
IT'S MY FAULT YOU AND DAD ARE DEAD. IF I HADN'T SHORT-CIRCUITED YOUR SUIT, YOU--
HUSH NOW, YOU WERE DOING WHAT YOU THOUGHT WAS RIGHT.
BUT IT WASN'T RIGHT. IT WA
STUPID.
YOU ARE JUST A CHILD. I SHOULD NEVER HAVE PUT YOU IN THAT POSITION.
NOW, LET'S GET OUT OF HERE. SOO
ENOUGH PEOPLE ARE GOING TO COM
INVESTIGATE THE DESTRUCTION OF A
FEDERAL FACILITY.

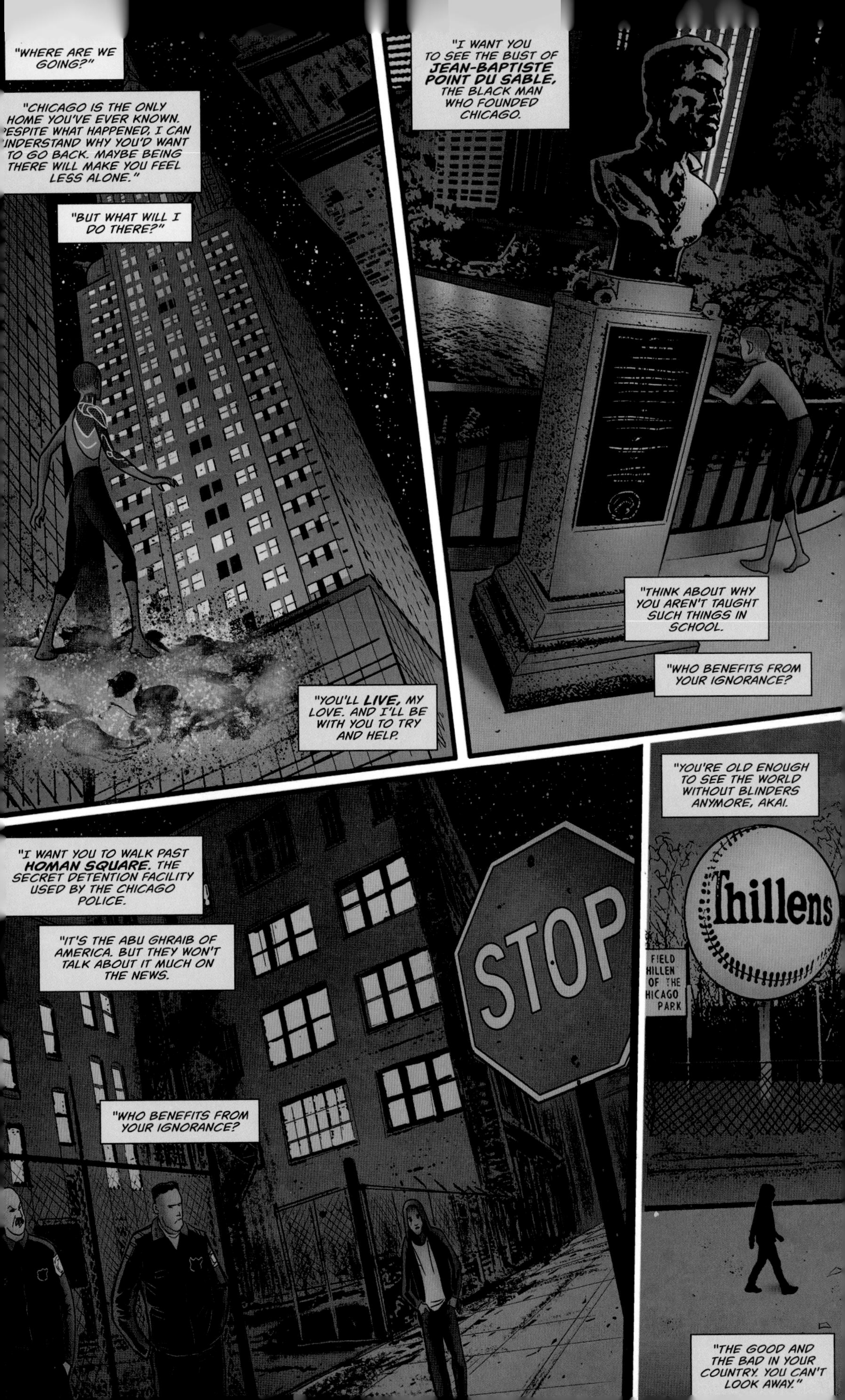
"WHERE ARE WE GOING?"
"CHICAGO IS THE ONLY HOME YOU'VE EVER KNOWN. ESPITE WHAT HAPPENED, I CAN INDERSTAND WHY YOU'D WANT TO GO BACK. MAYBE BEING THERE WILL MAKE YOU FEEL LESS ALONE."
"BUT WHAT WILL I DO THERE?"
"YOU'LL **LIVE,** MY LOVE. AND I'LL BE WITH YOU TO TRY AND HELP.
"I WANT YOU TO SEE THE BUST OF **JEAN-BAPTISTE POINT DU SABLE,** THE BLACK MAN WHO FOUNDED CHICAGO.
"THINK ABOUT WHY YOU AREN'T TAUGHT SUCH THINGS IN SCHOOL.
"WHO BENEFITS FROM YOUR IGNORANCE?
"I WANT YOU TO WALK PAST **HOMAN SQUARE.** THE SECRET DETENTION FACILITY USED BY THE CHICAGO POLICE.
"IT'S THE ABU GHRAIB OF AMERICA. BUT THEY WON'T TALK ABOUT IT MUCH ON THE NEWS.
STOP
"WHO BENEFITS FROM YOUR IGNORANCE?
"YOU'RE OLD ENOUGH TO SEE THE WORLD WITHOUT BLINDERS ANYMORE, AKAI.
Thillens
FIELD
HILLEN
OF THE
HICAGO
PARK
"THE GOOD AND THE BAD IN YOUR COUNTRY. YOU CAN'T LOOK AWAY."

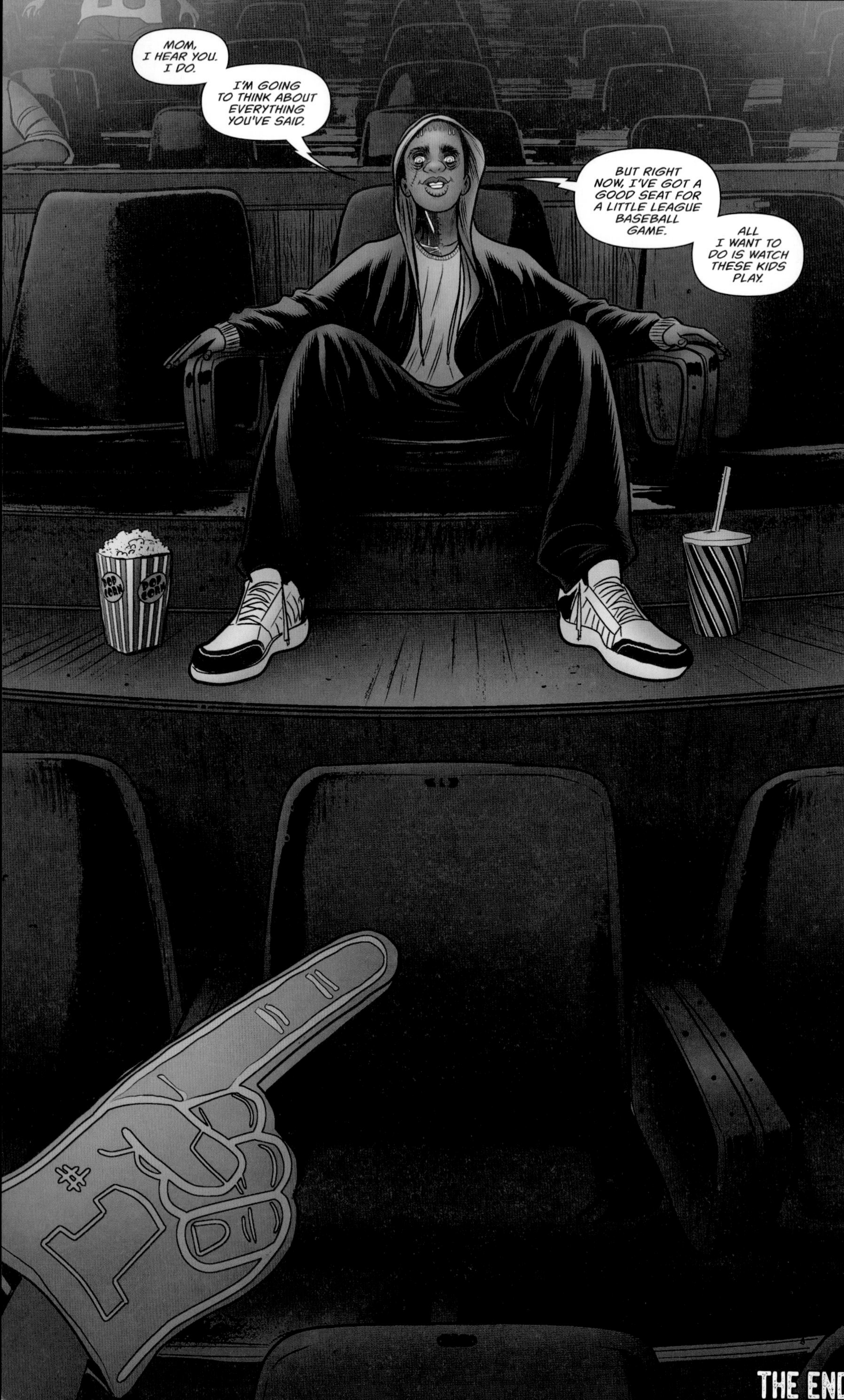
MOM, I HEAR YOU. I DO.
I'M GOING TO THINK ABOUT EVERYTHING YOU'VE SAID.
BUT RIGHT NOW, I'VE GOT A GOOD SEAT FOR A LITTLE LEAGUE BASEBALL GAME.
ALL I WANT TO DO IS WATCH THESE KIDS PLAY.
POP CORN
THE END

Mary Shelley died on February 1, 1851. She was fifty-three years old. After *Frankenstein* she went on to publish other books, but it's her first that made her famous. The great relationship of her life was with the poet Percy Shelley. They were together for only eight years and it was, to put it euphemistically, a complicated relationship. Nevertheless, after Mary died a surprising discovery was made among her effects. Mary Shelley had Percy Shelley's heart. Literally. He'd died three decades before her. The heart was found in her desk, wrapped in a silk shroud.

Percy drowned off the coast of Italy in 1822. His body had been cremated, but the heart wouldn't burn. That heart eventually made its way back to Mary, who was rumored not simply to have kept it in her desk but to have carried it with her everywhere. I love Mary Shelley for her novel first and foremost, but I adore her for this little factoid, too. What a hell of an interesting human being!

But beyond the admittedly gruesome aspect of that keepsake, the incident also makes me think of ideas like love and devotion. Mary became a widow at the age of only twenty-four, but Percy Shelley remained a central part of her life until her dying day. Percy's heart was only a reflection of the memory Mary Shelley held inside.

In her way this is all Dr. Baker is trying to do by reanimating the body of her son, Akai. She's bringing him back to life, but inside her he could never die. Of course, in real life there is no such magic, but how I wish such a thing could be. This comic was inspired by Mary Shelley's novel and by the regular waves of black people murdered, without consequence, by the police forces of the United States. Men and women who work on behalf of some of America's citizens at the cost of the lives of other American citizens.

As I write this I wonder which seems more fantastical: that a woman could bring her dead son back to life, or that our country might ever hold itself accountable for injustices it has perpetrated. Technology is improving at an astonishing rate; honest conversation—and actual change—move at a much slower pace.

For all this apparent pessimism, there's a reason Akai refuses cynicism in this comic, a reason why he won't succumb to rage. Because Akai Baker embodies the best that humanity has to offer. Despair doesn't do a damn thing. And fear only turns people into animals. But as long as we have kids like Akai in the world, there's still a chance for us. The trick, then, is to make sure that they actually are in the world, living, breathing, growing up, growing old.

VICTOR LaVALLE

ISSUE #1 COVER BY

MICAELA DAWN

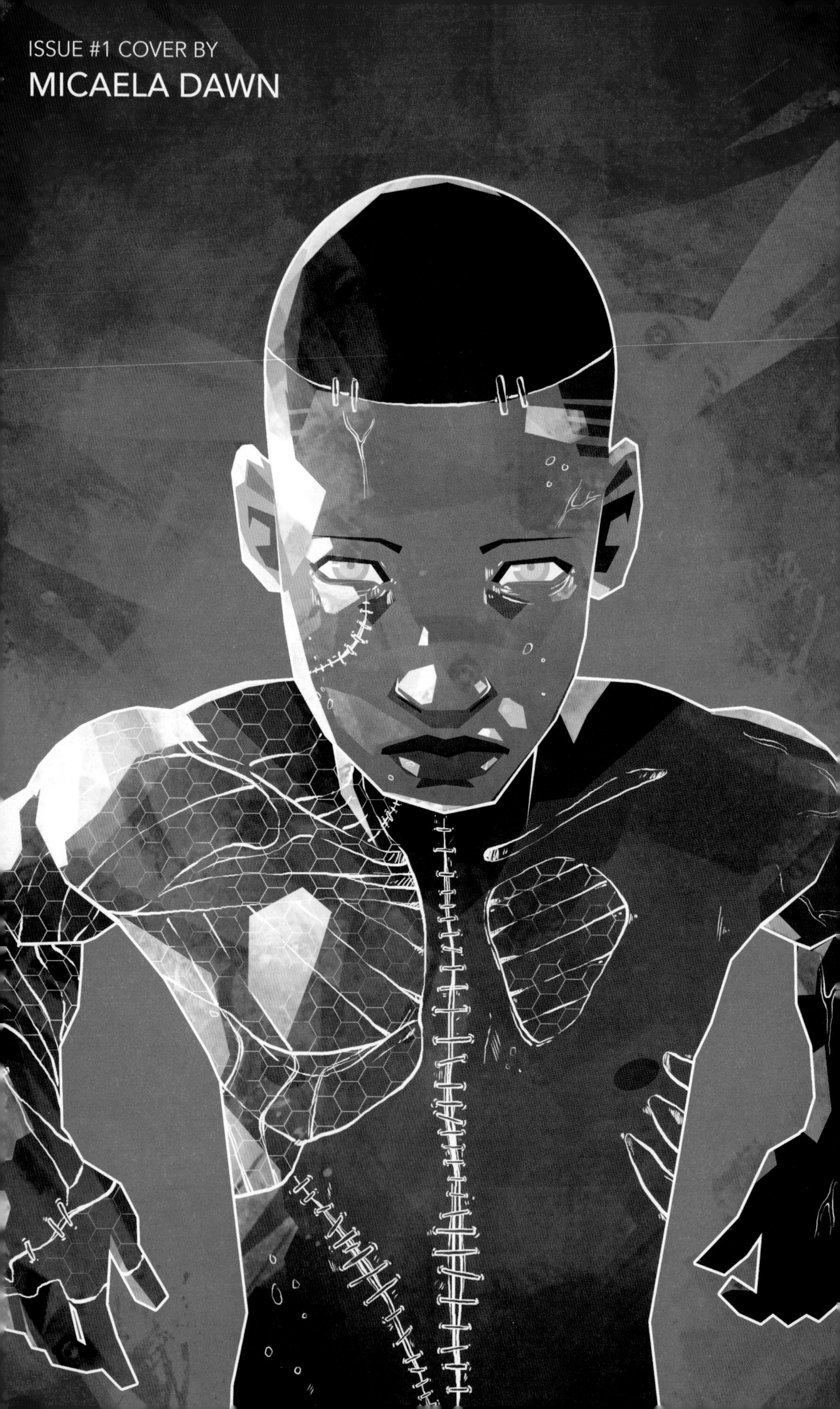

ISSUE #1 UNLOCKED RETAILER VARIANT COVER BY
BRIAN STELFREEZE

ISSUE #2 COVER BY

MICAELA DAWN

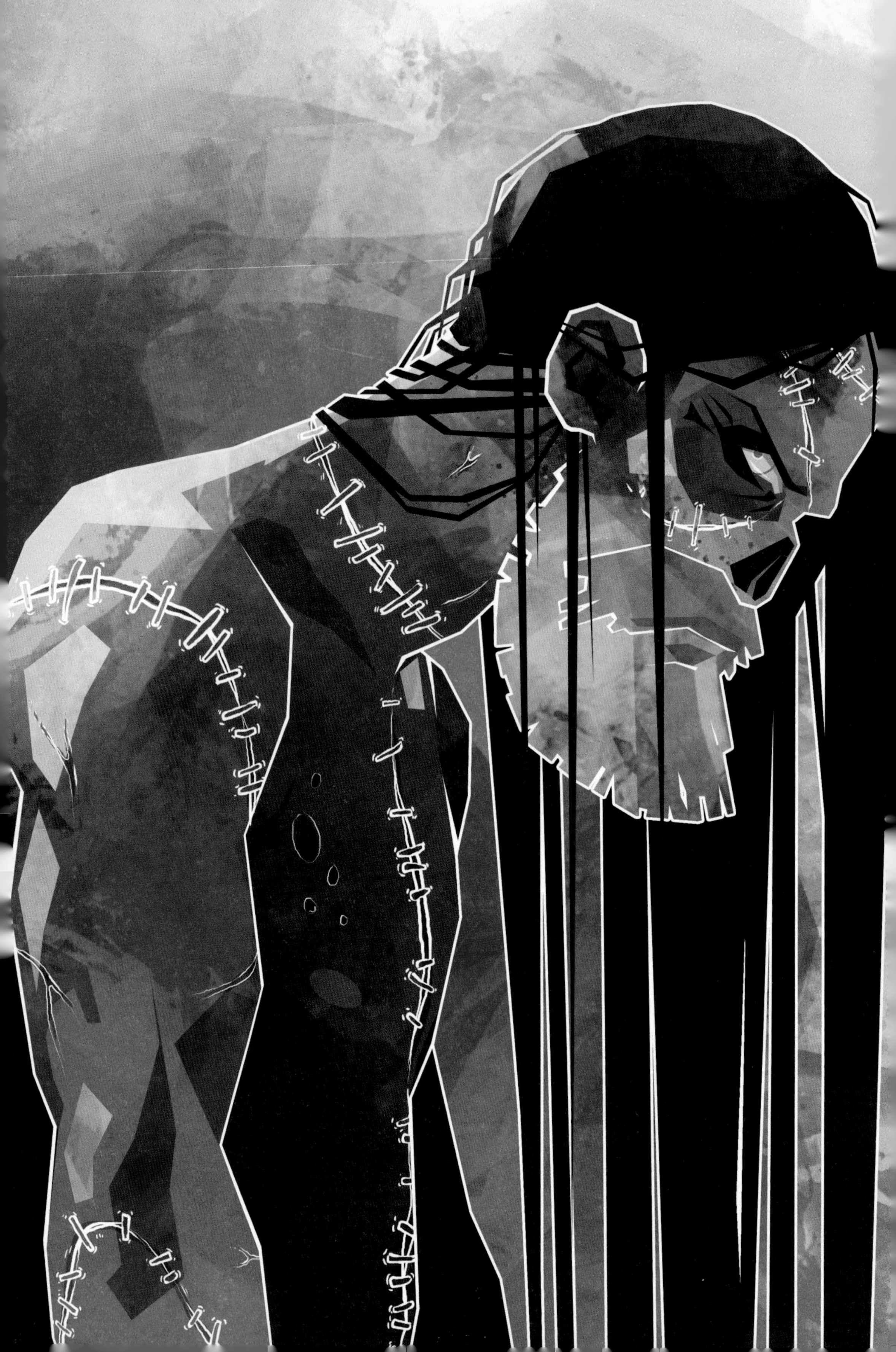

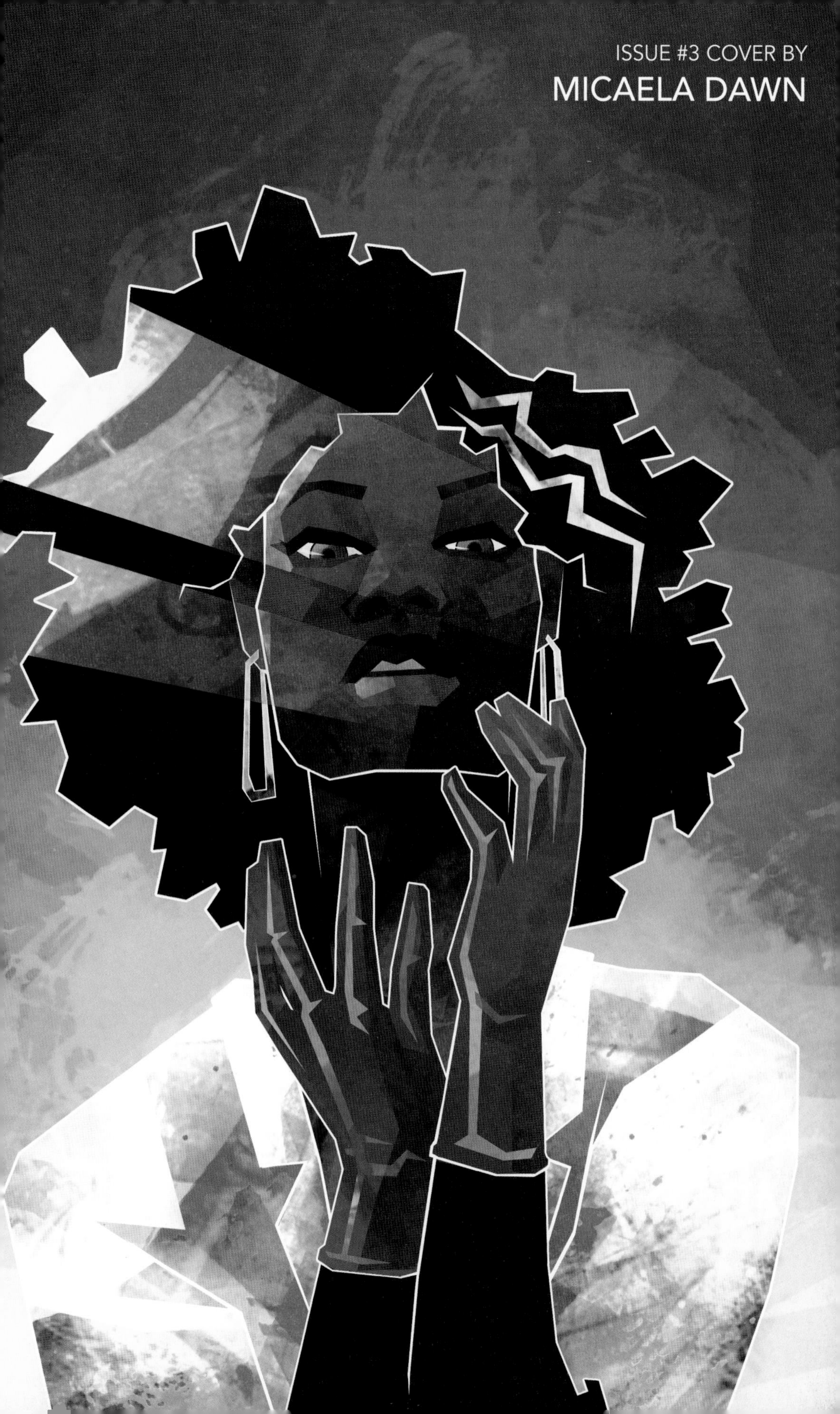
ISSUE #3 COVER BY
MICAELA DAWN

ISSUE #4 COVER BY

MICAELA DAWN

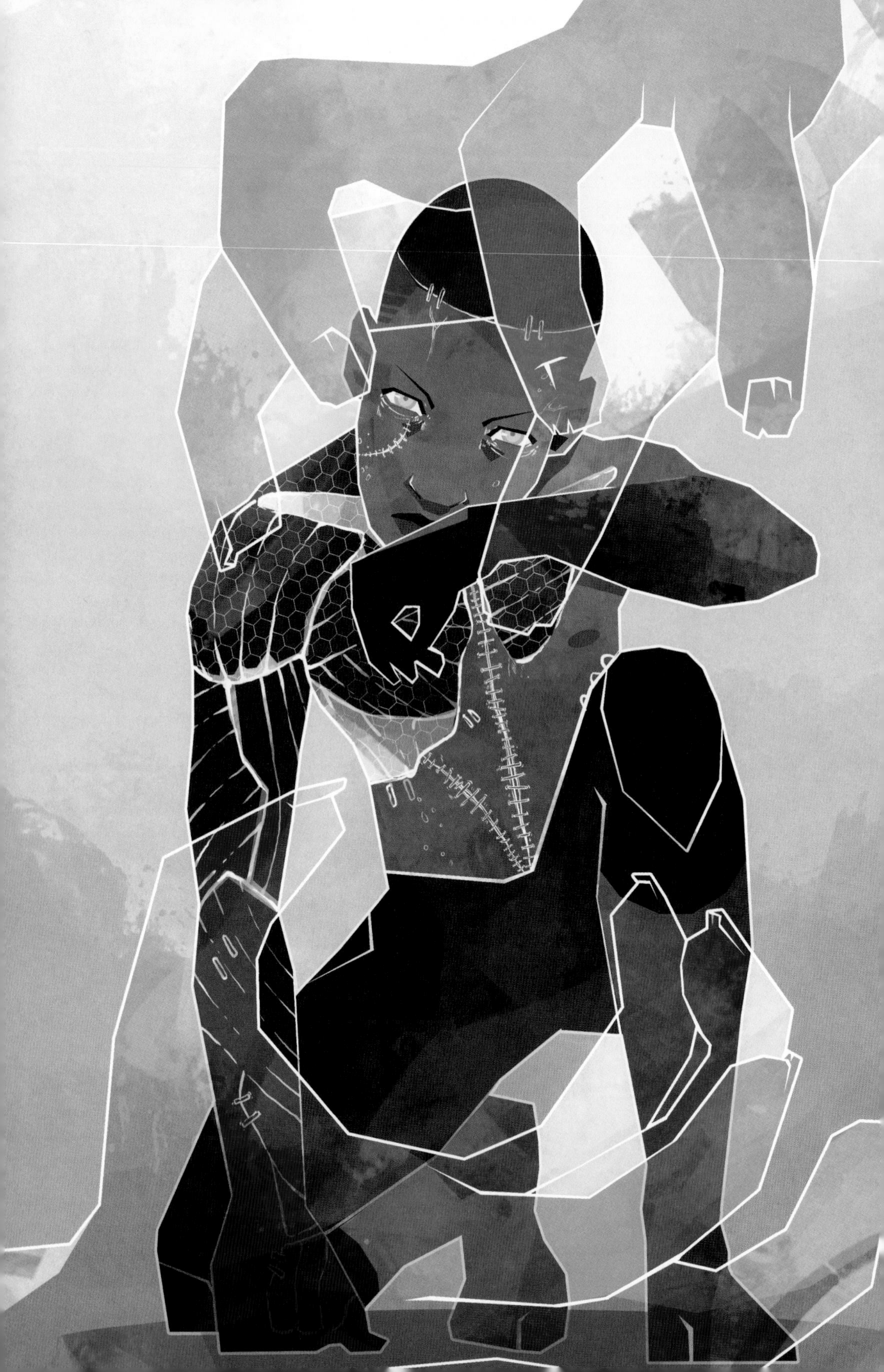

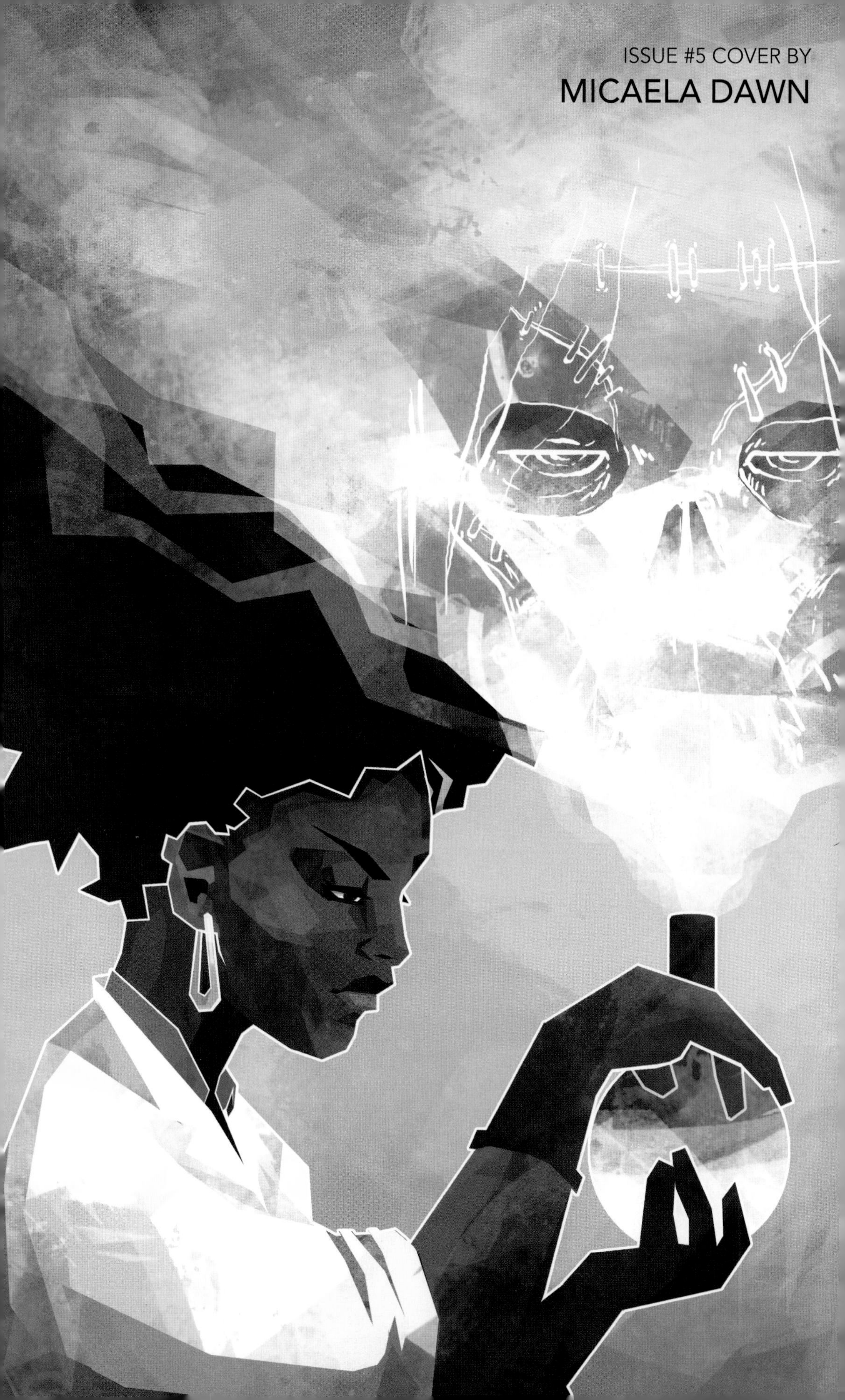

ISSUE #5 COVER BY
MICAELA DAWN

ISSUE #6 COVER BY

MICAELA DAWN

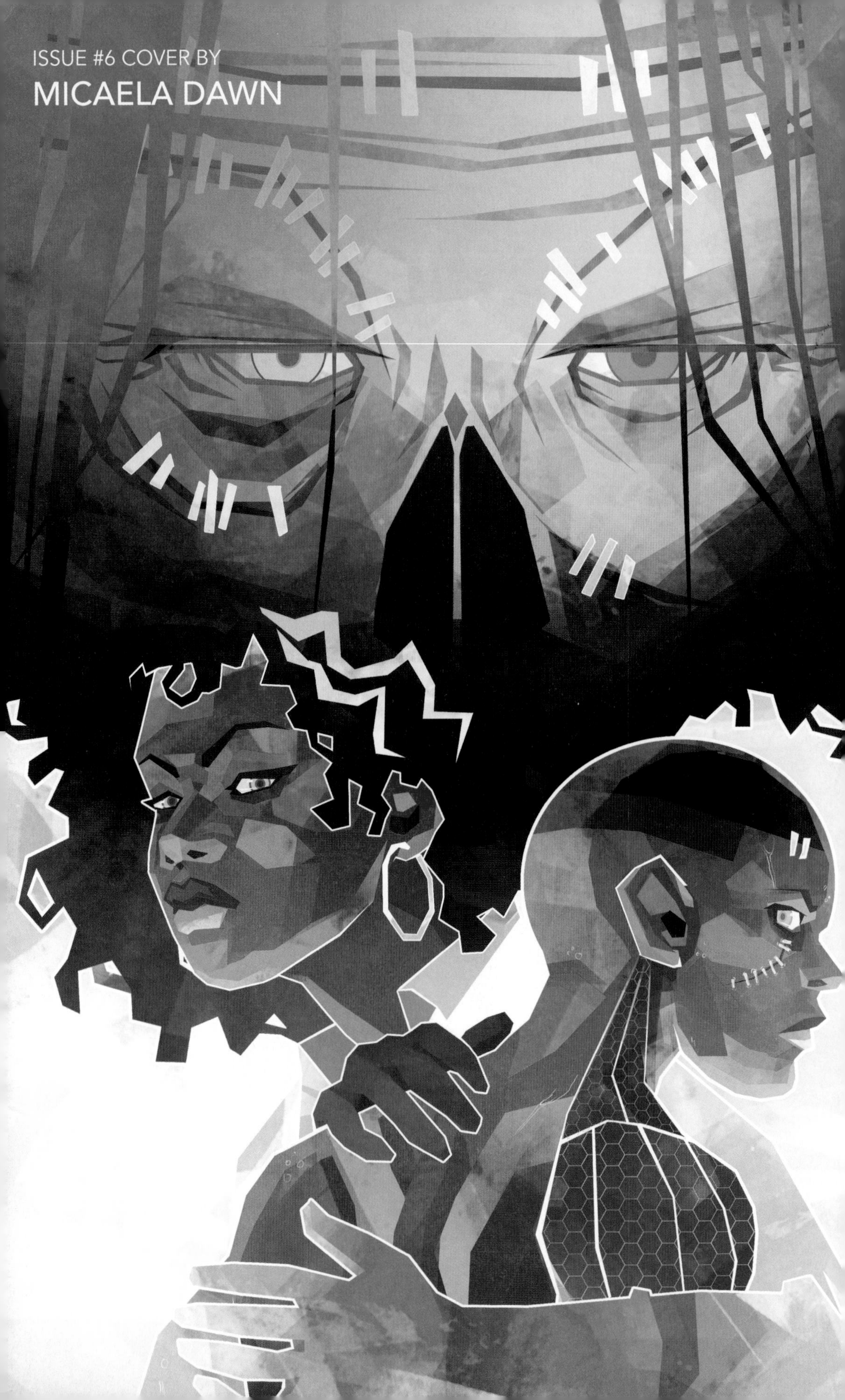

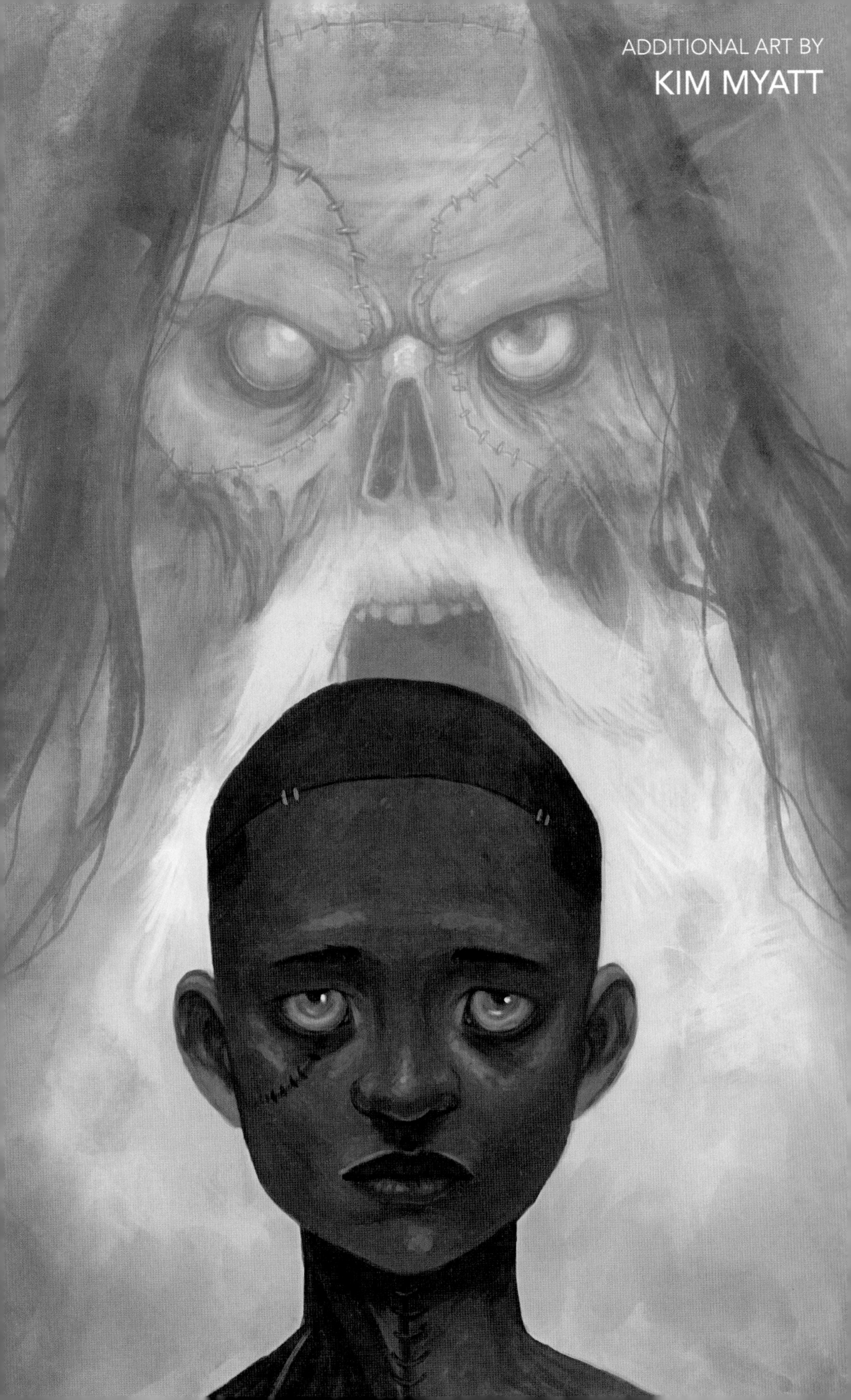
ADDITIONAL ART BY
KIM MYATT

CHARACTER DESIGNS BY
DAN MORA

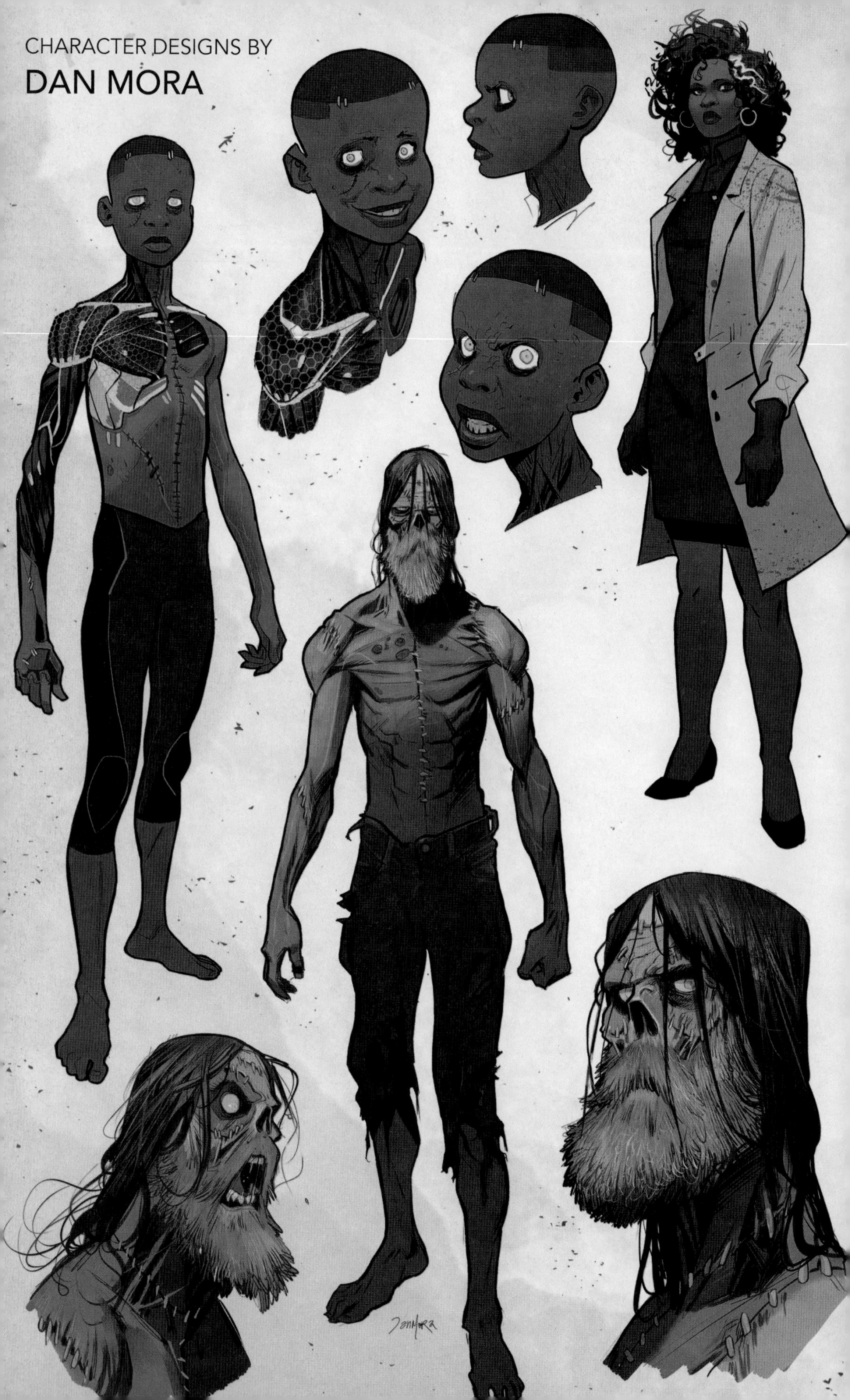
DanMora

VICTOR LAVALLE

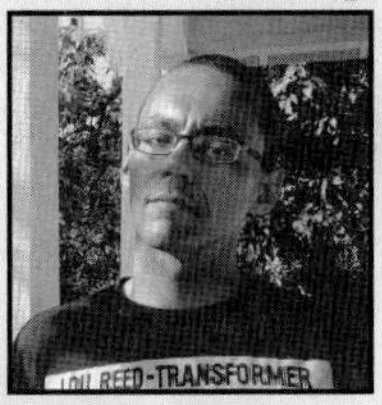
LOU REED-TRANSFORMER

Victor LaValle is the author of seven works of fiction including *The Ballad of Black Tom*, which is a finalist for a Nebula Award, a Hugo Award, a Bram Stoker Award, and the Theodore Sturgeon Award. His latest novel, *The Changeling*, was released in June 2017. His other books have won the American Book Award, the Shirley Jackson Award, a Guggenheim Fellowship, and the Key to Southeast Queens. He teaches at Columbia University and lives in New York City with his wife and kids.

DIETRICH SMITH

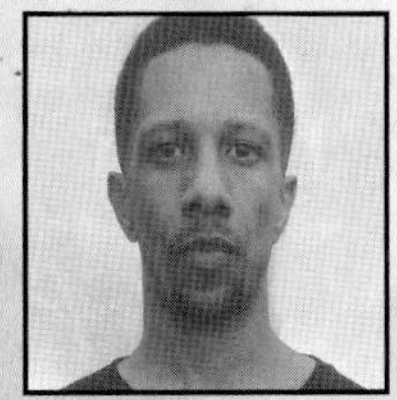

Born in the Yellowhammer State in 1973, **Dietrich Smith** is an illustrator and designer with work in the field of comics spanning over two decades. He studied at the College of Liberal Arts at Auburn University before becoming an Extreme Studios intern in the wild pin-up '90s. In the years that followed, he branched from comic books to TV animation as well as becoming involved in advertising, conceptual design, and children's books. Armed with knowledge of various styles, he serves as a consultant and a coach for artists, helping them further develop their potential. In his spare time he battles time travelers all around the globe.

JOANA LAFUENTE

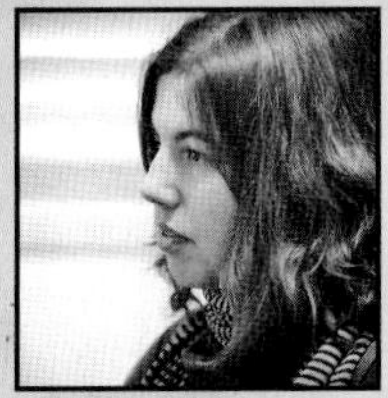

Joana Lafuente is a self-taught illustrator that has a Master's degree in computer engineering, but gave up on programming to follow her dream as an artist as soon as she could. She has been mostly working in comics, but not exclusively, having also worked for game and advertising companies.

JIM CAMPBELL

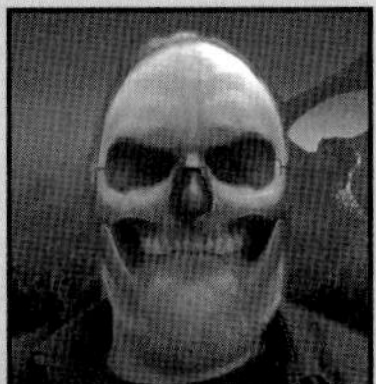

Jim Campbell has been lettering comics professionally for almost a decade, before which he worked in newspaper and magazine publishing for even longer. He knows more about print production than mortal man was meant to know and has also scanned more images than you've had hot dinners. Unless you're ninety years old. If you're very unlucky, he might start talking to you about ligatures.

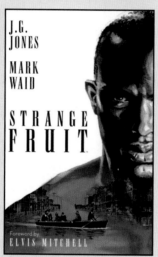
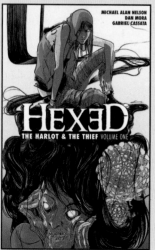
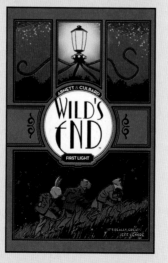